GREEK OLIGARCHIES

THEIR CHARACTER AND ORGANISATION

GREEK OLIGARCHIES

THEIR CHARACTER AND ORGANISATION

BY

LEONARD WHIBLEY, M.A.

FELLOW OF PEMBROKE COLLEGE,
CAMBRIDGE

CAMBRIDGE:
AT THE UNIVERSITY PRESS
1913

CAMBRIDGE
UNIVERSITY PRESS

University Printing House, Cambridge CB2 8BS, United Kingdom

Cambridge University Press is part of the University of Cambridge.

It furthers the University's mission by disseminating knowledge in the pursuit of
education, learning and research at the highest international levels of excellence.

www.cambridge.org
Information on this title: www.cambridge.org/9781316626177

© Cambridge University Press 1913

First published 1896
Reissued 1913
First paperback edition 2016

A catalogue record for this publication is available from the British Library

ISBN 978-1-316-62617-7 Paperback

PREFACE

THE following dissertation was awarded the *Hare Prize* in 1894. The pressure of other work obliged me to postpone the preparation of it for the press until last year.

For the study of Oligarchic Constitutions in Greece there are no adequate materials. No oligarchic state has left us any historical literature; nor have we the record of the internal working of any oligarchy: in this inquiry, as in most branches of Greek history, we realise how little we know of any Greek states other than Athens. Our conception of oligarchic government, its character and its method, cannot fail to be partial and incomplete. If we except Aristotle's masterly treatise on political ideas and political forms, information on oligarchic constitutions is scattered over a very wide field, extending from the Lyrical poets to Plutarch. Inscriptions yield less that is valuable than we should expect or desire.

The lack of positive knowledge induced me to devote the first chapter to an examination of the place occupied by Oligarchy and Aristocracy in the Greek classification of constitutions. By a study of the definitions, which are, like the political terminology of the Greeks, too often vague and uncertain, we are able to arrive at the impression produced on the minds of the Greeks by the different governments, and thus we catch a reflection of their real character. In the second and third chapters I have briefly discussed the causes of constitutional change and traced the development of constitutions, in order to show the place occupied by oligarchy in this process. Two Appendices deal with some problems of early A-thenian history. In the fourth chapter the varieties of Oligarchy are discussed, and the last chapter is devoted to the organisation of oligarchic government. It is followed by an Appendix on the revolution of the Four Hundred at Athens.

Of modern books, I have made constant use of the second volume of Gilbert's *Handbuch der griechischen Staatsalterthümer*, which contains an invaluable collection of material. Mr Newman's Introduction to the *Politics of Aristotle* I have found most useful and suggestive. I have cited in my notes the other modern works to which I am indebted.

In preparing the work for press it is my pleasure to acknowledge most gratefully the help of Mr W. Wyse, of Trinity College, one of the adjudicators for the prize, who put many valuable notes at my disposal, and the kindness of Mr R. A. Neil, of Pembroke College, and of Mr J. W. Headlam of King's College, who read my proofs and gave me the benefit of many criticisms and suggestions.

LEONARD WHIBLEY.

PEMBROKE COLLEGE, CAMBRIDGE.
February 3, 1896.

[In the citations of Aristotle's *Politics* I have followed the text of Susemihl's small edition, as well as his numbering of the books. The first volume of Mr Newman's *Politics* is cited as 'Newman, *Introduction*.' References to Dr Gilbert's *Handbuch* are to the second German edition.]

CONTENTS

CHAPTER I.

THE CLASSIFICATION OF CONSTITUTIONS: THE CLAIMS AND CHARACTER OF OLIGARCHY.

CHAPTER IV.

VARIETIES OF OLIGARCHY.

CHAPTER V.

ORGANISATION OF OLIGARCHIC GOVERNMENT.

CHAPTER I.

THE CLASSIFICATION OF CONSTITUTIONS: THE CLAIMS AND CHARACTER OF OLIGARCHY.

§ 1. *The Popular Classification of Constitutions.*

THE genius of the Greeks, which has given them a sure and lasting preeminence as political inventors and political theorists, made them conscious at a comparatively early date of the variety of governments under which they lived. The ruling element, as Aristotle says, must be one man, or a few men, or the multitude[1]: and this distinction, which has served ever since as the basis of classification, is recorded for the first time by Pindar in language that is neither technical nor precise[2]. In his words 'tyranny, the ravening host and the wise wardens of the city' denote monarchy, democracy and oligarchy: and the poet reveals his preference for the government of the few by the choice of the epithets that he employs[3]. Thus from

---

[1] *Pol.* iii 6 1279 a 25 πολίτευμα δ' ἐστὶ τὸ κύριον τῶν πόλεων, ἀνάγκη δ' εἶναι κύριον ἢ ἕνα ἢ ὀλίγους ἢ τοὺς πολλούς.

[2] *Pyth.* 2 86 ἐν πάντα δὲ νόμον..... | παρὰ τυραννίδι, χὠπόταν ὁ λάβρος στρατός, | χὤταν πόλιν οἱ σοφοὶ τηρέωντι. Homer *Il.* ii 204 οὐκ ἀγαθὸν πολυκοιρανίη· εἷς κοίρανος ἔστω, gives us the first reflection on Politics.

[3] The political application of the commonest moral epithets is found in Theognis, although he does not expressly moralize on forms of government.

the first we find constitutional forms and political parties described in moral terms, and this tendency did much to confuse the political terminology of the Greeks[4]. The use of such terms could never be altogether consistent, for the advocates of oligarchy and democracy used identical phrases of praise and abuse, and applied them, as might suit their purpose or occasion, to describe opposite parties and different forms of government[5].

There is no rhetorical commonplace so constantly employed as the comparison of the three constitutions or the contrast of the principles of oligarchy and democracy : it was a universal topic with the rhetors and sophists, who taught their pupils the stock descriptions of each constitution, and directed them to adapt their epithets and suit their conclusions to the taste of their audience[6]. By the time of Herodotus this criticism of constitutions was already in fashion, and the scientific terms of monarchy, oligarchy and democracy had been introduced[7]. The his-

[4] It will be seen below how inconsistent and ambiguous the use of many political terms is.

[5] It would be beside my purpose to discuss this subject here : but there is abundant evidence in the orators that the epithets and qualities, which are supposed to have acquired a special political application in the mouths of oligarchs, were employed in an absolutely opposite way by speakers wishing to say pleasant things to a democracy. Instances could be quoted of εὐνομία, εὐταξία and σωφροσύνη (the particular virtues of oligarchies) attributed to the democratic constitution: while πονηρία, μοχθηρία, ὕβρις and the like are supposed to be innate characteristics of oligarchy.

[6] Examples of this practice are quoted in the text: it is described in Isocr. xii 111 τοὺς τοιούτους ἐπειδὰν αἴσθωνται τοὺς τόπους προκατειλημμένους...ἐπὶ τὸν λόγον οἶμαι τρέψεσθαι τὸν περὶ τῶν πολιτειῶν.

[7] Thus μουναρχίη, τυραννίς, ὀλιγαρχίη occur in the debate in iii 80—82. He uses δῆμος there to describe democracy: but in vi 43 δημοκρατίη is found.

torian could not deny himself the pleasure of discussing
the question, which was then, perhaps for the first time,
agitating the minds of the Greeks, the question of the
best form of government[8]. The debate, attributed with
a grotesque inappropriateness to the three Persian nobles,
is nothing else than a representation of Hellenic institutions and a reflection of Hellenic ideas[9]. We find that
Herodotus introduces moral qualities in his definitions[10],
but they show a considerable power of scientific analysis
and include many of the characteristics essential to the
three constitutions[11].

Thucydides as far outstrips Herodotus in the science
of politics as in the art of history. He invented for
himself the canons of his art and the principles of his
philosophy, and having no predecessor he may have unconsciously formed the design of his work on the model of
the Greek drama. Thus the narrative, which we may
liken to the recitals of the messengers or the other episodes
of tragedy, is interrupted, while the orator performing the
function of the chorus introduces into the discussion of

[8] Cf. Newman, *Introduction* p. 85. 'The quest of 'a best constitution'
was a tradition of political inquiry in Greece. The question was apparently first raised by practical statesmen, and it was thus perhaps that
Herodotus came to imagine a group of Persian grandees discussing the
claims of monarchy, oligarchy and democracy.'

[9] The debate, as a whole, is unreal and impossible, but the characteristics attributed to the constitutions are entirely Greek and un-Oriental.

[10] Thus ὀλιγαρχίη is defined as ἀνδρῶν ἀρίστων ὁμιλίη (practically Aristotle's definition of ἀριστοκρατία): κακότης is regarded by Darius as inevitable in a democratic government.

[11] Thus ἰσονομία (cf. Thuc. iii 82) is attributed to democracy, and
Otanes says of it πάλῳ μὲν ἀρχὰς ἄρχει, ὑπεύθυνον δὲ ἀρχὴν ἔχει, βουλεύματα
δὲ πάντα ἐς τὸ κοινὸν ἀναφέρει. The description of tyranny is thoroughly
in accord with Greek sentiment.

particular events the searching analysis of motive, the
masterly application of general principles, which make
Thucydides an author for all time[12]. In the speeches,
moreover, there is a tragic irony, a foreknowledge of the
catastrophe which reminds us again of the analogy. The
splendid panegyric of Athens put into the mouth of Pericles is followed without a break by the narrative of the
plague—the first step in the downfall of Athens. The
assertion of the empire of force at Melos and the warnings
of the Melian speakers prepare the way for that master-
piece of tragic narrative, the story of the disaster in Sicily.
Hence though the speeches are often not inconsistent with
the character of the speaker and are appropriate enough
to the circumstances of the occasion[13], they may be regarded rather as containing the reflections of Thucydides
himself than as the actual words or thoughts of the orator
to whom they are attributed. Thucydides is nowhere
concerned with the comparison of the three constitutions,
but he shows that he has carried the analysis of constitutional forms much further than his predecessors. His
classification is more accurate, varieties of the main types
are distinguished[14], and the characteristics of the different
governments are drawn in more detail and with greater
precision[15].

[12] Thucydides rarely inserts his own comment on events. The most
noteworthy instance is the reflection on the στάσις at Corcyra (iii 82—3).

[13] Thucydides himself says (i 22) ὡς δ᾿ ἂν ἐδόκουν ἐμοὶ ἕκαστοι περὶ τῶν
ἀεὶ παρόντων τὰ δέοντα μάλιστ᾿ εἰπεῖν, ἐχομένῳ ὅτι ἐγγύτατα τῆς ξυμπάσης
γνώμης τῶν ἀληθῶς λεχθέντων, οὕτως εἴρηται.

[14] In i 13 τυραννίδες and πατρικαὶ βασιλεῖαι are distinguished. In iii
62 ὀλιγαρχία ἰσόνομος and δυναστεία are distinguished.

[15] Cf. the descriptions of the Athenian democracy (ii 38) and of the
moderate democracy at Syracuse (vi 39).

In these respects he anticipates Aristotle, and it is clear that the philosopher to a great extent follows the historian both in his phraseology and in his general descriptions. To Thucydides the Peloponnesian war was a conflict of political principles, a duel between oligarchy and democracy[16]: it was even more particularly a trial of strength between the free and popular constitution of Athens and the rigid, military aristocracy of Sparta. Hence he is haunted by the antithesis afforded by these two states; and it is scarcely an exaggeration to say that there are few speeches in which traces of this antithesis cannot be found, while it is emphasized or implied on occasions when the introduction of the contrast is inappropriate to the speaker and irrelevant[17].

To continue the examination of the popular classification: Thrasymachus in Plato's *Republic* refers to the three ordinary constitutions under the names of tyranny, aristocracy and democracy[18]. Isocrates enumerates them and further differentiates them by their ethical qualities—a distinction to which I refer below[19]. Aeschines introduces the comparison in order to draw conclusions in favour of the fairness and good order of democracy[20]. Demosthenes

[16] Cf. especially iii 82 1.

[17] The contrast of the character of the two states is natural and avowed in the speech of the Corinthians (i 68—71) and in that of Archidamus (i 80—85). In the praise of Athens by Pericles Sparta serves as a foil to her great rival (ii 35 ff., see especially chapters 37, 39, 40). The contrast does not seem so relevant in the mouth of Cleon (iii 37—40), but it is obviously implied though not avowed; for Cleon is made to repeat the description of the Spartans given by the Corinthians and Archidamus. Lastly, the comparison is made by Nicias (vi 11).

[18] i 338 D.

[19] xii 132—3. [Lys.] vi 30 enumerates δῆμος, ὀλιγαρχία and τύραννος.

[20] *In Timarch.* 4.

mentions all three forms and has much to say about the
relative merits of democracy and oligarchy[21].

These instances suffice to show that the threefold
division of constitutions was generally accepted.

§ 2.   *Classification of Constitutions by the Philosophers.*

The sophistic movement gave a great impetus to the
criticism of constitutional forms, and the philosophers also
devoted no little interest to the study of politics.   The
theory of Socrates is preserved for us in the pages of
Xenophon, the most faithful exponent of his master's
teaching[1].   Plato has different schemes in the *Republic*,
the *Politicus* and the *Laws*[2], and Aristotle in three passages
discusses the classification of constitutions[3].   Of later writers
Polybius[4], Plutarch[5] and Dion Chrysostom[6] follow Aristotle
in the main, with some variation of phraseology.   All
these writers, while distinguishing constitutions by the
number of those to whom sovereign power is entrusted,
recognise more than three varieties; and their classifica-

[21] The three forms are enumerated in xxiii 66.   The orator offers us
a good instance of the commonplace contrast of oligarchy and democracy,
for a somewhat frigid passage in which the two forms are compared
occurs both in xxii 51—2 and xxiv 163—4.

[1] *Mem.* iv 6 12.

[2] *Rep.* v 449 A; *Pol.* 291 ff.; *Laws*, 710 E.

[3] The scheme in the *Rhetoric* (i 8 1365) has a great resemblance to
the scheme in Xenophon, while it differs considerably from that in the
Politics (iii chs. 6—9), wherein Aristotle adopts in the main the classification of Plato in the *Politicus*.   There is a third scheme in the *Ethics*
(viii 12 1160) resembling the classification of the *Politics* with some
slight variations in the definitions.

[4] vi chs. 3—10.   [5] *De unius dom.* 3.

[6] iii 45—9.

tion, in so far as it differs from the popular theory, is based primarily on ethical considerations. The classifications of Plato and Aristotle must be discussed in some detail. The speculations of both writers are intimately connected with attempts to construct ideal states on the Greek model. Both of them observed the conditions that prevailed in the ordinary Greek communities; neither of them conceived of anything beyond the city-state. Even Plato's *Republic*, however impossible of realisation, does but depict the government of philosophers on the basis of the Lacedaemonian state[7]. Hence we may often discern real institutions underlying the ideal, and the Utopias of Plato and Aristotle, in so far as they reflect the political theory of the Greeks, have their value in the study of actual constitutions. At the same time the introduction of the ideal state, as the end of political enquiry, tended to divorce the classification of ordinary states from reality.

To Plato 'the ideal view of politics probably seemed the only view worth taking. Politics is to him a more concrete sort of Ethics[8]' and 'the construction of the ideal state is to him more or less an episode in an ethical inquiry[9].' The ideal state of the *Republic* embodies a constitution for Mars or Saturn, or, as Plato himself says, 'it exists nowhere on earth, but a pattern of it is laid up in heaven[10]'; 'it is suited only for gods or the sons of gods[11].' Real constitutions, when compared with this political paradise, can only appear ludicrous perversions of justice, and they are estimated fancifully enough in their

[7] Jowett, *Plato*[2], v p. xxxviii.

[8] Newman, *Introduction* p. 486.

[9] *Ib.* p. 455.   [10] *Rep.* ix 592 A, B.

[11] *Laws*, v 739 D; ix 853 C.

supposed order of deviation from the ideal. Thus 'the government of honour,' the description of which is based on the Cretan and Lacedaemonian states, ranks first of the perversions[12] : next comes oligarchy, the government of wealth, 'laden with divers evils[13],' and below these are democracy and tyranny. No attempt is made to distinguish the better forms of these constitutions from the worse : all are included in the condemnation.

In the *Laws*, a work written in all probability within the last ten years of Plato's life, when he had realised the hopeless impossibility of his ideal, we have his final thoughts on politics[14]. His classification of ordinary governments is not so clear as in the *Republic*. In one passage monarchy and democracy are ranked as 'mother forms' above other constitutions[15] : in another passage the rule of a perfect tyrant is said to be best[16], and existing governments are considered, according as they are capable of being transformed into this form[17]. He thus ranks them in the order of tyranny, monarchy, democracy and oligarchy. It seems that Plato had really changed his opinion of democracy and now set it above oligarchy, but he is still in irreconcilable hostility to ordinary forms of government. They do not deserve the names of 'constitutions,' they are factions governing without justice in the interest of the rulers[18]. The state that is to remedy the prevailing defects, if less ideal than the state of the *Republic*, is not more possible[19]. It is a government of

---

[12] *Rep.* viii 547—8.
[13] *Ib.* 544 A. It is described in 550 c.
[14] Newman, *Introduction* p. 434, n. 2.
[15] iii 693 D.   [16] iv 709 E.   [17] iv 710 E.
[18] iv 715 B.   [19] See Jowett, *Plato*[2], v p. xxxvii.

mixed aristocratic and democratic elements, but Plato cannot overcome his distrust of the people. He wishes to give the control of the government to a few wise men, and to leave to the multitude only such a semblance of power as shall soothe their discontent and prevent them from being dangerous.

Plato's description of actual constitutions in the *Politicus* is incidentally introduced to show how worthless they are in comparison with the rule of the perfect statesman. His enumeration is therefore intended to be complete, and it is certainly based on far more scientific principles than the classification in either of the other works. Starting with the criterion of number[20] he adds the ideas of force and consent (already mentioned in Xenophon's definition of monarchy[21]), of poverty and wealth[22], of lawlessness and respect for law[23]. These principles serve to divide constitutions into kingship and tyranny, aristocracy and oligarchy, and the two forms of democracy, both described by one name. Of these six governments monarchy and aristocracy have the first place, then come the two democracies, lastly oligarchy and tyranny. In the *Politicus*, as in the *Laws*, the philosopher deviates from the order of the *Republic* and gives a preference to democracy over oligarchy.

Plato, then, adopting the popular classification, adds certain ethical considerations, which serve to divide the better forms of each type from the worse.

[20] 291 D (μοναρχία, ἡ ὑπὸ τῶν ὀλίγων δυναστεία, ἡ τοῦ πλήθους ἀρχή).

[21] *Mem.* iv 6 12 βασιλεία is ἑκόντων τῶν ἀνθρώπων καὶ κατὰ νόμους; τυραννὶς is the opposite.

[22] It is not easy to see how poverty or wealth would serve to differentiate one kind of democracy from another.

[23] This principle also appears in Xenophon, *l. c.*

Aristotle followed Plato in the division of constitutions into six main forms. In the *Rhetoric* and the *Ethics* the discussion of the subject is incidental and subordinate to the main topic, and we may accept the scheme in the *Politics* as representing the more accurate and the more mature thought of the philosopher; the definitions in the other works we need only discuss in so far as they differ. In the *Rhetoric*—the earliest of the three works—where he argues that the orator must take into account the ἔθη καὶ νόμιμα of the constitution, he practically adopts the classification of Socrates as it is recorded by Xenophon[24]. Besides the double forms of monarchy and oligarchy he only mentions one form of democracy and defines it somewhat arbitrarily as 'the government in which office is assigned by lot.' In the *Ethics*[25], where he discusses varieties of friendship, the six forms of government are mentioned with the titles they bear in the *Politics*[26], but with slight variations in the definition. The principles of classification, finally adopted by him, lead him to distinguish three 'normal constitutions' and three 'perversions' or 'corruptions[27].'

The perversion is distinguished from the normal type by a difference of end. In the perversion the rulers rule

[24] *Rhet.* i 8 1365. The definition of ἀριστοκρατία corresponds to that given by Xenophon (*Mem.* iv 6 12). I discuss it below § 6.

[25] viii 12 1160. The definition of πολιτεία as τιμοκρατική differs from the definition of the *Politics*. See below § 5.

[26] iii chs. 6—9.

[27] Cf. *Eth. l. c.* πολιτείας δ' ἐστὶν εἴδη τρία, ἴσαι δὲ καὶ παρεκβάσεις, οἷον φθοραὶ τούτων. The idea of the 'normal' and the 'perverted' constitutions had been already suggested by Plato, though he regards all *actual* constitutions as perversions, in comparison with the ideal. Cf. *Rep.* v 449 A ὀρθὴ πολιτεία and ἡμαρτημέναι; *Polit.* 302 B; *Laws* iv 714 B.

for their own advantage and govern absolutely : in the constitution properly so called they rule for the common good²⁸.
Of this distinction we find traces in earlier writers²⁹. The
distinction thus drawn between the personal interests of
the rulers and the common interests of the state is of
great importance. Kant traced the origin of the state
' to the antagonism resulting from the fact that men have
both tendencies to social union and tendencies disruptive
of it, both general sympathies and private interests³⁰'; and
the same contrast was noticed by Napoleon III. 'There
exist,' he said, 'in every country two distinct and often
contrary interests, general interests and individual interests
—these may be denominated the permanent and the
transient interests³¹.' The statesman has no harder pro-
blem than the reconciliation of particular claims with
common advantage, and in a practical work on statesman-
ship, such as is the *Politics,* Aristotle was right to insist

²⁸ *Pol.* iii 6 1279 a 17. In the *Ethics l. c.* this criterion is applied to
monarchy (ὁ μὲν γὰρ τύραννος τὸ αὑτῷ συμφέρον σκοπεῖ, ὁ δὲ βασιλεὺς τὸ τῶν
ἀρχομένων) and suggested in the description of oligarchy.

²⁹ Cf. Thuc. iii 82 οὐ μέχρι τοῦ δικαίου καὶ τῇ πόλει ξυμφόρου προτιθέντες,
ἐς δὲ τὸ ἑκατέροις που ἀεὶ ἡδονὴν ἔχον ὁρίζοντες; [Xen.] *De Rep. Ath.* 1 13
οὐ τοῦ δικαίου αὑτοῖς μέλει μᾶλλον ἢ τοῦ αὑτοῖς συμφέροντος. The distinction
is drawn by Plato in the dialogue between Socrates and Thrasymachus
(*Rep.* i 338 D and 342 E). Cf. *Laws* iv 715 B ταύτας...φαμεν...οὔτ' εἶναι
πολιτείας οὔτ' ὀρθοὺς νόμους, ὅσοι μὴ ξυμπάσης τῆς πόλεως ἕνεκα τοῦ κοινοῦ
ἐτέθησαν. Cf. also Isocr. xii 132.

³⁰ Quoted by Newman, *Introduction* p. 33.

³¹ See *Des Idées Napoléoniennes* (English Translation 1840) p. 21.
Aristotle is not so precise in his definition, he does not distinguish the
temporary and the permanent interests. 'He does not appear to note
that the rule must be exercised not merely for the common advantage of
the existing generation, but for the advantage also of the unborn of
future generations.' (Newman, *Introduction* p. 252, n. 1.)

on it. But the motive of the ruler scarcely offers a satisfactory criterion to determine varieties of constitutions.
Montesquieu says of Aristotle's definition of monarchy ' he
makes five species; and he does not distinguish them by
the form of constitution, but by things merely accidental,
as the virtues and vices of the prince; or by things
extrinsic, such as tyranny usurped or inherited[32].' We
cannot tell *a priori* what ethical character a constitution
possesses; governments must be classified in accordance
with the form of their institutions, not the character of
their rulers. Moreover the principle leads Aristotle into
inconsistency[33], and he himself seems to have realised its
inadequacy, for in his detailed account of constitutions he
applies formal, rather than moral, principles of classification[34].

Aristotle supplies us with another test by defining the
common advantage to be identical with justice[35]; and the
normal states are those that pursue justice, the perversions
those that disregard it. If we define justice with Mill as
'the impartial administration of law,' we arrive at the
separation of states ruling with due observance of law
from those which rule absolutely without regard for law[36].

[32] *Esprit des Lois*, Bk xi § 9.

[33] Thus αἰσυμνητεία, which was essentially a government for the common good, is classed by Aristotle, *Pol.* iii 14 1285 a 31, with τυραννίς.

[34] Thus πολιτεία (the 'normal' democracy) is defined, either as the
government of those possessing arms, or as a constitution of mixed
democratic and oligarchic elements. Even ἀριστοκρατία can be brought
within formal definitions. See below § 6.

[35] *Pol.* iii 12 1282 b 17; *ib.* 13 1283 b 40. Thuc. and [Xen.] also
identify them. See above n. 29.

[36] Aristotle argues for the supremacy of law (*Pol.* iii 11 1282 b 2).
Thrasymachus (in Plato, *Rep.* i 338 c) defines justice as τὸ τοῦ κρείττονος

This distinction had already been drawn by other writers[37], and serves to distinguish absolute forms of government from constitutional forms, observing equal laws[38]. Thus tyranny, extreme oligarchy and extreme democracy contain despotic elements, alien from the idea of law, while kingship and the more moderate forms of oligarchy and democracy (including aristocracy and ' polity ') are characterised by respect for law and justice[39].

Another test has to be considered before our classification is complete. A constitution might be mixed, might contain elements which were characteristic of more than one of the main types of government.

Such constitutions were warmly praised by the political philosophers. The general tendency of constitutional development in Greece was towards the intensification of oligarchy and democracy, and in the fourth century the extreme forms were found almost everywhere[40]. But in the gradual evolution of democracy the constitution passed through a stage in which the old aristocracy was tempered

σνμφέρον (i.e. the interest of the ruler, not of the state). Plato, *Rep.* iv 433 A defines it as τὰ αὑτοῦ πράττειν καὶ μὴ πολυπραγμονεῖν (i.e. the correct apportionment and performance of special functions).

[37] Thuc. iii 62 contrasts ὀλιγαρχία ἰσόνομος with δυναστεία μὴ μετὰ νόμων. Cf. Xen. *Mem.* iv 6 12. Νόμος and ἀνομία differentiate constitutions in Plato, *Politicus* 291 E.

[38] The distinction is made clear in Aristotle, *Pol.* vi 4 1292 a 32 ὅπου γὰρ μὴ νόμοι ἄρχουσιν, οὐκ ἔστι πολιτεία. δεῖ γὰρ τὸν μὲν νόμον ἄρχειν πάντων, τῶν δὲ καθ' ἕκαστα τὰς ἀρχὰς καὶ τὴν πολιτείαν κρίνειν. In iii 4 1277 b 9 (ἀρχὴ πολιτικὴ) and 8 1279 b 16 (ἀρχὴ δεσποτικὴ) the two forms are described by the names usually employed.

[39] Constitutions according to law are not necessarily normal. The basis of government may be bad, and the respect for law will then only distinguish *degrees* of perversion.

[40] See chapter ii § 27.

with the new democracy, and for a time a moderate form
of government was maintained. Thus the Solonian constitution at Athens was described with universal approval[41];
and the same consideration will explain much of the
admiration that was lavished on the institutions of Lycurgus[42]. Thucydides departs from his usual attitude of
absolute impartiality to praise the mixed constitution
established at Athens in 411[43]; Plato made the ideal state
of the *Laws* a mixture of democracy, oligarchy and aristocracy; Aristotle devotes a large part of the sixth book to
the discussion of mixed forms and argues for their greater
justice and stability[44].

This consideration need not cause us to enlarge our
classification. Although some constitutions like that of
Solon might involve so even a balance of diverse elements,
that it would be difficult to define their character, we find
in most governments some one social element predominant;
and we are thus able to assign each to one of the ordinary
classes.

To sum up; we may accept in the main Aristotle's
classification. The ruling element will be one man, or

---

[41] Cf. Ar. *Pol.* ii 12 1273 b 38; Isocr. xii 131 (δημοκρατία ἀριστοκρατίᾳ
χρωμένη), Plato, *Laws* iii 698 B.

[42] The Spartan constitution was regarded as a combination of all other
forms.   See below § 3 nn. 15—20 and cf. Isocr. xii 153 (δημοκρατία
ἀριστοκρατίᾳ μεμιγμένη); Polyb. vi 10 6.

[43] viii 97 2.

[44] *Pol.* vi 8 1293 b; *ib.* 9 1294 a.   Cf. *ib.* 12 1297 a 7 ὅσῳ δ' ἂν ἄμεινον
ἡ πολιτεία μιχθῇ, τοσούτῳ μονιμωτέρα.   Tacitus (*Ann.* iv 33) took an
opposite view; 'cunctas nationes aut urbes populus aut primores aut
singuli regunt: delecta ex his et consociata reipublicae forma laudari
facilius quam evenire, vel si evenit, haud diuturna esse potest.'   Cf. Cic.
de rep. i 29 45.

a few men, or the multitude: and this element will either
rule absolutely, without regard to law, without the participation of other elements in the government, or rule
constitutionally, with due observance of law, under the
influence of other elements.   This classification was intended to apply only to the city-state, but though political
conditions have changed, and nations have taken the place
of cities as political units, modern political science has
little or nothing to add to the definitions of Aristotle[45].

§ 3.   *Oligarchy in a general sense.*

For practical purposes any study of Greek constitutions
may be limited to those included under the terms oligarchy and democracy, if we use the terms in a general
sense without implying any ethical meaning.   These, as
Aristotle himself says, are the constitutions that generally
prevailed[1], and many of the Greeks roughly classified all
governments as democracies or oligarchies[2].   Tyranny was
not regarded as a constitution, but as a temporary interruption of legal rule[3]: kingship 'was in the whole political
theory of antiquity only a form of aristocracy resting on

[45] Bluntschli, *The Theory of the State* p. 311, accepts Aristotle's classification, but adds to it 'Ideocracy' and 'Idolocracy,' constitutions 'in
which the supreme power has been attributed to some divine being or to
an idea.   The men who exercised power were regarded as the servants
and vice-regents of an unseen ruler.'   But whatever pretensions may
have been put forward, power was actually wielded by one or more men.
As Bluntschli says, both forms involve the rule of priests.   We may
fairly regard the governments as theocratic monarchies or aristocracies.

[1] *Pol.* viii 1 1301 b 39 μάλιστα δύο γίνονται πολιτεῖαι δῆμος καὶ ὀλιγαρχία.

[2] Cf. Ar. *Pol.* vi 3 1290 a 15: popular classification recognised only
oligarchy (including aristocracy) and democracy (including polity).

[3] *Ib.* vi 8 1293 b 29 διὰ τὸ πασῶν ἥκιστα ταύτην εἶναι πολιτείαν.

no separate and independent basis of its own[4].' In practice
also this holds good; for kingship, which is defined as the
government of willing subjects, requires the consent and
support of a class of nobles. The rise of aristocracies in
Greece involved the transfer of supreme power from the
king to the nobles, but the king was in many states
retained as the nominal head of the constitution[5]. Hence
it comes that Aristotle, leaving out of view the monarchies
in the semi-barbarous and backward states of Greece,
regards kingship merely as a life magistracy[6]. No one
would have thought of calling the Spartan constitution a
kingship, because it had two hereditary generals who held
office for life.

Classing kingship, therefore, with aristocracy and
omitting tyranny from consideration we have only left
the governments of the few and of the many: oligarchy
and aristocracy on the one hand and democracy and polity
on the other. Polity (which is discussed more fully below)
denotes either a moderate popular government or a government of mixed oligarchic and democratic elements. It
thus forms a link between oligarchy and democracy, and
in some constitutions the fusion of these elements is so

---

[4] Henkel, *Studien zur Geschichte der griechischen Lehre vom Staat*,
p. 57. Cf. Austin, *Jurisprudence* Lect. vi. 'Limited monarchy is not
monarchy. It is one or another of those infinite forms of aristocracy,
which result from the infinite modes, wherein the sovereign number may
share the sovereign power.' Aristotle ranks it with aristocracy (*Pol.* iii
16 1287 a 3 ὁ μὲν γὰρ κατὰ νόμον λεγόμενος βασιλεὺς οὐκ ἔστιν εἶδος πολιτείας; viii 10 1310 b 2 ἡ βασιλεία κατὰ τὴν ἀριστοκρατίαν ἐστίν) except in
the ideal form of παμβασιλεία (iii 14 1285 b 31).

[5] See § 24.

[6] Ar. *Pol.* iii 14 1285 a 6 αὕτη μὲν οὖν ἡ βασιλεία οἷον στρατηγία τις
αὐτοκράτωρ καὶ ἀίδιος ἐστίν.

complete that the same government may bear the name either of oligarchy or democracy[7]. There is, then, no sharp line of cleavage between oligarchies and democracies ; and different opinions might be held about the definition of a particular constitution. For where governments are classified according to the relative numbers of the ruling class and the entire community, some may regard as an oligarchy what others will consider a democracy[8], and Aristotle says that what in his day would have been called a polity, was in earlier times described as a democracy[9].

We must, therefore, arrive at a more precise definition of oligarchy. As the word implies, it originally denoted simply the government of the few, whatever the test was by which they were chosen from the many[10]. 'Aristocracy' was also used popularly to denote the same thing[11], and

[7] Ar. *Pol.* vi 9 1294 b 14.

[8] Cf. Austin, *Jurisprudence* Lect. vi.

[9] *Pol.* vi 13 1297 b 24 διόπερ ἃς νῦν καλοῦμεν πολιτείας, οἱ πρότερον ἐκάλουν δημοκρατίας. A good instance is afforded by Syracuse. It is clear from Thucydides (vi 39) that he regarded the constitution in 415 as a democracy: Aristotle (*Pol.* viii 4 1304 a 2) describes it as a polity. The term πολιτεία seems to have been in general use as a complimentary description of democracy. Cf. Ar. *Eth.* viii 12 1160 a 33 πολιτείαν αὐτὴν εἰώθασιν οἱ πλεῖστοι καλεῖν ; Harp. *s. v.* ἰδίως εἰώθασι τῷ ὀνόματι χρῆσθαι οἱ ῥήτορες ἐπὶ τῆς δημοκρατίας ; Dem. xv 20 ; Isocr. iv 125.

[10] Hdt. iii 80 uses ὀλιγαρχίη of the government of the ἄριστοι. Ar. *Pol.* viii 1 1306 b 24 defines aristocracy as a sort of oligarchy: vi 3 1290 a 16 the popular definition included aristocracy under the title ὀλιγαρχία. Plutarch *l.c.* uses ὀλιγαρχία to denote the *good* form.

[11] Thrasymachus in Plato, *Rep.* i 338 D. Thuc. iii 82 says that ἀριστοκρατία σώφρων was a party catchword of the oligarchs: but he himself uses ἀριστοκρατία in a general sense in viii 64. Cf. Xen. *Hell.* v 2 7 οἱ ἔχοντες τὰς οὐσίας...ἀριστοκρατίᾳ ἐχρῶντο.

2

' dynasty' was also employed in a general sense[12]. The writers, however, who differentiated constitutions by their ethical qualities used aristocracy to denote the good form of the rule of the few and oligarchy to denote the bad, though even in this respect the usage was not consistent[13].

Taking number only into account, we may define oligarchy as a form of government in which supreme power is held by a privileged class, small in proportion to the total number of free men in the state[14]. To complete our definition we must take into account the basis of privilege and of exclusion, a subject discussed in the following sections. The classification of Greek constitutions is complicated by the class divisions, which generally existed. The slaves or serfs may be omitted from consideration, but there existed in many states a class of free subjects, and this class we must regard in defining the character of a constitution. In so doing we may conflict with the usage of some Greek writers. The political theory of the Greeks was not clearly or consistently formulated, and we have a striking instance of the vagueness of Greek writers in their treatment of the Spartan constitution.

The Spartiates were a comparatively small part of the free population of Laconia, ruling not only over the Helots

---

[12] Plato, *Politicus* 291 D. It generally denotes a narrow and absolute oligarchy.

[13] Aristotle uses these terms in all three passages (quoted above). Plato, *Politicus* 301 A, also does so. In the *Republic* viii 545 c he uses τιμοκρατία to denote the first deviation from the ideal ἀριστοκρατία. Xen. *Mem.* iv 6 12 denotes the ordinary oligarchy by πλουτοκρατία; Plutarch *l.c.* uses δυναστεία.

[14] Professor Freeman, *Comparative Politics* p. 194, defined oligarchy as the constitution 'in which political rights belong to only a part of those who enjoy civil rights'; he should at least have said a minority.

who were serfs, but over the Perioeci who were subject
but not enslaved. Greek writers, in their general ignorance
of Lacedaemonian institutions, formed different concep-
tions of the constitution.   Some excluded the Perioeci,
others took them into account[15].   Aristotle tells us that
many wished to call the government a democracy, others
an oligarchy[16]: it was said to be compounded of oligarchy,
monarchy and democracy[17], and he defines it himself as a
mixture of aristocratic and democratic elements[18]. Isocrates
in the *Panathenaicus* defines the constitution of Lycurgus
as democracy mixed with aristocracy[19]; but in another
treatise he says that the Lacedaemonians were governed
by an oligarchy[20]. The uncertainty and inconsistency of
the Greek writers leaves us to form our own definition,
and in the light of present knowledge we conclude that
the Spartan constitution, so peculiarly compounded of
diverse elements as to evade exact definition, must alike
from the form of its institutions, the spirit of its administration, and the exercise of sovereign power, be
included among the oligarchies of Greece.   It is distinguished more particularly below as an aristocracy[21].

[15] Isocrates xii 178 calls the perioeci δῆμος, as if they were part of a
Spartan oligarchy.   Aristotle on the other hand (*Pol.* ii 6 1270 b 18)
confines this term to the Spartiates.

[16] *Pol.* vi 7 1294 b 19.

[17] *Ib.* ii 6 1265 b 35.

[18] *Ib.* vi 7 1293 b 16; cf. ii 9 1270 b 16 (owing to the power of the
Ephors) δημοκρατία ἐξ ἀριστοκρατίας συνέβαινεν; Plato, *Laws* iv 712 D.   In
Pol. viii 7 1307 a 34 and 12 1316 a 33 Aristotle describes the Spartan
constitution as an aristocracy.

[19] xii 153; cf. vii 61, xii 178.

[20] iii 24.

[21] See §§ 6 and 32.

§ 4. *Oligarchy in a special sense.*

I proceed to the more precise definition of the '*Government of the few.*' Oligarchy in general includes both oligarchy in a special sense and aristocracy, while polity, although classed by Aristotle with democracies, sometimes denoted the government of a minority, and must not, therefore, be omitted from consideration.

Aristotle recognises that *oligarchy* is distinguished from democracy by other principles than those of number, and at the outset he corrects his definition by adding the test of poverty and wealth[1]. Any constitution, in which wealth confers the privileges of citizenship[2], whether the rulers be few or many, must be regarded as an oligarchy[3]. He even argues that if a constitution existed in which a thousand wealthy men ruled over three hundred poor men, excluded from the rights of citizenship, no one would call it a democracy[4]. At the same time economic

---

[1] The difficulty of including the idea of both number and wealth in the definition of oligarchy and democracy is discussed in *Pol.* iii 8 1279 b.

[2] I use *citizen* throughout this essay in the strict sense given to the word by Aristotle, as one possessed of political privilege: πολίτης δ' ἁπλῶς οὐδενὶ τῶν ἄλλων ὁρίζεται μᾶλλον ἢ τῷ μετέχειν ἀρχῆς (*Pol.* iii 1 1275 a 22). Aristotle quotes other definitions, which he rejects. In iii 7 1279 a 31 he regards participation in the weal of the state as essential, but in iv 13 1322 a 33 he refers to 'citizens who share in the constitution' as if the title included others who were excluded. As he says (iii 1 1275 a 3) the citizen in a democracy would not be a citizen in an oligarchy. Whether the *title* would have been conferred on the unprivileged class in an oligarchy we do not know.

[3] *Pol.* iii 8 1280 a 1 ἀναγκαῖον ὅπου ἂν ἄρχωσι διὰ πλοῦτον ἄν τ' ἐλάττους, ἄν τε πλείους, εἶναι ταύτην ὀλιγαρχίαν.

[4] *Pol.* vi 4 1290 a 30; at the same time Aristotle (*ib.* b 15), citing the

forces lead to the concentration of wealth, and it may be assumed as a safe general rule that the rich are the few, the poor the many[5]. There is, perhaps, no absolute reason why wealth should be so important an element in the classification of constitutions ; but, as a matter of history, power in the Greek cities had passed into the hands either of the rich or of the many, and if we except the old, traditional aristocracies, all the constitutions known to Aristotle were based either on wealth (the defining principle of oligarchy) or liberty (the defining principle of democracy)[6].

The definition given in the *Politics* is consistent with the general theory of the Greeks. In the *Ethics*[7] Aristotle says 'wealth and ascendency[8]' are the basis of oligarchy : in the *Rhetoric* it is the government in which 'those who have the assessment' rule[9]. Xenophon, who uses the term plutocracy, gives the same definition. Plato in the *Republic* uses the same description and further says 'the

case of Colophon, where there was a *majority* of rich men, refuses to the constitution the title of oligarchy.

[5] *Ib.* 1290 b 2 λεκτέον ὅτι δῆμος μέν ἐστιν ὅταν οἱ ἐλεύθεροι κύριοι ὦσιν, ὀλιγαρχία δὲ ὅταν οἱ πλούσιοι, ἀλλὰ συμβαίνει τοὺς μὲν πλείους εἶναι, τοὺς δ' ὀλίγους. This may be accepted as the final definition. No rule can be laid down either for the amount of wealth required, or for the proportion of the ὀλίγοι to the rest of the population; but it is clear that the ordinary oligarchs expected the government to be in the hands of a small minority. Thus Thuc. viii 92 11 says the 400 at Athens would not appoint the 5000 τὸ καταστῆσαι μετόχους τοσούτους ἀντικρυς δῆμον ἡγούμενοι, i.e. to impart the government to about a fourth of the total citizen population would be 'downright democracy.' See also the next section.

[6] Ar. *Pol.* vi 8 1294 a 10.

[7] I refer throughout to the passages cited above § 2 n. 3.

[8] δύναμις (which I translate 'ascendency') is used in a special sense, which I discuss below, § 35 n. 7.

[9] οἱ ἀπὸ τιμημάτων.

rich rule and the poor man has no share[10].' In the *Politicus* he defines both aristocracy and oligarchy as the government of the rich. The element of wealth was therefore generally recognised as an essential condition of oligarchy.

§ 5.   *Polity.*

Of course there were governments based upon a money qualification which the Greeks did not regard as oligarchies. We are not able to determine the minimum amount of property qualifying for privilege in an oligarchy, but it is necessary to discuss how far we should include the *polity* within our general definition. The polity forms the link between oligarchy and democracy[1], and intermediate forms are naturally difficult to classify. But there is no doubt that, however he defines it, Aristotle ranks polity with democracy and not with oligarchy. In the first place it denotes the normal democracy, in which 'the multitude rules for the common interest[2].' Secondly, it denotes a mixed constitution inclining more to democracy than to oligarchy[3], or a mixed constitution of rich and poor[4]. Neither of these descriptions justifies us in associating it with oligarchy, but another definition employed by Aristotle shows that he conceived it to be a

---

[10] viii 550 c ἡ ἀπὸ τιμημάτων πολιτεία ἐν ᾗ οἱ μὲν πλούσιοι ἄρχουσι, πένητι δ' οὐ μέτεστιν ἀρχῆς. Throughout the description of oligarchy (550 c to 551 B) Plato lays the greatest stress on wealth and money making.

[1] *Pol.* ii 6 1265 b 27 μήτε δημοκρατία μήτε ὀλιγαρχία, μέση δὲ τούτων, ἥν καλοῦσι πολιτείαν. On the general use of the term see § 3 n. 9.

[2] *Pol.* iii 7 1279 a 37. Many other passages confirm this: cf. especially vi 3 1290 a 18.

[3] *Ib.* vi 8 1293 b 33.

[4] *Ib.* vi 8 1294 a 22.

government based on a moderate census, in which power
was entrusted to a minority. In three passages he defines
it as the constitution of those 'who bear arms[5],' and it is
obvious that he means those men of moderate property,
who were able to equip themselves and serve as hoplites[6].
This, either directly or indirectly, implies a property
qualification, and there are several passages in which it is
implied that the men of moderate property will be the
ruling element[7]. Lastly in the *Ethics* he defines it as a
'timocratic' constitution, based on the assessment of property, i.e. he applies to it the identical terms used elsewhere to define oligarchy[8].

Polity, then, was used to denote a moderate timocracy,
the constitution of the middle class. It is clear from the
few *data* that we have, that the hoplite census would
only admit a minority to privilege[9]. This minority would
however be so large, and the property qualification would

---

[5] *Pol.* ii 6 1265 b 28; iii 7 1279 b 3; iii 17 1288 a 12.

[6] Hoplite service, whether regarded as a duty or a privilege, was not
usually undertaken by poor men. Aristotle, *Pol.* vii 7 1321 a 12, says
τὸ γὰρ ὁπλιτικὸν τῶν εὐπόρων ἐστὶ μᾶλλον ἢ τῶν ἀπόρων. This is a care-
less statement at variance with his definition of the πολιτεία.

[7] Thus one method of forming a polity is to split the difference (of
τίμημα) between oligarchy and democracy: *Pol.* vi 8 1294 b 5. In viii 6
1306 b 9 the τίμημα must be so arranged in a πολιτεία as to admit οἱ
μέσοι.

[8] *Ethics l.c.* τιμοκρατική...ἐκ τιμημάτων, identical with the definition of
oligarchy in the *Rhetoric*, and with that implied throughout the *Politics*.

[9] Beloch, *Bevölkerung* p. 70 (to take the instance of Athens), concludes
that the proportion of hoplites to thetes at the beginning of the Peloponnesian war was about 15/16,000 to 19/20,000. If we are to lay any
stress on Lys. xx 14 (see below, Appendix C), there were perhaps 9,000
hoplites in 411, and the total number of citizens of full age must have
been over 20,000.

be so moderate, that Aristotle would refuse to include the constitution under the term oligarchy[10], but unless we accept his definition absolutely, we cannot omit from consideration a government analogous in every way to oligarchy, based upon the same kind of qualification and differing from it solely in degree.

Of governments based upon wealth there must have been many gradations from the moderate polity, in which perhaps almost half the freemen ruled, to the extreme, narrow oligarchy, in which a few men, concentrating all power in their own hands, controlled the government in their own interest.

§ 6.   *Aristocracy.*

The inconsistency and confusion of Greek political terminology is illustrated by the use of the title *Aristocracy.* While popular usage made it a mere equivalent for oligarchy[1], the philosophers chose the term to describe the ideal state[2], the only constitution, according to Aristotle, justly entitled to the name[3]. But it was in general

[10] He seems to have considered a high census essential to oligarchy. Thus in *Pol.* vi 11 1296 a 14 he tells us that the moderately wealthy citizens are found in greater numbers in democracies than in oligarchies. Cf. iii 5 1278 a 22 ἐν δὲ ταῖς ὀλιγαρχίαις...ἀπὸ τιμημάτων μακρῶν αἱ μεθέξεις τῶν ἀρχῶν. See above § 4 n. 5.

[1] See above § 3 n. 11.

[2] Plato *Rep.* iv 445 D applies the term ἀριστοκρατία to the ideal state, reserving τιμοκρατία (viii 547 D) to describe the better type of oligarchy which in the *Politicus* (301 A) is called ἀριστοκρατία. Aristotle uses ἀριστοκρατία for the best state, but he is not consistent.

[3] *Pol.* vi 7 1293 b 3 τὴν γὰρ ἐκ τῶν ἀρίστων ἀπλῶς πολιτείαν κατ' ἀρετὴν καὶ μὴ πρὸς ὑπόθεσίν τινα ἀγαθῶν ἀνδρῶν μόνην δίκαιον προσαγορεύειν ἀριστοκρατίαν.

use and was too convenient to be renounced, and Aristotle
himself applies it to actual as well as to ideal constitutions.
The normal government of the few he calls Aristocracy[4],
thereby putting it on a level with monarchy and polity:
the rule of the nobles in early Greece is similarly described[5], and there are passages enough in the *Politics* to
show that there were governments existing in his own
day, to which Aristotle would not deny the title[6].

Aristocracy, however, is usually defined by Greek
writers in moral terms, so that it is difficult to reduce it
to ordinary principles of classification. As the normal form
of the government of the few, it differs from oligarchy in
the political qualification. In place of wealth, the qualification of the oligarchy proper, 'virtue' or 'merit[7]' or
'education[8]' is substituted, and the ruling class is described
as 'the best[9],' 'the good[10],' 'the wisest[11]' or 'the men of
worth[12].' Any process of selection which tended to assign

[4] *Pol.* iii 7 1279 a 34 (he there shows that he is following popular
usage—καλεῖν εἰώθαμεν).

[5] The use of the title is implied in *Pol.* iii 15 1286 b.

[6] Aristocracies are spoken of as actual constitutions frequently in the
sixth and eighth books. Cf. for example viii 8 1308 a 3.

[7] *Pol.* vi 8 1294 a 10 ἀριστοκρατίας ὅρος ἀρετή. It is defined again and
again as the government κατ' ἀρετὴν or κατ' ἀξίαν. (See *Politics passim*
and *Ethics* l.c.)

[8] On παιδεία see below, nn. 25—28.

[9] *Pol.* iii 7 1279 a 34 (where another definition is suggested): cf. Hdt.
iii 81.

[10] *Pol.* iii 15 1286 b 4.

[11] Polybius vi chs. 3—10 defines aristocracy as the government administered ὑπὸ τῶν δικαιοτάτων καὶ φρονιμωτάτων κατ' ἐκλογήν.

[12] ἐπιεικεῖς (a word constantly used in this connection by Aristotle, cf.
Pol. iii 10 1281 a 28; 12 1283 a 16) is difficult to translate, as it seems
to combine a moral sense (fair, reasonable) with a social application
(respectable, decent).

power in accordance with merit was said to be aristocratic[13], and some constitutions, which in other respects might be regarded as oligarchies or democracies, by the exercise of this principle acquired an aristocratic element[14].

If we accept the definition in a purely moral sense it is obvious that the term aristocracy can only have an ideal application. Virtue in the abstract can only be made the test of citizenship in Utopia; in the world of facts there is no infallible means of excluding the base and worthless. In a political connexion virtue must bear a relative and conventional sense, and I proceed to enquire what formal tests can be applied to define the actual aristocracy. The virtue of the citizen, as Aristotle says, is relative to the state[15]; and the term may be used in a conventional sense to denote the qualities, which may be predicated of a ruling class[16]. In this sense it is the attribute of power, and the qualities implied are generally the qualities of the warrior and the ruler. Considered historically these were found in the early constitutions only in certain

[13] *Pol.* vi 7 1293 b 10 ὅπου γε ἀριστίνδην αἱροῦνται τὰς ἀρχὰς αὕτη ἡ πολιτεία ἀριστοκρατικὴ καλεῖται; cf. ii 11 1273 a 25. The election of archons described in Ar. *Ath. Pol.* 8 2 (cf. Philoch. 58, F. H. G. i 394) was aristocratic and the process of δοκιμασία was, in intention, aristocratic.

[14] Cf. *Pol.* viii 7 1307 a. The Solonian democracy was regarded as having an aristocratic character (Isocr. xii 131): Pericles claims the same character for the fully developed democracy (Thuc. ii 37 ἕκαστος...ἀπ᾽ ἀρετῆς προτιμᾶται).

[15] *Pol.* iii 3 1276 b 30 τὴν ἀρετὴν ἀναγκαῖον εἶναι τοῦ πολίτου πρὸς τὴν πολιτείαν. Cf. vi 7 1293 b 6.

[16] It is obvious that ἀρετή is used in a restricted sense; Aristotle (*Pol.* iii 12 1283 a 20) mentions δικαιοσύνη and πολεμικὴ ἀρετή as the attributes of the ἐπιεικεῖς (the ruling class of an aristocracy). Xen. *Resp. Lac.* 10 7 alludes to πολιτικὴ ἀρετή. So Montesquieu (Preface to *Esprit des Lois*) uses virtue in an absolutely arbitrary sense.

privileged families, who were the foremost in war and alone entitled to have any share in the government[17]. Constitutions in which power was transmitted by hereditary descent marked a stage of political development. They were called aristocracies; and the rulers arrogated to themselves the titles of 'best' and 'good'; and expected that their subjects should so regard and so describe them[18]. In the absolute separation of social classes such an identification of power with virtue[19] was natural and to a certain extent reasonable[20].

Many governments, in which power was restricted to certain noble families, survived in later times, and unless they had degenerated into the narrow and oppressive type known as a 'dynasty[21],' they would naturally be described as aristocracies. If, then, we consider the historical application of the word it appears at first sight strange that Aristotle did not introduce the qualification of noble birth in his definition of aristocracy. But the political

[17] The diffusion of '$ἀρετή$' among a larger number led to the institution of aristocracies; on these constitutions see § 24.

[18] The use of moral titles to denote social classes is found even in Homer and Hesiod. It needs no illustration. Cf. Grote ii p. 64 'The epithets of good and just are euphemisms arising from submission and fear.'

[19] Cf. De Parieu, *La Science Politique*[2] p. 56 'L'aristocratie a toujours en fait désigné le gouvernement des plus puissants plutôt que celui des plus vertueux.'

[20] Freeman, *Comparative Politics* pp. 266—7 'In aristocratic commonwealths...there was for ages something which it needed no great straining of language to call the rule of the best. Morally best I do not say, but best so far as this, that narrow as was the government of those commonwealths, fenced in as the state was within a circle of exclusive houses, these houses at least knew how to rule, and how to hand on the craft of the ruler from generation to generation.' Mr Warde Fowler, *The City State* pp. 93 ff., ranks the merits of the aristocracy even higher.

[21] See § 35 below.

development of the Greeks had tended in most states to transfer privilege from birth to wealth or to numbers; in others in which the privilege of birth was still maintained the government had become narrow and despotic. Noble birth had lost its glamour, and Aristotle, though he does not overlook its political importance, prefers to define it in terms of the qualities, which it most generally implied. Thus he defines it as hereditary virtue[22] or as the conjunction of virtue and ancient wealth[23]: and in explaining the varieties of oligarchical constitutions he enumerates as qualities of the notables wealth, good birth, virtue and education[24]. Of these qualities wealth is the characteristic of the oligarchy proper, and one of the attributes of good birth. Virtue, as we have seen, stands for certain qualities of the ruling class, but education adds a new element for consideration.

We know of no instance in which education in the sense of general culture formed a qualification for citizenship, but in certain states of Greece, of which Sparta and Crete were the most eminent[25], a rigid system of training

[22] *Pol.* iii 12 1283 a 36 ἀρετὴ γένους.

[23] *Ib.* vi 8 1294 a 21 ἀρετὴ καὶ πλοῦτος ἀρχαῖος; viii 1 1301 b 3 προγόνων ἀρετὴ καὶ πλοῦτος. It is worth noting that ἀρετή and ὄλβος (ancestral wealth) are the attributes constantly mentioned by Pindar as essential to success in the games, which was, in his time, the ambition of the aristocratic houses of Greece.

[24] *Pol.* vi 4 1291 b 28 τῶν δὲ γνωρίμων πλοῦτος εὐγένεια ἀρετὴ παιδεία. Cf. *ib.* 12 1296 a 17 where the elements of 'quality' in a state are described as πλοῦτος παιδεία εὐγένεια. Diod. i 28 5 in defining the Eupatrids as ἐν παιδείᾳ μάλιστα διατετριφότες ascribes to them one of the usual characteristics of nobility.

[25] Sparta and Crete both kept up a rigid system of training under state control. We do not know whether such a system was maintained elsewhere; but it is quite possible that some of the Dorian colonies (such

under state control was maintained. This training, carried
out in accordance with traditional rules[26] and directed to
inculcate habits of patriotism and obedience and to fit the
citizen for the duties of war, was supposed to be productive
of 'political virtue[27].' Governments, therefore, based on
such a system of training were properly classified as
aristocracies, and their characteristic features did in fact
supply the terms of a definition of aristocracy both to
Xenophon and to Aristotle[28].

This brief survey suffices to show that the Greek conception of aristocracy does permit us to apply formal
principles of classification; that constitutions based on
birth or training might both be included among the
'governments of virtue,' and inasmuch as the system of
training was usually maintained only within a privileged
class the Greek definition of aristocracy, in its application

as Thera) and some of the smaller Dorian states (such as Epidaurus)
may have practised it.

[26] The training was based upon 'ordinances' (νόμιμα), which I take to
denote traditional (and probably unwritten) laws. Cf. *Eth.* x 9 1179 34
αἱ μὲν γὰρ κοιναὶ ἐπιμέλειαι δῆλον ὅτι διὰ νόμων γίνονται. On νόμιμα cf.
the passages quoted in note 28, and the descriptions of Sparta quoted
below § 32.

[27] Omitting the particular evidence of Sparta (on which see § 32
below), Ar. *Pol.* vi 7 1293 b 12 talks of states that make κοινὴ ἐπιμέλεια
ἀρετῆς. Cf. iii 12 1283 a 25 on the association of παιδεία and ἀρετή.
Mr Hicks in his note says that Aristotle uses the words interchangeably.

[28] Xen. *Mem.* iv 6 12. In an aristocracy offices are appointed ἐκ τῶν
τὰ νόμιμα ἐπιτελούντων. (These are the rules of training.) Ar. *Rhet.* i 8
1365 b 34 adopts and enlarges this definition. ἀριστοκρατία ἐν ᾗ οἱ κατὰ
παιδείαν (διανέμονται τὰς ἀρχάς). παιδείαν δὲ λέγω τὴν ὑπὸ τοῦ νόμου
κειμένην. οἱ γὰρ ἐμμεμενηκότες ἐν τοῖς νομίμοις ἐν τῇ ἀριστοκρατίᾳ ἄρχουσιν.
ἀνάγκη δὲ τούτους φαίνεσθαι ἀρίστους. Cf. *Pol.* vi 15 1299 b 25 οἱ πεπαι-
δευμένοι are described as the governing class in an aristocracy. We may
compare the importance attached to education in the ideal states of both

to actual constitutions, does not differ seriously from our own.

§ 7. *Aristocracy, Oligarchy and Polity.*

I have now concluded the definition of the three terms applied to 'the government of the few.' We trace a radical distinction between aristocracy, the government based on ' virtue,' and oligarchy, the government based on wealth. It is unnecessary to emphasize the contrast. The old aristocracies of birth and training, the origin of whose institutions was lost in a period of mythical romance, were preserved by the prescription of social and religious privilege from change or revolution; they held aloof from commerce and made their whole life a preparation for war[1].

Of the oligarchies based on wealth some few perhaps had been developed without violence out of the older aristocratic governments: but most of them were the offspring of revolutions, creations designed to meet new social conditions or instituted on the first foundation of a commercial colony. Wealth was the principle of the constitution, and wealth the aim of the citizens. A majority of freemen, who lacked the qualifying amount of property, were altogether excluded from citizenship, while the government was controlled by a small number of citizens, whose efforts were often directed to make still

Plato and Aristotle. Cf. also Ephorus 67, F. H. G. i 254, who traces the ill-success of the Boeotians to the fact that they had no ἀγωγὴ or παιδεία.

[1] I am speaking of aristocracies in the period after constitutional development was completed. In the earlier period there were many aristocracies actively engaged in trade, both in Greece and the colonies. See § 25, n. 14.

more narrow the circle of the governors. Analogous to this government but on a more equitable basis was the polity, a constitution resembling oligarchy in the exclusion of the poor and in the privilege ascribed to property, but differing from it in the low census required and the proportionately larger number included within the citizen body.

§ 8.   *The basis of Oligarchy and Democracy.*

All constitutions, according to Aristotle, are based on some principle of justice or equality[1]; in other words there must be in the governing body some qualification, which forms the basis of privilege, some one respect in which all citizens, *qua* citizens, are equal[2]. The democrat claimed that all the freemen of the state were equal : he, therefore, based his claim on 'freedom[3].' Equality, however, is not a mere question of number: states are based on 'qualities,' as well as 'quantity[4]'; and there is as much injustice in giving equality of privilege to unequals, as in denying it to equals[5]. The truth is well expressed

[1] *Pol.* viii 1 1301 a 26.

[2] *Pol.* vi 11 1295 b 25 βούλεται δέ γε ἡ πόλις ἐξ ἴσων εἶναι καὶ ὁμοίων ὅτι μάλιστα. Cf. Isocr. iii 15 αἱ ὀλιγαρχίαι καὶ δημοκρατίαι τὰς ἰσότητας τοῖς μετέχουσι τῶν πολιτειῶν ζητοῦσι, καὶ τοῦτ' εὐδοκιμεῖ παρ' αὐταῖς, ἢν μηδὲν ἕτερος ἑτέρου δύνηται πλέον ἔχειν.

[3] See below § 9.

[4] *Pol.* vi 12 1296 b 16 ἔστι δὲ πᾶσα πόλις ἔκ τε τοῦ ποιοῦ καὶ ποσοῦ: *ib.* viii 1 1301 b 29 ἔστι δὲ διττὸν τὸ ἴσον· τὸ μὲν γὰρ ἀριθμῷ τὸ δὲ κατ' ἀξίαν ἐστίν.

[5] *Pol.* iii 9 1280 a 11 δοκεῖ ἴσον τὸ δίκαιον εἶναι καὶ ἔστιν ἀλλ' οὐ πᾶσιν ἀλλὰ τοῖς ἴσοις. Cf. Plato *Rep.* viii 558 c (of democracy) ἰσότητά τινα ὁμοίως ἴσοις τε καὶ ἀνίσοις διανεμόμενοι. Cf. Isocr. iii 14 δικαιότατον τὸ...μὴ τοὺς ἀνομοίους τῶν ὁμοίων τυγχάνειν.

by Montesquieu. 'There are always persons,' he says,
'distinguished by their birth, riches, or honours: but
were they to be confounded with the common people
and have only the weight of a single vote, like the rest,
the common liberty would be their slavery and they
would have no interest in supporting it....The share they
have, therefore, in the legislature, ought to be proportioned
to their other advantages in the state⁶.'

The three qualities, which claim equality of privilege,
are freedom, wealth and virtue (of which the two latter in
combination include the idea of good birth⁷). But good
birth and virtue are rare, and therefore democracy and
oligarchy are the common types of constitution⁸; and the
issue is limited to the rival claims of freedom and wealth.
The democrats from being equal in respect of freedom
regard themselves as entitled to absolute equality: the
oligarchs from being unequal in the matter of property
regard themselves as generally unequal and therefore seek
to have an advantage in the state⁹. The contest thus lies
between those who claim general equality and those who
claim general inequality; in other words between the
greater number and the greater property¹⁰.

The demands of oligarchy and democracy were irreconcilable: each asserted an indefeasible right to power:

⁶ *Esprit des Lois* Book xi c. 6. This corresponds to Aristotle's theory
of political justice. Cf. Ar. *Pol.* viii 3 1303 b 6 στασιάζουσι...ἐν ταῖς δημοκρατίαις οἱ γνώριμοι, ὅτι μετέχουσι τῶν ἴσων οὐκ ἴσοι ὄντες.

⁷ *Pol.* vi 8 1294 a 19.

⁸ *Pol.* viii 1 1301 b 39.

⁹ *Pol.* viii 1 1301 a 29.

¹⁰ *Pol.* vii 3 1318 a 18 φασὶ γὰρ οἱ δημοτικοὶ τοῦτο δίκαιον ὅ τι ἂν δόξῃ
τοῖς πλείοσιν οἱ δ' ὀλιγαρχικοὶ ὅ τι ἂν δόξῃ τῇ πλείονι οὐσίᾳ...ἔχει δ' ἀμφότερα
ἀνισότητα καὶ ἀδικίαν.

and to the impossibility of compromising the dispute we
may trace the bitterness and permanence of party strife
throughout Greek history.

§ 9. *The character of Democracy.*

It will scarcely be possible to form a just idea of
oligarchic sentiment without briefly considering the theory
of the democrats, which was rejected so vehemently by
the oligarchs. Democracy rested on the two principles of
'liberty' and 'equality[1].' Liberty has been explained to
mean free birth (the respect in which all citizens of a
democracy were equal)[2]. But the term was used to denote
a great deal more than that. It implies above all the
right of the free man to have his voice in the control of
the state, to be free from subjection to a superior class:
in fact the self-government of the many[3]. At the same
time it includes the greater measure of individual freedom
and independence from restraint, which distinguished the
Greek democracies from other constitutions[4].

[1] *Pol.* vi 4 1291 b 34 (ἐλευθερία καὶ ἰσότης). Cf. Thuc. ii 37 (τὸ ἴσον...
ἐλευθέρως πολιτεύομεν); Dem. xxi 67.

[2] Newman, *Introduction* p. 248 n. 1.

[3] The definition I give in the text is borne out by Aristotle, *Pol.* vii 2
1317 b 2 ἐλευθερίας δὲ ἓν μὲν τὸ ἐν μέρει ἄρχεσθαι καὶ ἄρχειν, *ib.* 11 ἓν δὲ τὸ
ζῆν ὡς βούλεταί τις. 'Ελευθερία frequently means 'self-government of the
people,' while δουλεία denotes subjection to a ruling class. Cf. [Xen.]
Resp. Ath. 1 9 ὁ δῆμος οὐ βούλεται...δουλεύειν (= be subjects of an
oligarchy) ἀλλ' ἐλεύθερος εἶναι καὶ ἄρχειν. Contrast *ib.* 3 11. Cf. Thuc.
viii 68 4 (where ἐλευθερία = self-government) and contrast iv 85; vi 40 2;
Xen. *Hell.* ii 3 24; Plato *Rep.* v 463 A B.

[4] Cf. Aristotle quoted in n. 3 and *Pol.* viii 9 1310 a 30 (δοκεῖ) ἐλεύθερον
καὶ ἴσον τὸ ὅ τι ἂν βούληταί τις ποιεῖν. Plato *Rep.* viii 562 lays stress on the
excess of liberty in democracies. Cf. Thuc. ii 39; vii 69 (ἡ ἐν αὐτῇ ἀνεπί-
τακτος πᾶσιν ἐς τὴν δίαιταν ἐξουσία); Dem. xxv 25. Cf. § 12 n. 17.

Equality implies first of all that in the collective exercise of power the voice of the majority shall prevail[5]. Aristotle is inclined to set a high value on the collective wisdom of the people[6], and it is a universal principle of democracy that 'government should rest on the active consent of the citizens[7].' But democracy tends to assert a second principle, which is of more importance: that 'any one self-supporting and law-abiding citizen is on the average as well qualified as another for the work of government[8].' This principle found a limited application in some Greek democracies, but Aristotle asserts the danger of admitting the people to the chief offices of government[9]. Thucydides represents Pericles as asserting that at Athens, while poverty was no bar to public service, men were advanced to honour on the claim of ' virtue ' (using the word as a protest against its oligarchic associations[10]). Athenagoras in defining democracy is made to assign privilege both to wealth and to wisdom, and to leave only the collective decision to the people[11]. We see, then, that the democratic idea of equality admitted of degrees. While it was considered essential that the people should possess collective power in the assembly and the law courts, it was only in the more highly-developed democracies that the equal qualification of all

---

[5] Ar. *Pol.* viii 9 1310 a 28 Democracy is defined $\tau\hat{\varphi}\ \tau\grave{o}\ \pi\lambda\epsilon\hat{\imath}o\nu\ \epsilon\hat{\imath}\nu a\iota$ $\kappa\acute{\nu}\rho\iota o\nu\ \kappa a\grave{\imath}\ \tau\hat{\eta}\ \grave{\epsilon}\lambda\epsilon\nu\theta\epsilon\rho\acute{\iota}\grave{q}.$ Cf. *ib.* vii 2 1317 b 5—10.

[6] *Pol.* iii 11 1281 a 40.

[7] Sidgwick, *Elements of Politics* p. 584.   [8] *ib.*

[9] *Pol.* iii 11 1281 b 25.

[10] ii 37.

[11] vi 39. This, it is true, is a description of a moderate democracy, not fully developed.

citizens for administrative office was recognised and enforced[12]. The principle of election by the vote of the people gave a better chance to men of wisdom and ability, and so far prevented the theory of equality being carried to logical absurdity. But though there were some offices, and these usually the most important, which were in all constitutions elective, the introduction of the lot was an assertion of the absolutely equal qualification of all citizens for the duties of the magistracies to which it was applied. The lot, then, was the sign that the principle of equality was duly recognised, and it was regarded as so essential a characteristic of democracy[13] that it was by some writers introduced into the definition of this constitution[14].

§ 10. *The character of Oligarchy.*

I proceed to consider the grounds on which the oligarchic ruler based his claim to power. While the democrat asserted the equal right of all free burghers not only to determine the policy of the state but to take his turn or stand his chance of exercising the active duties of government, the oligarch, equally with

[12] I should say that I am here referring to the method of election, not to the eligibility of citizens for office. It was a general characteristic of democracy that most magistrates at any rate should be elected ἐκ πάντων. Cf. Aristotle *Pol.* vii 2 1317 b for this and for the general characteristics of democracy.

[13] See J. W. Headlam, *Election by Lot* p. 12 ff. He lays stress (p. 32) on another aspect of the lot: it prevented the magistrate getting power at the expense of the Assembly. Cf. Ar. *Pol.* vii 2 1317 b 20.

[14] In the *Rhetoric* i 8 1365 b 32 Aristotle defines democracy as the Constitution ἐν ᾗ κλήρῳ διανέμονται τὰς ἀρχάς. Cf. Hdt. iii 80 πάλῳ μὲν ἀρχὰς ἄρχει.

the aristocrat, maintained that only a part of the community was qualified for political duties or justified in exercising political power. They adopted the hypothesis that certain classes which might be qualified by birth and wealth, or birth and training, or by wealth alone, were fit to rule over others, who were not fit to rule. As long as aristocracy lasted, the authority of the rulers was not questioned. They were separated from their subjects by ineradicable class divisions: their rule was consecrated by prescription and they alone knew the secrets of government. In such a society, as long as the position of the rulers is not challenged, their sovereignty needs no explanation; it would be impossible to imagine any other distribution of power[1].

But in course of time other social forces became dominant: the basis of privilege was widened; wealth took the place of birth, and the oligarch regarded himself as the heir of the aristocrat and asserted in virtue of his property an exclusive claim to rule. His claim did not go unchallenged. Aristocracy had been hedged by a divinity that prevented assault; it survived because it was not assaulted. But oligarchy rose on the downfall of aristocracy: it had won its position by force and by force it must maintain it or lose it. The 'age of discussion' began with the first break-up of the old governments, and henceforth constitutions had to struggle for existence. What then was the justification of oligarchy? The oligarchs reasserted the claims of the aristocrats. In wealth and in the power that it gives they were on the same level, and they were not concerned to recognise

[1] On the early aristocracies and the transition to oligarchy, see ch. ii § 24.

other differences. In early days, they might argue, power
was entrusted to 'the few,' and in every state 'the few'
are 'wiser' and 'better' than 'the many': 'the wise' and
'the good' are intended by nature to govern 'the base'
and 'the mean.' There is of course the fatal fallacy
underlying this theory, that it assumes that the few *rich*
are identical with the few *wise*; but it is typical of
oligarchic sentiment and it colours all oligarchic literature,
although it was rejected and reversed by the democrats[2].

[2] I am obliged to omit from consideration the most interesting
question of the political sentiment of Greek literature: but without
touching on details, a few general points may be noted. The early
writers with the exception of Hesiod took an aristocratic standpoint;
and after political change had begun they remained the champions of
aristocracy, opposed alike to tyranny, the rule of the many and the rule
of wealth. (Cf. Solon, Theognis and Alcaeus.) After democracy and
oligarchy had become the prevalent forms of government, the oligarch
tried to assert the same claim as the aristocrat; and just as he used
ἀριστοκρατία to denote ὀλιγαρχία so he was inclined to identify the few
with οἱ καλοὶ κἀγαθοί, οἱ χρηστοί, οἱ δυνατοί, the many with οἱ πονηροί, οἱ
μοχθηροί and the like: and to credit himself with εὐνομία, σωφροσύνη etc.
and his opponents with ὕβρις and other evil qualities. Some of these
terms almost lost their moral meaning and became simply party catch-
words; but the democrats used many of them with an absolutely opposite
application, hurling back on the oligarchs the very terms of abuse
applied to themselves and using every epithet of praise to describe
democracy (see above § 1 n. 5). If we consider the writers, who were
neither oligarchs nor democrats by sympathy (such as Thucydides, Plato,
and Aristotle), we find that they have censure enough for democracy.
'History is a sound aristocrat,' and most of these writers, living in
Athens, must have been keenly alive to the faults of democracy: but
History is no oligarch, and it would not be difficult to show that Greek
literature is even less in sympathy with oligarchy than it is with democracy.

§ 11. *Material claims of the Oligarch.*

This self-laudation, while it throws some light on the
mental attitude of the oligarchs, has little bearing on
their claims to rule. Their claims were both material
and moral. On the former they assumed that they were
better qualified to serve the state both in person and
property, and, to invert the modern apophthegm, they
might argue that property has its rights as well as its
duties. We know that in Athens the burden of taxation
was mostly borne by the rich, and we may conclude that
in the oligarchies also the rich were the chief contributors
to the revenue of the state[1]. We have only to consider
the enormous influence which phrases like ' taxation and
representation' have wielded in the modern world to
realise that to the oligarch this fact would seem to
constitute an indefeasible right to rule, and there are
many instances in which we find the claim asserted[2].

The rich man served the state also in person as a
hoplite, while the poor man fought, not at all or only as a
light-armed soldier; and the fact that the poor were thus
unable to protect their fatherland in war, must have

[1] In Ar. *Pol.* vi 4 1291 a 33 οἱ εὔποροι are defined as τὸ ταῖς οὐσίαις
λειτουργοῦν.

[2] Good instances occur in connection with the establishment of the
Four Hundred. Thus it was proposed to entrust power τούτοις οἳ ἂν
μάλιστα τοῖς τε χρήμασι καὶ τοῖς σώμασιν ὠφελεῖν οἷοί τε ὦσιν (Thuc. viii 65:
cf. Ar. *Ath. Pol.* 29). The conspirators were ready ἐσφέρειν ἐκ τῶν ἰδίων
οἴκων προθύμως...ὡς οὐκέτι ἄλλοις ἢ σφίσιν αὐτοῖς ταλαιπωροῦντας (Thuc.
viii 63). The claim is very prominent in the speech of the Boeotians
(Thuc. iii 65); they argue that a minority of rich men, *having a greater
stake in the city* (πλείω παραβαλλόμενοι) had a right to betray it in order
τὰ ἄξια ἔχειν. Cf. Ar. *Pol.* iii 12 1283 a 31.

seemed to the oligarch an unanswerable argument for his permanent exclusion from privilege[3]. Even to-day the ability at need to serve in the army is regarded by many as an essential condition of political enfranchisement[4], and in the city state of Greece, which was ever prepared for war, there was even stronger reason for such a provision[5]. But though the argument might be used against the poor, we must not forget that the ordinary oligarchy excluded from power many men who served as hoplites, and it was only in the polity that the qualification was sufficiently low to admit this class.

§ 12. *Moral claims of the Oligarch.*

The oligarch based his claim on other grounds. He argued, in effect, not only that he had a better right, than the poor man, to govern the state, but that he was better qualified to do so; while other classes were disqualified, alike physically and morally, from discharging political duties. I have pointed out that the oligarch assumed a moral and mental superiority, and there were, of course, elements of culture to which only the rich man could

[3] The satirical pamphlet on the Athenian Constitution practically assumes that public service should mean political power, and the author explains that the principle is really recognised at Athens, for the δῆμος are the source of the city's power more than the γενναῖοι and πλούσιοι and ὁπλῖται ([Xen.] *Resp. Ath.* 1 2).

[4] We may compare the conscription. The inability to serve furnishes a common argument against the enfranchisement of women.

[5] Cf. Freeman, *Comparative Politics*, p. 197 'In all primitive societies the distinction between soldier and civilian is unknown. Hence the army is the assembly, the assembly is the army.' Cf. the same author *Sicily* ii p. 62 where he argues (from Diod. xii 19) that it was originally the custom to wear arms in the assembly as a badge of citizenship.

attain¹: but the great advantage (according to the ideas
of the Greeks) possessed by the man of property lay in his
having leisure to practise the arts of war and of government, while the poor man not only lacked leisure, but was
obliged to follow employments, which were disqualifying
and degrading to body and mind. This subject is so
intimately connected with the attitude of the Greeks to
industry and commerce that we must briefly consider it.

In this matter we must distinguish the sentiment of
the old military aristocracies from that of the commercial
oligarchies. It has been suggested that the origin of the
contemptuous feeling for industry and trade should be
traced to the age of the migrations when the victorious
invaders possessed themselves of the best land and left
menial occupations to the subject-races². Hence a general
characteristic of the old military aristocracies was a definite
division of classes, which resulted in the practical exclusion
of the artisan and trader from the government. Some
states actually made 'money-making' a disqualification,
or forbade the 'banausic' arts to their citizens; an aristocracy, according to Aristotle, would render it impossible
for the labourer or mechanic or trader to be a citizen³;

¹ Cf. Ar. *Pol.* vi 8 1293 b 37 τὸ μᾶλλον ἀκολουθεῖν παιδείαν καὶ εὐγένειαν
τοῖς εὐπορωτέροις.

² Cf. Büchsenschütz, *Besitz und Erwerb* pp. 255 ff. See also Goll,
*Kulturbilder*³ pp. 162 ff. and Newman, *Introduction* pp. 98 ff.

³ Ar. *Pol.* iii 5 1278 a 19 'In an aristocratic state, in which power is
given κατ' ἀρετὴν and κατ' ἀξίαν, the βάναυσος and the θὴς cannot be citizens,'
οὐ γὰρ οἷόν τ' ἐπιτηδεῦσαι τὰ τῆς ἀρετῆς ζῶντα βίον βάναυσον ἢ θητικόν. Cf.
viii 12 1316 b 2 ἐν πολλαῖς τε ὀλιγαρχίαις οὐκ ἔξεστι χρηματίζεσθαι. Xen. *Oec.*
4 3 ἐν ἐνίαις μὲν τῶν πόλεων, μάλιστα δὲ ἐν ταῖς εὐπολέμοις δοκούσαις εἶναι,
οὐδ' ἔξεστι τῶν πολιτῶν οὐδενὶ βαναυσικὰς τέχνας ἐργάζεσθαι. Cf. Hdt. ii
167. For the few known particular instances of this prohibition see ch.
v § 50.

and in the ideal states of Plato and Aristotle the separation of the ruling class from those engaged in trade or the manual arts was rigidly carried out[4].

On the other hand the oligarchies of wealth could not exclude the rich traders and craftsmen[5], for they were commercial communities bent upon money-making and probably holding trade higher in esteem than it was held in a democracy of aristocratic feeling like Athens[6]: but for the artisan working for a wage the oligarch had the utmost contempt.

The Greeks regarded *leisure* as a necessary condition of a good life, and as in itself a source of happiness[7]. They had no feeling in favour of ' work for work's sake ': work was for them only the means and leisure the end[8]. Leisure was a necessity, not only for the proper training of the hoplite, which must have required constant practice[9], but above all for the due discharge of political duties[10]. The philosophers tended to make government

[4] The assignment of special functions to different orders in the state is the keynote of the *Republic*. Cf. especially iii 415 B C. In the *Laws* v 741 E Plato forbids money-making to the citizens; while Aristotle forbids the citizens of his ideal state to live a βίος βάναυσος or ἀγοραῖος or even to be γεωργοί (*Pol.* iv 9 1328 b 39). Cf. *Pol.* iii 5 1278 a 8 ἡ δὲ βελτίστη πόλις οὐ ποιήσει βάναυσον πολίτην.

[5] Cf. Ar. *Pol.* iii 5 1278 a 21 ἐν δὲ ταῖς ὀλιγαρχίαις θῆτα μὲν οὐκ ἐνδέχεται εἶναι πολίτην...βάναυσον δὲ ἐνδέχεται πλουτοῦσι γὰρ καὶ οἱ πολλοὶ τῶν τεχνιτῶν.

[6] Cf. S. H. Butcher *Aspects of the Greek Genius*[1] p. 73.

[7] *Pol.* v 3 1338 a 1 τὸ δὲ σχολάζειν ἔχειν αὐτὸ δοκεῖ τὴν ἡδονὴν καὶ τὴν εὐδαιμονίαν καὶ τὸ ζῆν μακαρίως.

[8] *Pol.* iv 14 1334 a 14 τέλος γὰρ σχολὴ ἀσχολίας.

[9] Plato *Rep.* ii 374 B C D asks ἡ περὶ τὸν πόλεμον ἀγωνία οὐ τεχνικὴ δοκεῖ εἶναι; Cf. Newman, *Introduction* p. 113.

[10] Cf. Aelian *V. H.* x 14 ἡ ἀργία ἀδελφὴ τῆς ἐλευθερίας. Ar. *Pol.* iv 9

and even citizenship a profession[11]; and though we need not suppose that any state reached this ideal, yet the rich man was able to find leisure for the discharge of his political duties, while the poor man could ill afford to sacrifice the time[12].

The quality which the Greeks called βαναυσία involved more than the denial of leisure; it implied positive defects which degraded the banausic man. Aristotle gives a definition of the term. 'That work or art or science must be considered banausic, which unfits the body or mind of free men for the employment and practice of virtue. Wherefore such arts as cause a worse condition of the body and works done for profit, we call banausic. For they deprive the mind of leisure and debase it[13].'

In their effects on the body banausic arts were regarded as a positive disqualification for the practice of warlike pursuits[14]. To this feeling, combined with the natural feeling of superiority felt by the rich towards the poor, we may attribute to a great extent the contempt of the higher classes for the lower orders[15].

1329 a 1 δεῖ γὰρ σχολῆς καὶ πρὸς τὴν γένεσιν τῆς ἀρετῆς καὶ πρὸς τὰς πράξεις τὰς πολιτικάς.

[11] Plato *Rep.* 374 E; *Laws* 846 D E.

[12] This explains the importance to democracies of pay in the law courts and assembly.

[13] *Pol.* v 2 1337 b 8: cf. iv 9 1329 a 20.

[14] Cf. Plato *Rep.* ii 374 C D and especially *ib.* vi 495 D; Xen. *Oec.* 4 2 αἵ γε βαναυσικαὶ καλούμεναι (τέχναι)...καταλυμαίνονται τὰ σώματα...ἀναγκάζουσαι καθῆσθαι καὶ σκιατραφεῖσθαι, ἔνιαι δὲ καὶ πρὸς πῦρ ἡμερεύειν. Cf. Bacon *Essay* 29 (quoted by Newman, *Introduction* p. 105) 'Sedentary and within door arts...have in their nature a contrariety to a military disposition.'

[15] Some of the epithets of abuse throw some light on class feeling. Thus δειλὸς (which occurs in Homer, Hesiod and Theognis) was chosen,

But the effects of banausic employments on the mind were considered more serious. They enslaved the soul[16]; they reduced those who practised them to the level of the non-citizens, the slaves and aliens; they deprived them of freedom of action and compelled them to live at the disposal of others[17]. They were, in fact, assumed to degrade the mind as they degraded the body and to render men unfit for the duties of political life[18].

The oligarch assumed then that wealth and leisure were necessary conditions of citizenship : that they conferred higher political ability than could be possessed by those who were compelled to gain a living by the exercise of laborious arts. The aristocrat went further and regarded money-making, whether pursued by industry or by commerce, as unworthy of a free man and as a positive disqualification for citizenship. In this respect, also, there was a marked contrast between the military aristocracy and the commercial oligarchy : for the former set a ban upon the arts and professions by which the latter was maintained ; and the sentiment of the philosophers in this respect is entirely aristocratic[19].

perhaps because it implied a craven, 'warless' man. So πονηρὸς and μοχθηρὸς may originally have had the same idea as βάναυσος.

[16] Xen. *Mem.* iv 2 22.

[17] Ar. *Rhet.* i 9 1367 a 31 ἐλευθέρου τὸ μὴ πρὸς ἄλλον ζῆν. (The same passage furnishes a humorous illustration of Greek feeling. It was considered the mark of a free man at Lacedaemon to wear the hair long οὐ γάρ ἐστιν κομῶντα ῥᾴδιον οὐδὲν ποιεῖν ἔργον θητικόν.) Cf. *Pol.* v 2 1337 b 17.

[18] Xen. *Oec.* 4 2 τῶν δὲ σωμάτων θηλυνομένων καὶ αἱ ψυχαὶ πολὺ ἀρρωστότεραι γίγνονται.

[19] Plato and Aristotle do not regard χρηματισμός with more favour than they regarded industry generally. In this respect they were entirely at variance with oligarchic sentiment.

But both constitutions agreed in requiring for citizenship some definite qualifications other than free birth, and in thus drawing an absolute line between citizen and non-citizen. They differed from democracy, moreover, in their whole conception of the method of government; and in every detail of the constitution, in the appointment of magistrates, in the powers conferred upon them, in the question of sovereignty, they showed their divergence from the democratic theory. But the full treatment of these subjects must be reserved to a later chapter[20].

[20] See chapter v.

CHAPTER II.

THE CAUSES OF CONSTITUTIONAL CHANGE.

§ 13. *The Variety of Greek Constitutions.*

IT would be difficult to assign a cause for the countless variety of constitutions that were to be found in the different Hellenic communities. The fact that each city formed an independent state and pursued its own political development made constitutional experiments easy and frequent; and the character of the Greeks and their political ability ensured an originality and diversity in these experiments.

'Infinite time,' says Plato, 'is the maker of cities'; and the origin of the old traditional monarchies and aristocracies is as difficult to trace in Greece as elsewhere. Many Greek states could, however, set dates to the invention of their constitutions: they recorded the time when some lawgiver cleared away the fabric of the old institutions to build up a new government on new principles that broke entirely with the past. Moreover the Greek cities could not all boast prehistoric foundations: the colonies, which sporadically diffused Greek influence from the eastern shores of the Pontus to Massalia, from Thrace to Libya, were planted at dates which the Greeks

themselves pretended to fix, and many of them at a time
when constitutional changes had already begun in Greece.

Hence there is a radical distinction to be drawn
between the old constitutions of prehistoric origin, consecrated by prescription, and the governments, invented in
a later age, founded on the deliberate principles of a lawgiver or instituted in imitation of the laws of some other
state. The 'historical constitutions,' gradually and spontaneously developed, had a far greater chance of permanence than the 'constitutions of recent invention[1].'
Governments like those of Sparta and Crete owed a
great deal of the credit which they enjoyed with the
Greeks to their stability. New ideas had not proved
able to break their continuity; status and custom had
not given place to contract and progress[2]. But in other
states the course of civilisation and the alteration of
political conditions had brought in the age of discussion;
social forces had been given free play, constitutional changes
were frequent and produced the diversity of governments,
which formed a striking contrast to the uniformity of type
in the early states.

§ 14.   *The Causes determining the form of a Constitution.*

All constitutions are the result either of spontaneous
growth or of deliberate invention: in either case they
must be adapted to the community in which they exist.
Forms of government are not equally applicable to all
states; and it is only their relative fitness that preserves

[1] On the 'historical' and the '*a priori* constitutions' see Maine,
Popular Government p. 172.

[2] See Bagehot, *Physics and Politics, passim.*

the old constitutions from change in the one case, or renders the new constitutions acceptable in the other. There must be a predominance of consent, and in case the community be divided, the supporters of the government must be stronger than its opponents[1]. They must also have force to maintain it; for 'force is an absolutely essential element of all law whatever. Law is nothing but regulated force, subjected to particular conditions[2].' Those classes, then, in which this element of force resides will naturally predominate and we arrive at the principle enunciated (with qualifications) by J. S. Mill: 'The government of a country, it is affirmed, is in all substantial respects fixed and determined beforehand by the state of the country in regard to the distribution of the elements of social power. Whatever is the strongest power in society will obtain the governing authority; and a change in the political constitution cannot be durable unless preceded or accompanied by an altered distribution of power in society itself.' Mill further defines the elements of power to be (besides the strength of numbers) property and intelligence and organisation; and the power must be not quiescent but active power, actually exerted[3]. If we add to this definition the element of prescription, the strength which the undisputed possession of authority gives to a class, which has been for some time in control of government, we may accept

[1] Ar. *Pol.* vi 12 1296 b 14 δεῖ γὰρ κρεῖττον εἶναι τὸ βουλόμενον μέρος τῆς πόλεως τοῦ μὴ βουλομένου μένειν τὴν πολιτείαν: cf. iv 9 1329 a 11; viii 9 1309 b 16. Xen. *Hell.* ii 3 19 Theramenes says ὁρῶ δύο ἡμᾶς τὰ ἐναντιώτατα πράττοντας, βιαιάν τε τὴν ἀρχὴν καὶ ἥττονα τῶν ἀρχομένων κατασκευαζομένους.

[2] Sir J. F. Stephen, *Liberty Equality and Fraternity*[2], p. 239.

[3] *Representative Government* ch. 1.

and apply the principle. Aristotle was not far from
realising the same theory. He, also, traces the varieties
of constitutions to varieties in the social system; every
city has different elements and classes[4]: there are rich
and poor; some are armed, some unarmed; there are
differences in the working classes, differences in the
notables[5]; and changes in the strength of social classes
tend to bring about changes in the constitution[6].

§ 15. *Changes of Constitutions effected from within.*

Constitutional changes either proceed from within the
community or are imposed from without: they are caused
either by the conflict of social forces or by the violent interference of a foreign power[1]. To consider first the
changes promoted from within, it is obvious that the
history of constitutions reflects the general history of the
race; and constitutional developments must be traced to
the movements, social and economic, military or religious,
which mark the progress or decline of a nation. These
movements will be alluded to more fully in the next
chapter, but a few general points may be noticed.

It follows from the definition of oligarchy and democracy as the governments of the few rich and of the many

[4] *Pol.* vi 12 1296 b 16 ἔστι δὲ πᾶσα πόλις ἔκ τε τοῦ ποιοῦ καὶ τοῦ ποσοῦ.
λέγω δὲ ποιὸν μὲν ἐλευθερίαν πλοῦτον παιδείαν εὐγένειαν, ποσὸν δὲ τὴν τοῦ
πλήθους ὑπεροχήν.

[5] *Pol.* vi 3 1289 b 27.

[6] *Pol.* viii 3 1302 b 33. What Aristotle says (*ib.* vii 1 1317 a 20) of
varieties of democracy, is true of other constitutions also. Variation is
due (1) to difference in the population, (2) to different combinations of
the elements of government.

[1] Ar. *Pol.* viii 7 1307 b 20 πᾶσαι δ' αἱ πολιτεῖαι λύονται ὁτὲ μὲν ἐξ αὐτῶν,
ὁτὲ δ' ἔξωθεν. Cf. also Plato *Rep.* viii 556 E.

poor that *economic changes* must have been the most
frequent cause that gave birth to these constitutions and
effected revolutions in them. Originally land was the
sole source of wealth and each state was for the most
part self-sufficient and self-supporting. While this condition prevailed power remained with the landowners, but
the diffusion of the Greek race in colonies, the spread of
commerce and navigation, the introduction of money as a
medium of exchange, altered the distribution of wealth
and tended to raise the commercial and industrial classes
to an equality with the landholding aristocracy. Henceforth economic forces had free play, and to these forces the
changes in the strength of classes must be chiefly attributed. Aristotle mentions the narrowing of oligarchies
caused by the concentration of property in the hands of a
few[2]; and the gradual development of democracy, as a
consequence of the alteration in the value of money[3].
Another cause of change lay in the actual decrease of the
numbers of different classes. Instances are quoted of the
loss suffered by the better classes in war leading to
democracy[4], while the tendency within governments
based on birth was to narrow the number of the privileged.

Military changes have often been instrumental in
effecting political revolutions. On the one hand the

[2] *Pol.* viii 7 1307 a 29.

[3] *Pol.* viii 6 1306 b 9.

[4] *Pol.* viii 3 1302 b 33 γίνονται δὲ καὶ δι’ αὔξησιν τὴν παρὰ τὸ ἀνάλογον
μεταβολαὶ τῶν πολιτειῶν. He refers to the disproportionate increase of the
δῆμος and cites instances of the losses of the γνώριμοι in war; and then
says σύμβαινει δὲ καὶ ἐν ταῖς δημοκρατίαις, ἧττον δέ· πλειόνων γὰρ δὴ τῶν
εὐπόρων γινομένων ἢ τῶν οὐσιῶν αὐξανομένων μεταβάλλουσιν εἰς ὀλιγαρχίας καὶ
δυναστείας. He cites several instances; cf. also *Ath. Pol.* 26 1.

W. 4

military superiority of an invading race, either in tactics
or in equipment, may make them masters of the state,
and to this superiority the 'aristocracies of conquest'
within Greece owed their origin. On the other hand
military causes may affect the strength of classes within
states. Aristotle associates oligarchy with cavalry and
hoplites, democracy with light-armed troops and the
fleet[5]; the introduction of hoplite tactics led to the admission of more men to citizenship[6]; the rise of maritime
power favoured the advance of democracy[7], and at a later
date the introduction of mercenary soldiers broke down in
some degree the power of the richer classes, who had
previously formed the main strength of the hoplites.

Religion is a force of the utmost importance in an
early state of society. There is then no clear separation
of the sacred and the profane; and in Greece the rulers
were also the priests. Under these conditions the political
power of the nobles cannot be broken, as long as they
alone can mediate with the gods: and it needed the break-
up of religious privilege and the introduction of new cults
to dissolve the old aristocracies and render democracy
possible[8]. Closely connected with this movement was
the overthrow of tribal organisation and of local influence.

The causes hitherto considered in this section have

[5] *Pol.* vii 7 1321 a 6 ff.

[6] *Pol.* vi 13 1297 b 23 τῶν ἐν τοῖς ὅπλοις ἰσχυσάντων μᾶλλον πλείους
μετεῖχον τῆς πολιτείας.

[7] *Pol.* viii 4 1304 a 22. See [Xen.] *Resp. Ath.* 1 2.

[8] On this subject the monograph of Fustel De Coulanges *La Cité
Antique* should of course be consulted, although the author tends to
exaggerate the importance of religious forces by excluding other considerations.

been those which operated mainly on social forces. But
when once the old aristocracies had been broken down
and the era of political conflict had begun, there were
factions to be reckoned with in every state. Parties in
Greece, so far as they were definitely distinguished, were
divided mainly by constitutional preferences. I called
attention in the last chapter to the irreconcilable con-
tentions of numbers and property, of oligarchs and
democrats; and this opposition was the cause of that
deeply-rooted political malady, which the Greeks called
στάσις[9]. In almost every state the two factions were to be
found; and unless one of them had a decisive superiority
over the other[10], there was a constant struggle for political
power, the government being the prize at stake[11]. In
the bitterness of party feeling help was sought by the
disaffected from other states, and in this way 'influences
from without' cooperated with 'causes from within.'

§ 16. *Changes of Constitutions effected from without.*

In the early period of Greek History the most important changes were effected by the conquest of an invading
race, who dispossessed or reduced the previous inhabitants

[9] Plato *Rep.* viii 545 D πᾶσα πολιτεία μεταβάλλει ἐξ αὐτοῦ τοῦ ἔχοντος
τὰς ἀρχάς, ὅταν ἐν αὐτῷ στάσις ἐγγένηται. Thucydides (iii 82) gives the
most forcible and incisive description of στάσις.

[10] This was the case at Athens for almost the whole history of her
democracy. There was, of course, the antithesis of oligarchs and democrats there (cf. Plut. *Per.* 11), but as I have argued in a previous essay,
Political Parties, pp. 34—5, parties there were divided more by questions
of the day than by fixed principles.

[11] Thuc. iii 82 οἱ γὰρ ἐν ταῖς πόλεσι προστάντες μετ' ὀνόματος ἑκάτεροι
εὐπρεποῦς, πλήθους τε ἰσονομίας πολιτικῆς καὶ ἀριστοκρατίας σώφρονος προτι-
μήσει, τὰ μὲν κοινὰ λόγῳ θεραπεύοντες ἆθλα ἐποιοῦντο.

and established their own power, as an aristocracy, ruling
in virtue of their conquest and of their power to maintain
what they had won. In later times there are few instances
in which conquest reduced a people to a state of absolute
subjection, but in many cases the form of the constitution
was determined either by the active interference of a
foreign power or by the support given to one faction in
the state against the other[1].

Hence the constitutional changes of the weaker states
were closely connected with the supremacy of different
powers, and Persia, Athens, Sparta, Thebes and Macedon
all had their influence on the constitutions of many cities[2].
This is but one instance of the *assimilation of constitutions*, which tended to introduce some unity of form into
the numberless states of Greece. Besides the assimilation
of subject to ruler, we may note the influence of the same
tendency in tribal federations, like those of Thessaly,
Boeotia or Crete[3], in political alliances[4], in towns not

---

[1] Cf. Plato *Rep.* viii 556 E ἡ πόλις…ἔξωθεν ἐπαγομένων ἢ τῶν ἑτέρων ἐξ
ὀλιγαρχουμένης πόλεως ξυμμαχίαν ἢ τῶν ἑτέρων ἐκ δημοκρατουμένης…αὐτὴ
αὐτῇ μάχεται. Ar. *Pol.* viii 7 1307 b 20 αἱ πολιτεῖαι…λύονται…ἔξωθεν,
ὅταν ἐναντία πολιτεία ᾖ, ἢ πλήσιον ἢ πόρρω μὲν ἔχουσα δὲ δύναμιν. The
Peloponnesian war affords many illustrations of this.

[2] Cf. Ar. *Pol.* vi 11 1296 a 32 ἔτι δὲ καὶ τῶν ἐν ἡγεμονίᾳ γενομένων τῆς
Ἑλλάδος πρὸς τὴν παρ' αὐτοῖς ἑκάτεροι πολιτείαν ἀποβλέποντες οἱ μὲν δημοκρατίας ἐν ταῖς πόλεσι καθίστασαν, οἱ δ' ὀλιγαρχίας. For the particular
influence of Athens and Sparta see below § 18.

[3] Crete offers a good instance. Although there was no permanent
union of the Cretan cities, their constitutions were so homogeneous that
Aristotle and other ancient writers habitually talk of 'Cretan' magistrates
and institutions. Swoboda, *Griechische Volksbeschlüsse* p. 30, calls attention to the 'local style' of the Cretan decrees.

[4] Athens and Sparta afford the best illustration. See below § 18 n. 3.
There was a double influence at work, for states sought the alliance of

connected by any bond save that of locality[5] and in colonies.

§ 17. *Constitutions in the Colonies.*

The constitutions of the different colonies were new creations, not developed from preceding historical conditions, but instituted concurrently with the foundation of the state. Colonies were cities without a past and offered therefore the best ground for constitutional experiments. Under normal circumstances it would be natural for the colonists to transfer to their new home the political ideas and institutions of the mother city. It is easier to reproduce than to innovate ; and in the absence of contrary motives, if circumstances permitted, the government of the colony was a reflection of that of the metropolis. But it might be impossible or undesirable to adhere to the social divisions or political organisation, that had been left behind. Many colonies were composed of citizens of mixed race ; and this would prevent them from establishing the social or tribal divisions of the mother country : others again were founded by a class in revolt against the aristocracy ; and these would be unlikely to recognise the privilege of noble birth. Many of the colonies, therefore, adapted the constitution to the new conditions, and there were special

cities of similar constitution, and worked at the same time to establish their own form of government among their allies.

[5] The towns of Italy and Sicily offer an instance of states politically independent of one another adopting similar institutions. Cf. Swoboda *op. cit.* p. 30. This was in part due to the influence of lawgivers, on which see below § 20.

forms of government, produced by these conditions, which lasted for a long time in the colonies[1].

§ 18.   *The influence of Athens and Sparta.*

The establishment of democracy at Athens and her rise to power in the fifth century led to a rivalry and division of empire between that city and Sparta. Henceforth there were two great powers in Greece, who sought by supremacy or federation to unite other states with themselves and thus to correct in some degree the permanent tendencies to separate autonomy, which prevailed generally in Greece. Many motives combined to effect such a cleavage, Athens and Sparta were opposed in every way, by race, by traditions, by character and by policy: but there was no stronger force at work than the opposition of principles of government. Sparta in character and constitution presented a form of aristocracy, almost unique in Greece, but in the general antithesis of democracy and oligarchy, minor differences were forgotten, and the Peloponnesian confederacy included commercial states, like Corinth and Megara, which, in many ways, must have felt more in sympathy with the enterprise and energy of Athens, than with the barbarous military system of Sparta[1]. The two leading states

[1] Of forms of government specially found in colonies we may note the 'oligarchies of first settlers, of the kingly house, and of fixed number.' See Chapter iv.

[1] Corinth and Megara were doubtless thrown into alliance with Sparta by a feeling of commercial rivalry towards Athens (Megara in fact must have been democratic when she joined the confederacy); and they can have had little community of sentiment with Sparta. At the same time the oligarchs of Corinth, for example, would have been loath

appeared at once as the champions and standards of the political principles that they professed. Within their own confederacies it was only natural that they should foster the governments with which they were in sympathy; and alliance with one or other of the great powers often determined for lesser states the fate of their constitution[2]. In the fifth century, when the empire of Greece was divided between Athens and Sparta, each state strove to introduce some uniformity of constitution into their own alliance, and in case of faction their support was assured to the party representing their own principles[3]. By the beginning of the Peloponnesian war the only members of the Delian confederacy that are known to have been oligarchic were Lesbos and Chios[4]. The rest were subject to Athens, and had either adopted a democratic constitution or had had institutions similar to those of Athens forced upon them[5]. In the Peloponnesian con-

to enter into union with a state so active in the support of democracies as Athens.

[2] The fate of Cos may be regarded as typical. We first hear of it as governed by a tyrant under Persian sway; it was probably democratic while in the Delian confederacy, oligarchic at the end of the war, democratic and in the Athenian alliance after Cnidus, oligarchic after revolt from Athens in 357. (I have accepted the inferences drawn by Gilbert, *Handbuch* ii pp. 172—3.)

[3] Ar. *Pol.* viii 7 1307 b 23 οἱ μὲν γὰρ Ἀθηναῖοι πανταχοῦ τὰς ὀλιγαρχίας, οἱ δὲ Λάκωνες τοὺς δήμους κατέλυον. See § 26.

[4] Mitylene was oligarchic (cf. Thuc. iii 27). Chios Gilbert (*Handbuch* ii p. 153) thinks was democratic. There is, I think, no evidence for this; and the narrative in Thuc. iv 58, viii 24 and 38 seems to me to imply the existence of oligarchy.

[5] The events of the first half of the fifth century, the delivery from Persia, the overthrow of the tyrants, the spread of trade etc., must have favoured democracy. In many states we can trace the deliberate introduction of Athenian institutions; and Miletus had even adopted

federacy Sparta left autonomy to her allies[6], but she
took good care that they should be governed by oligarchies
well disposed to herself[7], and it is clear that democracy
was an 'inconvenient' form of government, the correction
of which was demanded by Spartan interests, wherever
it was possible[8]. At the beginning of the war Megara,
Elis and Mantinea were her only democratic allies of
importance. The Peloponnesian war was a conflict between the opposing principles of the two governments[9],
and as the fortunes of either side rose or fell, the cause of
democracy or oligarchy was advanced. But even after
Athens and Sparta had ceased to exercise supremacy
over other states, they still remained the refuge and
support of democrats and oligarchs[10]; and while their
help was always ready to further the cause that they

the Athenian tribes and demes. (The evidence, which is epigraphic, is
quoted by Gilbert, *Handbuch* ii p. 141 n. 1.) Interference with constitutions was especially forbidden in the second Athenian Confederacy:
C. I. A. ii 17 (Hicks, *Inscriptions* 81).

[6] Sparta always posed as the champion of autonomy. See § 49 n. 8.

[7] The principle is stated by Thuc. i 19. Cf. i 76 where the Athenians
say ὑμεῖς γοῦν, ὦ Λακεδαιμόνιοι, τὰς ἐν τῇ Πελοποννήσῳ πόλεις ἐπὶ τὸ ὑμῖν
ὠφέλιμον καταστησάμενοι ἐξηγεῖσθε. Cf. also i 44.

[8] Thuc. v 81 2 (In Argos) ὀλιγαρχία ἐπιτηδεία τοῖς Λακεδαιμονίοις
κατέστη. Cf. *ib.* 82 1. I think ἐπιτήδειος and ἀνεπιτήδειος must have been
cant oligarchic terms, used to describe people or governments not in
sympathy with oligarchy. Besides the two passages cited above we find
ἐπιτήδειος used in the same association in i 19; i 144 (σφίσι...ἐπιτηδείως
αὐτονομεῖσθαι); viii 63 4 (Alcibiades was considered οὐκ ἐπιτήδειος...ἐς
ὀλιγαρχίαν); 70 2 and ἀνεπιτήδειος in viii 65 2.

[9] I have collected some evidence on this subject in *Political Parties*,
pp. 32—4 and notes.

[10] This is illustrated by the history of the fourth century. Cf. Isocr.
iv 16 τῶν γὰρ Ἑλλήνων οἱ μὲν ὑφ' ἡμῖν, οἱ δ' ὑπὸ Λακεδαιμονίοις εἰσίν· αἱ γὰρ
πολιτεῖαι, δι' ὧν οἰκοῦσι τὰς πόλεις, οὕτω τοὺς πλείστους αὐτῶν διειλήφασιν.

professed, they offered models of imitation to other states[11].

§ 19. *The admiration for the Spartan Constitution.*

The other Greeks combined with one consent to praise the Spartan constitution. It must be said that their admiration would probably not have been so unqualified had they had a better acquaintance with its principles or a personal experience of its working. The policy of secrecy, the exclusion of strangers, the little intercourse that the Spartans ever had with other Greeks, covered Sparta in a veil of mystery, which concealed her faults and exaggerated her virtues. People were familiar, at least by repute, with the famous institutions of Lycurgus, and the rigorous practice of virtue, by which every Spartiate devoted himself to the service of his fatherland. They were impressed by the success of the state in war, by the glorious position she won for herself in Greece, and above all they marvelled at the long continuance of her constitution, amidst the constant changes and revolutions of the democracies and oligarchies of other states. They did not realise the sacrifices demanded by the system; the galling tyranny of the military training; the suppression of individuality; the renunciation of the graces of life; the squalid barbarity of many of her customs, and the inward corruption of the very principles she professed. It was not till late in the fourth century, when Sparta lost even her military supremacy, that people began to find her

[11] The influence of Sparta will be discussed more fully. On Athens cf. Dem. xxiv 210 πολλοὶ τῶν Ἑλλήνων πολλάκις εἰσὶν ἐψηφισμένοι τοῖς νόμοις χρῆσθαι τοῖς ὑμετέροις, ἐφ' ᾧ φιλοτιμεῖσθε ὑμεῖς, εἰκότως.

out[1] and to recognise how little worthy she was of the
extravagant praises bestowed upon her.

But before the downfall of Sparta her government com-
manded almost universal admiration. Aristotle speaks
of earlier writers who left all other constitutions out
of view while they praised that of Lacedaemon[2]. Plato
spoke of ' the generally-praised Cretan and Lacedaemonian
constitutions ': and though he is by no means blind to
the faults of Sparta his ideal state is built upon a similar
framework[3]. Thucydides refers to the long continuance
of a well-ordered constitution at Sparta[4], and Xenophon
makes Critias (himself the author of the first treatise
on the Spartan state) refer to the general opinion that
the government of Sparta was the best[5].

But although admired it is doubtful whether the
Spartan constitution was imitated. Pindar refers to the
city of Aetna being founded ' in laws of the norm of
Hyllus ' and remaining ' under the ordinances of Aegi-

[1] Cf. Ar. *Pol.* iv 14 1333 b 21 καίτοι δῆλον ὡς ἐπειδὴ νῦν γε οὐκέτι
ὑπάρχει τοῖς Λάκωσι τὸ ἄρχειν, οὐκ εὐδαίμονες, οὐδ' ὁ νομοθέτης ἀγαθός.

Sir Frederick Pollock, *History of the Science of Politics* p. 11 n. 1,
expresses himself on the Spartans with a frankness that is refreshing.
' The Spartans have had their day of glorification from rhetoricians and
second-hand scholars. To me they have always appeared the most
odious impostors in the whole history of antiquity,...with all their pre-
tentious discipline they produced in the whole course of their wars only
two officers, who are known to have been gentlemen, Brasidas and
Callicratidas.'

[2] *Pol.* vi 1 1288 b 41; iv 14 1333 b 12. The political theorists of the
fourth century regarded Sparta as the ideal military state; see Meyer,
Geschichte des Alterthums ii p. 564.

[3] *Rep.* viii 544 c. See Newman, *Introduction* pp. 400—1.

[4] i 18; cf. iii 57.

[5] Xen. *Hell.* iii 3 4. Xenophon himself wrote a panegyric of the
Lycurgean state (*Resp. Lac.*).

mius'⁶: and he describes Aegina as governed under
'the norm of Hyllus and Aegimius⁷.' But these are
probably merely conventional methods of praise; a
government founded on so rigid a system, as that of
Sparta, was not for general application. There were
colonies in which we can trace the existence of the
so-called Dorian tribes, the division of classes, as in
the Dorian states and other Dorian institutions⁸: but
the essential features of a military aristocracy, based
on a strict training, the separation of classes and occupations Sparta shared, so far as we know, only with Crete.

§ 20. *Lawgivers.*

The method by which important changes of constitution were effected in early times was most often the
appointment of a single man, entrusted with full powers
to revise the constitution and to draw up a code of laws.
The practice was so fully in accord with Greek sentiment
that the earliest constitutions were often connected with
the name of some individual, although they may have
arisen naturally and spontaneously from the circumstances
of the community¹. In the history of early societies a time
comes when it is felt necessary to reduce the old unwritten laws to order and to publish them, when revised,
in a code². In Greece this work was usually effected in
each state by a single man, and as the development of

⁶ *Pyth.* i 61.
⁷ *Fr.* 4 (Böckh).
⁸ Cf. Heraclea in Pontus, Byzantium, Chalcedon.
¹ Cf. the unsolved question of Lycurgus and his work.
² Maine, *Ancient Law* pp. 14 ff.

society had made reform essential, such an one was usually
given indefinite powers to readjust the constitution. Even
in later times when further reforms were necessary the
same process was sometimes employed. The absolute
authority entrusted to the legislators induced Aristotle
to regard men of this class as tyrants[3], although their
appointment was intended to prevent tyranny by a
reconciliation of factions. Either a citizen was chosen
to reform the constitution of his own state, as Draco,
Solon and Cleisthenes at Athens, Pittacus at Mitylene,
Epimenes in Miletus, and Zaleucus in Locri ; or a stranger
was called in, as one who would be free from party feeling
and might introduce the institutions of some more wisely
ordered state. Thus Charondas legislated for many of
the states of Sicily and Italy[4]; Philolaus of Corinth for
Thebes[5] and Demonax of Mantinea for Cyrene[6]. In the
consideration of lawgivers we must not omit the founders
of colonies: the oecist must often have been aesymnete,
and nothing affords a better proof of the political talent of
the Greeks than the institution of well-ordered and syste-
matic government in so many colonies.

In some cases we can trace the influence of philosophers
on legislation. Pythagoras affords a notable instance of
the philosopher in politics, but his action was directed
more to influence the rulers than to alter the constitu-

[3] Ar. *Pol.* iii 14 1285 a 30, (the office of αἰσυμνήτης is defined as
αἱρετὴ τυραννίς); *ib.* ii ch. 12 gives a general account of the ancient
legislators. Cf. Plato *Rep.* x 599 D E.

[4] See Plato cited in the last note.

[5] Ar. *Pol.* ii 12 1274 a 22 and 31.

[6] Hdt. iv 161, Demonax seems to have made some effort to adapt
Spartan institutions to the needs of Cyrene.

tion[7]. Strabo suggests that the good order of Elea was due to Parmenides and Zeno[8]. There were political theorists before Socrates; but the most prominent of them, the Sophists, were 'in the anti-social camp[9].' The masters of political philosophy came too late for their teaching to be realised in practice, if we except the attempt of Dion to found a philosophic state[10] and the possible influence of philosophic ideals on such men as Epaminondas[11], Archytas and Timoleon.

One other factor of constitutional change must not be omitted; the pretence of a return to an 'ancestral constitution[12].' It is easier to effect a revolution, if it be represented as a return to the past; and though the Greeks were not particularly moved by sentimental admiration for the archaic, the fiction of the restoration of ancient forms of government was put forward especially by oligarchs who wished to overthrow the later growths of a democracy[13].

[7] Newman, *Introduction* p. 377. Pythagoras breathed 'a new and more ethical spirit into the rule of the Few.'

[8] Strabo vi 252.

[9] Newman, *Introduction*, p. 391.

[10] Plut. *Dion* 53.

[11] Ar. *Rhet.* ii 23 1398 b 18 'Thebes never flourished till she was ruled by philosophers.'

[12] Cf. Ar. *Pol.* ii 8 1268 b 26 ff. on οἱ πάτριοι νόμοι.

[13] The oligarchies at Athens were established under a pretext of the restoration of the old democracy. Cf. Ar. *Ath. Pol.* 29 3; 34 3; Xen. *Hell.* ii 3 2; iii 4 2; Diod. xiv 3.

CHAPTER III.

The Historical Development of Constitutions.

§ 21. *The origin of Constitutions.*

I PROCEED to consider the process of constitutional development, tracing in a brief outline the general course of political change and dwelling only on such matters as illustrate the genesis or character of oligarchies.

The Greek writers gave different accounts of the cycle of governments. With Plato[1] and Polybius[2] the order is drawn up more in accordance with the relative merit of the different forms than in agreement with their succession in point of time. Aristotle's account is nearer to facts but it is too absolute[3]; as all states did not go through the same cycle in the same order: but there is still enough truth in it to make it applicable to the majority of those constitutions which did pass through the ordinary stages of development.

---

[1] Plato *Rep.* viii 544 c (criticised by Ar. *Pol.* viii 12 1316 b).

[2] Polyb. vi 4 7; vi 9 10; αὕτη πολιτειῶν ἀνακύκλωσις, αὕτη φύσεως οἰκονομία. Machiavelli, *First Decade of T. Livius* ch. 2, also describes 'the sphear and circle in which all Republics have, and do move' and his order of succession is also *a priori*.

[3] Ar. *Pol.* iii 15 1286 b.

Aristotle starts with the heroic age, and we also must assume it as 'a primary fact for the purpose of following out its subsequent changes' without speculating on 'its antecedent causes and determining conditions[4],' while we leave the difficult subject of the government of the tribal community out of view[5]. Aristotle was aware that other forms of union had preceded the state of the Homeric age, and his account of village settlements and their government at the beginning of the first book is not out of harmony with modern theories. It is important, however, to keep clearly before us that cities were generally formed by the coalescence of several communities : that each, in fact, was a federation of smaller aggregates, which were in many cases tribal unions[6]. This is a fact of the utmost importance for the comprehension of early constitutions, in which the conflict of city and tribe was waged throughout the whole of the period of aristocracies.

§ 22.   *The Heroic Monarchy.*

The heroic monarchy, as depicted in the Homeric poems, contains both in the powers of government and in the social classes the germs of later forms of consti-

[4] Grote ii p. 59—'To conceive absolute beginning or origin is beyond the reach of our faculties: we can neither apprehend nor verify anything beyond progress or development or decay.' In pushing our investigations back we must ultimately come to facts which defy analysis or explanation. The origin of social classes is one of these facts. Cf. Freeman, *Comparative Politics* pp. 247 ff.

[5] On this see W. W. Fowler, *The City State* ch. 2.

[6] De Coulanges, *La Cité Antique*[12] pp. 143—4.

tution[1]. We find that the orders of society are divided almost as definitely as castes, and these must be accepted as established institutions, the origin of which, like the origin of classes in general, is beyond our power to explain. The king and the chiefs form together the first class of nobles. The king is supreme in power and honour, but he differs from the other chiefs only in degree, not in kind[2]. King and nobles share the knowledge and practice of law and the science of things divine. The king is the chief leader in war, the nobles are the great warriors fighting from their chariots in front of the host of the commons, who hurl their weapons from a distance.

But king and nobles are separated by a broad distinction from the two other classes. Of these the general mass of freemen, practising different crafts[3] or cultivating their own lots of land, rank next in importance. Below them come the poor freemen, *Thetes,* working for hire, chiefly on the lands of other men[4]. They were paid in

---

[1] I assume that the picture of government and society presented by Homer corresponded in the main with the actual state of Greece in the so-called 'Achaean' period. There is an excellent sketch of Homeric Society in Grote Part i ch. 20.

[2] The nobles like the king are called βασιλῆες and ἄνακτες, while the superior *degree* of the kingly race is declared by the title βασιλεύτερος (Il. ii 101; ix 160) or βασιλεύτατος (xx 34). In Cyprus in historical times the actual kings were called βασιλεῖς, their kindred ἄνακτες (Aristotle F. H. G. ii 203); βασιλίδαι was the name of the nobility in some states.

[3] δημιοεργοί.

[4] Photius *s.v.* θής defines them as οἱ ἔνεκα τροφῆς δουλεύοντες. On these and the other class see Grote ii pp. 97—100.

The classes in Homer correspond with the general division of 'estates' in the European nations. Bluntschli, *Theory of the State (Engl. Trans.)* pp. 113 ff., distinguishes (1) The priests and nobles (who in some states formed two separate classes), (2) the freemen, who as a rule

kind, so that they could not save or accumulate, and as their employment was irregular they were in evil plight, almost as dependent on their masters as the bought slaves (of whom there were but few), while misfortune might reduce them eventually to serfdom.

Society was organised on a patriarchal basis. Many petty chieftains, ruling each over his family and dependents[5], each having his hill fort[6] and each sovereign in his own small domain, paid homage to such an overlord as Agamemnon. Herein the close connection of monarchy and aristocracy is made manifest. The nobles, supreme and independent princes in their own domain[7], in the united state formed an aristocracy in which all were subject to the king's authority, while in their relation to

were the owners and tillers of the soil and also took part in trade, (3) the estate of dependents occupied with the lower needs of life. Their freedom and their rights are less than those of the second class. We may compare the class divisions in Attica: it seems doubtful whether there is any essential distinction between classes 2 and 3.

[5] The petty chieftains ruled over the tribal communities, formed of the ruling γένος and its dependents or slaves. The head of the tribe exercised authority over the rest. Cf. Abbott, *History of Greece* ii p. 11, 'Patriarchal monarchies derived their origin from the authority of the father over his children; of the chief over his tribe. They were hereditary and continued to be so, as long as certain gifts, sacerdotal or judicial, were considered necessary in a king and peculiar to a family.'

[6] Ar. *Pol.* vi 11 1330 b 19 ἀκρόπολις ὀλιγαρχικὸν καὶ μοναρχικὸν...ἀριστοκρατικὸν δὲ...μᾶλλον ἰσχυροὶ τόποι πλείους. The excavations of the strongholds of the Peloponnese point to the existence of a number of strong castles, in which the ruling families dwelt.

[7] This will explain the appropriateness of the titles βασιλῆες and ἄνακτες applied to them. It is not therefore necessary to suppose that such titles were only applied 'in the later passages of the Epos.' Each head of a γένος was a βασιλεὺς in his own domain: but in relation to their overlord they were γέροντες, βουληφόροι, ἡγήτορες or μέδοντες.

each other they stood on the same level of privilege[8].
Their acknowledgment of one chief as superior to the
rest may be the justification of Aristotle's statement that
the heroic king ruled over willing subjects and obtained
his position by being the benefactor of his people in the
arts of peace or war[9].

The government of the united state included three
different powers, the monarch, the council of the nobles,
the assembly of the commons; but it is necessary to
insist that there was nothing like a formal constitution
at this period. 'There was,' as Grote says, 'no scheme or
system, no idea of responsibility; the obedience of the
subject depends on personal feeling and reverence for the
chief[10].' The king, who enjoyed a sort of 'divine right[11],'
alone exercised individual authority, based on the ascendency of himself and his race, and though he required the
consent and support of the other orders and usually observed the precedents and traditions of his ancestors, it is
a mistake to say, as Thucydides and Aristotle do, that his
powers were limited or defined[12].

There was no division of political functions between
different magistrates as there was in later times. War,
justice and religion were the three spheres of government,
and in all the king was supreme[13], though he might

[8] One account that Aristotle gives of the origin of Aristocracy is συνέ-
βαινε γίνεσθαι πολλοὺς ὁμοίους πρὸς ἀρετὴν (*Pol.* iii 15 1286 b 12).

[9] *Pol.* iii 14 1285 b 6.

[10] ii p. 61.

[11] The σκῆπτρόν τ' ἠδὲ θέμιστες came from Zeus.

[12] Thuc. i 15 (ἐπὶ ῥητοῖς γέρασι); Ar. *Pol.* iii 14 1285 b 5 (κατὰ νόμον)
and 21 (ἐπὶ τισὶ δ' ὡρισμένοις) both transfer the ideas of a later age to a
primitive, undefined government. The idea of νόμος is post-Homeric.

[13] Ar. *Pol.* iii 14 1285 b 9. It is characteristic of De Coulanges (*op.*

delegate part of his powers or take advice from his council.

The functions of the Council, in later times the chief organ of aristocratic and oligarchic government, were purely consultative : but the monarchy rested on the support of the nobles, so that it was necessary to seek their advice and to treat it with respect.

The Assembly of the Commons seems to have been alike devoid of power or influence. It formed 'a medium of publicity without any idea of responsibility,' 'an assembly for the discussion of the chiefs in the presence of the people, an opportunity for promulgation and record[14].' The people expressed their approval or dissent of the matters which the king or the nobles brought before them by shouting. The place of the Assembly in the constitution is illustrated by the method of administering justice. Whether the king himself pronounce judgment or whether the power be exercised by the chiefs, the trial seems always to have taken place in the *agora*, which thus served the purpose of publicity[15].

The Homeric constitution represents in its king, its council and its assembly, the organs of government afterwards found in all Greek states : magistrates, $\beta o \nu \lambda \dot{\eta}$ and $\dot{\epsilon} \kappa \kappa \lambda \eta \sigma i a$. Where a single magistrate controlled the state, monarchy (whether constitutional or despotic) was found. In the oligarchies and aristocracies the council represented

cit. p. 204) to say 'the principal function of a king was to perform religious ceremonies.' As a matter of comparison his command in war was most important.

[14] Grote ii p. 69.

[15] Besides Homer cf. Hesiod *Op.* where the δωροφάγοι βασιλῆες give judgment (l. 39), apparently in the agora (l. 29).

the privileged class and directed the government in their
interest.   In the democracy the people made known their
will in the assembly : but the assembly was no longer the
mute, submissive gathering of the legendary age, but a
sovereign body, in which speech was the right of all, and
speech the motor of government[16].

§ 23.   *Transition from Monarchy to Aristocracy.*

The transition from monarchy to aristocracy took
place at an early period of history ; the accounts of it are
largely legendary, and much room is left for speculation
as to the occasion and cause.   But one point is equally
certain and important.   If we put aside aristocracies
founded on conquest, the change involved no break of
continuity, no revolution of ideas : it was rarely violent,
most often gradual, and sometimes almost imperceptible[1].
The explanation lies in the similar character of kingship
and aristocracy in Greece.   ‘Aristocracy,’ as Montesquieu
described it, ‘is a monarchy with several monarchs’: no
violence was done to men’s ideas when the chieftains
resolved on an equal division of power among themselves.
The change was in the interests of the nobles, not of the
commons.   ‘The revolution was not the work of the
lower classes, who wished to overthrow the constitution of society, but of the aristocracy who wished to
maintain it[2].’

[16] παρρησία was a universal principle of democracy.   Cf. the description given by Dem. xix 184 ἔστ’ ἐν λόγοις ἡ πολιτεία.

[1] In the light of the Aristotelian treatise on the Athenian constitution, it would be difficult, for instance, to mark the date of the end of
βασιλεία at Athens.

[2] De Coulanges, *op. cit.* p. 301.

The causes of the change can only be considered most generally. Aristotle talks of kings surrendering part of their powers of their own accord[3], of a general spread of 'virtue,' which induced men to found a common constitution[4]. Both of these explanations point to the loss of prestige by the king, which brought the overlord to the same level as the chiefs. Elsewhere he mentions military changes which put power int. the hands of 'the knights[5],' who must probably in this connexion be identified with the nobles. It was possible too that a weak, unwarlike man might become king, and inasmuch as the chief duty of the monarch was to command in war, his authority would be lost, if he proved unfitted for his duties[6]; or a time of peace might come when no general was required.

Another cause that can be traced is connected with the union of smaller communities to form larger political organisations. Such a process, which the Greeks called συνοικισμός, abolished the separate authority of a number of petty princes[7], who were compensated for their loss of independence by the grant of aristocratic privileges in the new state. Whether the chief power were still held by a king in the new state, mattered little: for the privileges of the nobles limited his au-

[3] *Pol.* iii 14 1285 b 15.

[4] *Pol.* iii 15 1286 b 8 quoted above § 22 n. 8. The passage continues οὐκέτι ὑπέμενον ἀλλ' ἐξήτουν κοινόν τι καὶ πολιτείαν καθίστασαν.

[5] *Pol.* vi 13 1297 b 16.

[6] The cause assigned for the appointment of the πολέμαρχος at Athens by Ar. *Ath. Pol.* 3 2 is διὰ τὸ γενέσθαι τινὰς τῶν βασιλέων τὰ πολεμικὰ μαλακούς.

[7] Bekker *Anecdota* p. 257 Εὐπατρίδαι οἱ...μετέχοντες βασιλικοῦ γένους preserves a faint trace of the origin of the Athenian nobility from the families, which had formerly held kingly rank. See also Plut. *Thes.* 32.

thority, and the essential conditions of an aristocracy must have been fulfilled[8]. This process was the triumph of the city over the tribe, and it can be best illustrated in the history of Athens[9]: but the history of the same State shows the repugnance of the nobles to the loss of their former local sovereignty, and the tendency to recur to the system of separate tribal settlements[10].

A special form of aristocracy arose by the transfer of supreme power from the single monarch to the kingly family, who of their own numbers formed an aristocratic class. This subject I discuss more fully below[11].

Distinct from all these causes is the conquest of a land by an invading race, who, through superiority of tactics or better equipment[12], overcame the former inhabitants of a district, and reduced them to serfdom or subjection, while the invaders formed a ruling class. Whether the form of the constitution was monarchic or not, we may regard it as possessing the essentials of an aristocracy in the superior privilege of the conquerors in relation to the conquered. The Dorian migration established throughout the Peloponnese a number of states of aristocratic constitution; and

[8] It seems clear that at Athens the Eupatrids formed a power in the state distinct from the king, exercising a check on the absolute authority of the monarch. This may be the explanation of the persistent legends that Theseus established a 'democratic constitution' and offered a 'government without a king.'

[9] See Appendix A below.

[10] See Appendix B below.

[11] See chapter iv § 33.

[12] The Dorians perhaps had both advantages. Thus they are credited with the introduction of the hoplite tactics, which overcame the system of chariots and light arms; and there is some ground for supposing that the Dorians were 'men of iron' who overcame the 'men of bronze.'

the same origin must be attributed to the governments of Thessaly and Boeotia.

§ 24. *Changes of Government incident on the establishment of Aristocracy.*

From the description just given of the transition to aristocracy it may be inferred that the constitutional changes required were neither many nor important. The essence of the change was the assertion of the authority of the class of nobles, as against the single monarch or the magistrates. Hence the Council assumed a greater importance under the aristocracy, while the assembly of the commons seems to have had even less weight than it possessed under the monarchy. The fate of the king differed in different states. As has been pointed out, the title βασιλεὺς in Greek is a term elastic in its application[1]; and the title was often retained after monarchy was really abolished. The βασιλεὺς might become a temporary or a responsible magistrate, or several βασιλῆες might take the place of one[2].

In some states new magistrates with special titles were instituted to receive some part of the king's power. Thus at Athens the polemarch and the archon shared the functions of government with the king, and in the course of time the king became the least important of the three. At Megara there was a legend of a similar division of duties between king and general[3]. Gradually the duties

[1] Holm, *Griechische Geschichte*, i p. 318.

[2] The division of the kingly power is illustrated by the double kingship at Sparta (which diminished the importance of the office). But the origin of this institution is prehistoric. See also chapter iv § 33.

[3] Paus. i 39 6.

of administration were distributed among a still greater number of magistrates, and Aristotle classifies the titular kings of later times either as life-generals or as ritual magistrates[4].

In point of tenure Athens shows the transition from the hereditary king for life to the elected and annual magistrate, and at Athens too we hear of the responsibility of the kings being asserted. Probably the council in many states gained the right to control the magistrates.

§ 25. *Transition from Aristocracy to Oligarchy.*

The transition to aristocracy from monarchy, while it involved a formal change of constitution, was effected without doing violence to the general sentiment of the age; but the institution of oligarchy, even if it required no change in the external form of government, was connected with the most momentous social movements and with an absolute revolution in the thoughts of men.

In the aristocratic society classes were fixed with something of the rigidity of castes; the rulers formed a close corporation, marrying only within their own order[1], maintaining a monopoly of the secrets of government, keeping within their own circle judicial, military and religious functions, and exercising an absolute rule over submissive subjects. Their authority was, in most states,

---

[4] *Pol.* iii 14 1285 b 14.

[1] There is not very much evidence: but such a provision is usually characteristic of a close aristocracy. Hdt. v 92 asserts it of the Bacchiads at Corinth, and we may infer it of Megara from Theognis (see n. 19). Cf. the prohibition of *connubium* at Rome.

consecrated by the prescription of centuries; in others
sanctified as effectively by the right of conquest[2]. Respect for their rule was instinctive: they were 'the good'
and 'the best': their subjects the 'base' and the 'craven.'
To refuse them obedience was a sin[3], for they were descendants of the gods, who had given them both their power
and their wealth[4], and with whom they alone could
mediate.

To overthrow this government and set oligarchy in its
place was to substitute wealth for 'virtue[5],' to ignore the
power of the gods and drive them from the earth[6], to give
to might the place of right, to abolish privilege and let
social forces have unchecked play.

Changes so momentous and so destructive to their
pretensions could not be accepted by the nobles without a
bitter struggle; and the echoes of this conflict are preserved for us in the verses of the lyrical poets, all of them
aristocrats, many of them spendthrift and ruined, who
curse the power of wealth, and the rise of base men, and
mourn the lost privileges of 'the good.' Nowhere do we

[2] Bluntschli, *Theory of the State*, p. 247 'Ancient peoples regarded
war as a great international lawsuit, and victory as the judgment of God
in favour of the victor.'

[3] Cf. Xen. *Resp. Lac.* 8 5 οὐ μόνον ἄνομον ἀλλὰ καὶ ἀνόσιον τὸ πυθοχρή-
στοις νόμοις μὴ πείθεσθαι.

[4] No evidence is required for the belief that power comes from the
gods. It is inherent in the constitution of early society. Land, regarded
as the true form of wealth, is said to be given by the gods and is therefore
distinguished from other kinds of property. Cf. Solon fr. 13 9—13;
Theogn. 197—202.

[5] Cf. Plato *Rep.* viii 550 E and 551 A on the contrast of πλοῦτος and
ἀρετή, especially τιμωμένου δὴ πλούτου ἐν πόλει καὶ τῶν πλουσίων ἀτιμοτέρα
ἀρετή τε καὶ οἱ ἀγαθοί.

[6] Theogn. 1135—50. 'The gods have left the earth.'

get a more vivid representation of the revolution, or a better reflection of contemporary opinion, than in the pages of Solon and Theognis, the one a mediator between the past and the future, striving to unite the discord of factions and to restore peace and order to the state; the other an irreconcilable enemy of the changes that were being effected, refusing to accept the inevitable, and still maintaining the cause of the old aristocracy. There is uncertainty about both the date of Theognis and the constitution of Megara : he lived in an age of revolutions, and his poems may refer to more than one form of constitution; but his general attitude seems to be that of an aristocrat protesting against plutocracy, of a bitter opponent of the new-made rich who have risen to power and honour[7].

It is a circumstance peculiarly appropriate to the character of oligarchy that its origin can be traced to the invention of money more than to any one other fact; it

---

[7] We may assume that the Dorian aristocracy of birth at Megara was overthrown by Theagenes, and not restored after his expulsion. Probably an oligarchy of wealth followed (referred to by Plut. *Q. G.* 18), succeeded soon after by a violent democracy, after which oligarchy was probably restored (Welcker refers Ar. *Pol.* viii 5 1304 b 35 and vi 15 1300 a 17 to this period, but they seem to suit the events of 424 B.C. better). We do not know exactly at what stage Theognis was writing : his tone seems more natural in an oligarchy of wealth, than in a democracy. At any rate aristocracy was not far back in the past, and the poet shows the aristocratic loathing of the commons, rich and poor.

F. Cauer, *Parteien und Politiker in Megara und Athen*, discusses the overthrow of aristocracy at Megara and its causes with much ability : but I cannot agree with his theory that we can assign different poems of Theognis to different dates, and thereby trace a definite change in his position. Herr Cauer assumes a transition from personal and political friendship with the lower classes to the violent championship of the aristocracy. This speculation seems to me far-fetched and unnecessary.

was the redistribution of wealth, due to trade and industry, and only rendered possible by the introduction of coinage, which raised new social classes to power in the state. But these material causes required the contribution of moral causes. What had hitherto been considered the absolute right of the aristocracy came to be regarded as an odious privilege : and the revolution of ideas involved in this could not be effected without deep changes of sentiment in matters of government and religion, in fixed customs and social divisions.

These changes probably did not take place until the rule of the nobles had proved oppressive to the excluded[8]. A close society, based upon hereditary succession and maintained by intermarriage, tends naturally to become narrower, and as it becomes narrower to become also more despotic. When land is the only source of wealth, the landowners are apt to make an oppressive use of their monopoly, to enforce the laws of debt to their own purpose, to try and reduce the other classes to a still worse subjection[9]. Such an abuse of power raised a bitter feeling against the aristocracy ; and we may see in this degeneracy of government the basis of the ethical distinctions drawn by Plato and Aristotle between aristocracy and oligarchy. Oligarchy is the perverted form of a good

[8] On this see W. W. Fowler, *The City State*, pp. 119 ff.

[9] The laws of debt both at Athens and Rome were wrested so as to introduce a practical state of serfdom. I think the Eupatrid landowners at Athens were endeavouring before Solon's legislation to reduce the Thetes to the condition of the Lacedaemonian Helots. Cf. the description in Ar. *Ath. Pol.* 2 § 2 (ἐδούλευον οἱ πένητες τοῖς πλουσίοις); § 3 (τὸ δουλεύειν). This explains the importance of his prohibition τὸ μὴ δανείζειν ἐπὶ τοῖς σώμασιν (9 § 1) which is described as the most democratic measure of all.

government, and Aristotle explains that it came into being
at a time when the rulers became 'worse,' and used their
power to make money[10]. As long as land was the chief
or only form of wealth, the other classes must have been
in a state of dependence on the nobles, who owned most
of the land[11]. Some of the commons worked land belonging to the nobles, others served for hire, and as they
were paid in kind they could never accumulate wealth or
attain independence.

But the growth of trade and navigation, which succeeded the spread of colonies, introduced new methods of
producing wealth; deprived land of its exclusive importance, and exalted industry and commerce. One thing
more was essential to dissolve the 'law of *status*'[12]: the
introduction of a proper medium of exchange. The transition from barter to a money currency, which took place
in Greece about the beginning of the seventh century,
effected an economic revolution. Before this transition
had taken place it must have been impossible to effect a
proper division of employments or to give to industry its
due reward[13].

Trade in many Greek states was not essentially un-

[10] *Pol.* iii 15 1286 b 14 ἐπεὶ δὲ χείρους γενόμενοι ἐχρηματίζοντο ἀπὸ τῶν
κοινῶν, ἐντεῦθέν ποθεν εὔλογον γενέσθαι τὰς ὀλιγαρχίας. Cf. Plat. *Rep.* viii
550 ε.

[11] The possession of land is implied in Aristotle's definition of εὐγένεια
(discussed in § 6) and in many cities was one of the conditions of political
privilege. See ch. iv. § 30.

[12] Bagehot, *Physics and Politics* p. 29. 'In early times the guiding
rule was the law of *status*. Everybody was born to a place in the community: in that place he had to stay: in that place he found certain
duties which he had to fulfil, and which were all he needed to think of.'

[13] Cf. Ar. *Pol.* i 9 1257 a 35.

aristocratic.   Many of the colonies governed by close aristocracies were most active in the pursuit of commerce.
The chief epoch of colonisation, which was undertaken to
a great extent to promote and protect commercial interests, is earlier than the period of oligarchic government;
and there are many particular instances of aristocracies
generally or of particular nobles engaging in trade[14].   But
trade and industry, unlike property in land, could not be
limited to a class : other people besides the nobles might
accumulate wealth.   The introduction of money, a measure
which has always proved to the advantage of industry,
tended to emancipate the hired labourers from their thral-
dom and rendered the exchange of property easy, so that,
while it was possible for the commons to rise to wealth, it
was equally possible for the nobles to lose their substance
by rash speculation or to waste it in luxurious living.
Lastly, the importation of corn from abroad had its inevitable effects on agriculture[15].

The general diffusion of wealth, involving the im-
poverishment of some nobles and the enrichment of some
of the commons[16], produced a state of political inequality
which demanded redress.   The same causes were not
equally effective in all states.   In some trade never
attained to importance; class distinctions were rigidly
kept up and the old aristocracies survived[17].   But in

[14] The commercial activity of the aristocracies is obvious in the
colonies.   Cauer *id.* p. 21 argues that the nobles of Megara were
especially interested in foreign trade.   Of individual examples we may
cite Solon (Plut. *Sol.* 2) and Sappho's brother (Strabo xvii 808).

[15] See Cauer *id.* pp. 18—9 and Busolt *Staatsaltertümer*^{2} pp. 33—4.

[16] This is the burden of the plaint of Theognis, cf. 315 πολλοί τοι
πλουτοῦσι κακοί, ἀγαθοὶ δὲ πένονται.

[17] The commercial oligarchy was never established in Sparta or
Thessaly.

most states the power of wealth could not be resisted[18]:
the economic revolution led first to social, then to political changes. Intermarriage between the classes became
general[19], the commons were admitted to serve in the
army[20], and in some states the balance of power had
already shifted from birth to wealth before the people
were conscious of change, and the only course possible
was to recognise the accomplished fact and widen the
basis of government[21].

Such were the social and economic changes which
rendered possible the transition from aristocracy to oligarchy. But the transition was seldom effected immediately. The nobles did not surrender their privileges
without resistance, and the contest between birth and
wealth generally led to a state of faction, the issue of
which was almost invariably in the seventh and sixth
centuries a tyranny[22]. The commons, strong in numbers

---

[18] Cf. Theognis *passim*, especially 700 πλήθει δ' ἀνθρώπων ἀρετὴ μία
γίνεται ἥδε | πλουτεῖν : and the sentiment χρήματ' ἀνήρ, which occurs in
Alcaeus fr. 49 (Bergk); Pindar *Isth.* 2 11. The whole of lyrical poetry
bears witness to it.

[19] Theognis 183 ff. We may infer the same result for other states.

[20] The introduction of hoplite tactics probably rendered it necessary
to open the army to such of the commons as could furnish the equipment.
In a time of perpetual war the state could not afford to maintain aristocratic distinctions.

[21] The constitution of Draco at Athens, as discussed in Ar. *Ath. Pol.*
4 2 (ἀπεδέδοτο ἡ πολιτεία τοῖς ὅπλα παρεχομένοις), if we place any reliance
on the account, may have been only the legal recognition of changes
already accomplished. (This would explain the pluperfect ἀπεδέδοτο.)

[22] I do not know that there is any instance recorded besides that of
Athens in which oligarchy succeeded aristocracy without the intermediate stage of tyranny. But at Athens the constitution of Solon never
got to work, and it needed the tyranny of Pisistratus to break the power
of the nobles and clear the ground for a government on a fresh basis.

and wealth but without leaders or organisation, could only overthrow the aristocracy by reviving monarchy. And the tyrants almost without exception used their position to break the power of the nobility and to deprive them of their privilege and prestige[23]. Tyranny had but a short reign in Greece, but it was rarely, if ever, possible to establish the old aristocratic constitution after it was once overthrown[24]: in most states of the mainland oligarchy was introduced[25], in some democracy succeeded directly to tyranny[26].

I have postponed until now the consideration of one factor which must have been of momentous consequence in the struggle between the old government and the new. The struggle between the tribe and the city, which has been said to characterise early periods of history, had here to be fought out to the death : for both the political privileges and the personal influence of the nobles depended on the tribal organisation of the state, and it proved vain to abolish the privileges of birth, without touching the sway of the great families. In almost all Greek states the ascending series of house, clan and tribe

[23] E. Curtius in *Hermes* x p. 232 thinks Corinth was an exception. 'The Corinthian tyranny was distinguished from other tyrannies in having no democracy behind it: it maintained many of the conservative principles of the former oligarchy (of birth).'

[24] Hdt. iii 50 mentions Procles, a tyrant of Epidaurus; Epidaurus afterwards was governed by an aristocracy. Ar. *Pol.* viii 12 1316 a 34 mentions the tyranny of Charilaus at Sparta passing into aristocracy : but this was probably not a tyranny of the ordinary type.

[25] Oligarchy succeeded tyranny at Megara, Sicyon and Corinth.

[26] Democracy was instituted after the tyranny at Athens and in many of the towns of Ionia, where Greek tyrants had ruled in the interests of Persia.

may be traced[27].   Originally, no doubt, these divisions
were based on common descent[28] and, at a time when only
the nobles were admitted to privilege, they were naturally
adopted as political divisions and came to be recognised
as essential parts of the constitution.   But these divisions
had a religious as well as a political function.   Each tribe,
each clan and each house had its own religious cult, and
even if members of the other orders were admitted to the
sacred rites, the nobles were alone qualified to mediate
with the gods, just as they alone could represent the State
in divine affairs.   Lastly the so-called houses were associated with certain districts of the country[29], in which
the nobles must have exercised sway over such members
of the other orders as were settled there[30], and it was as
necessary to break down their local ascendency as it was
to abolish their political privilege.

The natural method of admitting the commons to the
state was to open the γένη to them, and still to retain the

[27] The divisions were usually called γένος or πάτρα, φρατρία or συγ-
γένεια and φυλή.   See Gilbert, *Handbuch* ii pp. 302 ff. and Dicaearchus
quoted there.

[28] The names of the different Athenian γένη were all patronymic.

[29] Many villages in Attica bore the names of noble γένη.   The local
factions of the sixth century each had noble leaders.

[30] The nobles would not lightly surrender their absolute dominion
within their own γένος.   They had the aristocratic feeling against
centralisation and were constantly asserting the rights of the γένος
against those of the state.   Cf. De Coulanges, *op. cit.* p. 312 'The
overthrow of royalty had resulted in the revival of the rule of the
γένος: the families had resumed their life of isolation : each had begun
again to form a petty state with a Eupatrid as chief and a crowd of
clients and serfs as subjects.'   He assumes that the Thetes had been
reduced to serfdom long before Solon.   I do not think there is any
evidence for this.

γένη and the larger organisations in which they were
grouped as parts of the constitution. This step can be
traced at Athens, where the fiction of common worship
took the place of kinship as a qualification for the
membership of a γένος, at least as early as the constitution of Solon, and the γένη were by this means thrown
open to the two lower classes besides the Eupatrids.
But this measure left both the power of the nobles within
the γένη and their local influence undiminished. Citizenship was no longer limited to a class, but it was based on
the membership of a religious corporation, in which Eupatrid influence was dominant and of which a Eupatrid was
the hereditary head. The people were still in vassalage;
the extension of the franchise failed to emancipate them
from the sway of their lords, and the instance only shows
us how useless are democratic reforms in a society, which
remains thoroughly aristocratic in spirit and organisation.
The history of the sixth century is but the record of the
factions of noble families, and it was not till Cleisthenes
took decisive measures to abolish, root and branch, the
tribal organisation as part of the constitution, to substitute purely artificial divisions for the old system of
house, clan and tribe, and to prevent by the most
elaborate institutions any possibility of local factions, that
the democratic constitution of Solon could be realised[31].

[31] On the position of the γένη in the Athenian state see Appendix B,
where also the character and importance of the reforms of Cleisthenes
are discussed. The importance of such measures was clearly realised by
Aristotle. Cf. *Pol.* vii 4 1319 b 19 ἔτι δὲ καὶ τὰ τοιαῦτα κατασκευάσματα
χρήσιμα πρὸς τὴν δημοκρατίαν τὴν τοιαύτην, οἷς Κλεισθένης τε Ἀθήνησιν ἐχρή-
σατο βουλόμενος αὐξῆσαι τὴν δημοκρατίαν, καὶ περὶ Κυρήνην οἱ τὸν δῆμον
καθιστάντες. φυλαί τε γὰρ ἕτεραι ποιητέαι πλείους καὶ φρατρίαι, καὶ τὰ τῶν
ἰδίων ἱερῶν συνακτέον εἰς ὀλίγα καὶ κοινά, καὶ πάντα σοφιστέον, ὅπως ἂν ὅτι

The instance of Athens shows us how important it was to dissolve the old tribal associations and how hard it was to effect their dissolution.   In most cases the tyranny performed this useful service : for the tyranny was called into being in the interests of the commons to break the power of the nobles, and this could only be done by depriving the old tribes of their dominant position.   We cannot tell by what particular means this was accomplished : in many cases the nobles were banished, in others, as at Sicyon, they were degraded[32].   We have evidence of disputes between the privileged and the excluded in other states[33], instances of the creation of artificial divisions in place of old tribal systems[34]; but even in default of positive evidence, we know that the change must have been accomplished before oligarchy was possible : and it is important to remember that the overthrow of these aristocratic privileges was as necessary a condition of oligarchy as of democracy.

The measures I have been discussing involved religious changes.   It was by a religious fiction that the commons were admitted to the γένη at Athens ; and the new poli-

μάλιστα ἀναμιχθῶσι πάντες ἀλλήλοις, αἱ δὲ συνήθειαι διαζευχθῶσιν αἱ πρότεραι.
Such measures were equally necessary before an oligarchy could succeed an aristocracy.

[32] Hdt. v 68.

[33] Such disputes were especially frequent in the colonies between the later immigrants and the original settlers.   See Ch. iv § 31.

[34] Busolt, *Die Lakedaimonier* p. 184, argues that ten local tribes took the place of nine birth tribes at Elis.   The inference is drawn from Paus. v 9 6.   A similar change in the tribal organisation at Cyrene is related by Hdt. iv 161, and the passage of Aristotle quoted in n. 31 probably refers to this (though Gilbert, *Handbuch* ii p. 230, assigns it to a later development of democracy mentioned by Heraclides, F. H. G. ii 212).

tical organisations had their religious side ; new cults had
to be instituted for the local tribes and demes. It was
essential that the religious privilege of the nobles should
be abolished not only in the tribe and its subdivisions but
also in the state generally. Hence the overthrow of aristocratic government was marked by the introduction of
new gods and new worships : and the efforts made by the
tyrants to gain the support of great religious organisations
show how keenly they realised the strength of religious
elements in political affairs.

§ 26. *Development of constitutions in the fifth century.*

The transition to oligarchy was usually accomplished
after an interval of tyranny. Tyrannies were prevalent
in Greece in the seventh and sixth centuries, and the
latter century witnessed the birth of democracy, the great
rival of oligarchy. It would involve a deviation from the
subject of this essay to discuss the causes which produced
democracy : democracy only concerns us as the alternative
to oligarchy. I have already referred to the cleavage of
Greek states in accordance with their form of government,
and to the influence of Athens and Sparta as the respective
champions of democracy and oligarchy, of 'liberty and
equality' on the one hand, of 'good order and good sense'
on the other[1].

Their influence may be illustrated from the events of
the fifth century. Apart from the Delian and the Peloponnesian confederacies, in which, as I have shown above,
each power exerted a steady pressure in favour of its

---

[1] ἐλευθερία and ἰσονομία opposed to εὐνομία and σωφροσύνη.

own principles, we may note the establishment of democracy in Argos and Megara, which should probably be
regarded as a consequence of their alliance with Athens[2],
and it is usually assumed that democracies were established
in Boeotia after the battle of Oenophyta[3]. During the
Peloponnesian war Athens strove to forward the cause of
democracy, by alliance with democratic states[4] or by
forcible methods[5], while the Spartans used their power
to strengthen the hands of the oligarchs in many cities[6].
The Sicilian disaster was followed by the revolt of many
Athenian allies, most of them establishing oligarchies immediately on revolt[7]; and after the crushing defeat of
Aegospotami Lysander imposed absolute and violent
oligarchies on almost every state in Greece[8]. In some

[2] The break-up of the general union of Greece, and the formation of
separate alliances, which dates from 461, accentuated the constitutional
differences. The existence of democracy at Megara in 427 is attested by
Thuc. iv 66, and Argos, which had been aristocratic in 480 (Hdt. vii 149),
was democratic in 421 (Thuc. v 31). Gilbert, *Handbuch* ii p. 70 and
p. 77, is probably right in suggesting that the change of constitution was
connected with their alliance with Athens.

[3] The evidence is hardly strong enough for the conclusion. See
Busolt, *Geschichte* ii[1] p. 493 n. 5, p. 494 n. 1.

[4] The coalition of Athens, Argos, Elis and Mantinea in 419 B.C. was
a combination of democracies.

[5] The plan of Demosthenes against Boeotia was concerted with
democratic partisans: and it was doubtless intended to establish
democracies.

[6] Examples of Spartan influence are, the restoration of oligarchy at
Megara (Thuc. iv 74): the establishment of the shortlived oligarchy at
Argos (Thuc. v 81): the strengthening of the oligarchy at Sicyon (Thuc.
v 81): the interference with the constitution in Achaea (v 82).

[7] Thuc. viii 64.

[8] Plut. *Lys.* 14 κατέλυε τὰς πολιτείας καὶ καθίστη δεκαδαρχίας. Cf. Xen.
Hell. iii 5 12—13; Diod. xiv 10.

cities his work was undone by the Spartan government[9], but in many oligarchies lingered on until Spartan power was shattered by the defeats of Cnidus and Leuctra.

§ 27. *Development of constitutions in the fourth century.*

The political state of Greece in the fourth century shows a marked change from its condition in the fifth century. Neither Sparta nor Athens had the ascendency which she had hitherto enjoyed; other states rose to power and in general the lesser cities were left free to control their constitutions as they liked. One general tendency was the intensification of democracies and oligarchies: extreme forms of both these types were developed towards the end of the century[1], and the philosophers, familiar with narrow oligarchies and tyrannical democracies, impressed with the rarity of moderate and legal governments[2], came to regard all existing constitutions as perversions[3] and turned with relief to the study of the ideal.

[9] Xen. *Hell.* iii 4 2.

[1] Cf. Newman, *Introduction* pp. 417—8. 'The Greek states were ruled either by harsh soldiers, pugnacious and keen for distinction like the Spartans, or by rapacious oligarchs, demagogues or tyrants....We know from Aristotle that moderate forms of oligarchy and democracy did exist, but he dwells on the intolerance of compromise and the determination not to share power with others.'

[2] See Ar. *Pol.* vi 11 1296 a 1. He discusses the extreme forms δῆμος ἔσχατος, ὀλιγαρχία ἄκρατος and τυραννίς; he talks of the rarity of moderate forms, and sums up the matter (l. 40) ἤδη δὲ καὶ τοῖς ἐν ταῖς πόλεσιν ἔθος καθέστηκε μηδὲ βούλεσθαι τὸ ἴσον, ἀλλ' ἢ ἄρχειν ζητεῖν ἢ κρατουμένους ὑπομένειν.

[3] To Plato all ordinary constitutions are perversions: even to Aristotle ἀριστοκρατία (which should mean the normal oligarchy) scarcely exists save as an ideal, while δημοκρατία had such evil associations that πολιτεία had to be employed to denote the normal democracy.

While one tendency of the age was to intensify the character of existing governments, the current set in favour of democracy rather than of oligarchy. The effective causes were various. The decline of Sparta, the break-up of her alliance, and the loss of her empire, set free a number of states, in which oligarchy had only been maintained by force. The most powerful and the most unscrupulous champion of this form of government was deprived of influence.

Alterations in the relative strength of classes must have been caused by the Peloponnesian war, which involved the decrease in the number of the better classes and the loss of much of their property[4]. Connected with this was the introduction of mercenary forces, which diminished the importance of the citizen soldier.

Economic causes tended to the same result. Trade became of increased importance, and trade is, in general, ultimately favourable to democracy. Hence came the growth of large trading cities, in which the people learnt to know their power and to divide the public funds by a system of state-socialism. It may have been this tendency which led Aristotle to the conclusion that 'in a large town it is difficult for any constitution save democracy to exist[5].'

The effect of the critical events of the fourth century may be briefly dismissed. The battle of Cnidus set free the islands and the Greek cities of Asia[6] and was un-

---

[4] Ar. *Pol.* viii 3 1303 a 8 (of Athens).

[5] *Pol.* iii 15 1286 b 20. Thucydides (vi 39 2) says practically the same thing, ἃ ὑμῶν οἱ δυνάμενοι (= oligarchs) προθυμοῦνται ἀδύνατα ἐν μεγάλῃ πόλει κατασχεῖν.

[6] Xen. *Hell.* iv 8 1.

doubtedly followed by the overthrow of many of the Lysandrian oligarchies[7]. The work was to a large extent undone by the peace of Antalcidas, which delivered over the Greeks of Asia to Persia. Persian dominion was maintained in them by means of oligarchies or tyrannies, which were overthrown by Alexander[8].

The democratic revolution at Thebes in 379 was in every way important. The Boeotian towns adopted the constitution of their capital, and when once Thebes had gained supremacy in Greece, she used her power to establish democracies[9]. The battle of Leuctra broke for ever the ascendency of Sparta: most of the Peloponnesian states renounced their allegiance and a series of revolutions led to the general triumph of democracy[10]. In 356 the Social war set free the Athenian allies to mould their constitutions to their own liking, and many seem to have established oligarchies without delay[11]. These events and

[7] There is little positive evidence: but many states attached themselves to the Athenian alliance immediately after Cnidus: and we may assume that the democracies, which can be traced in many of them soon after, now took the place of the decarchies. The narrative of Diodorus xiv 84 implies this.

[8] Plut. *Alex.* 34 mentions the overthrow of tyrannies: Arrian i 18 1—2 of oligarchies.

[9] Although Thebes did not interfere with the autonomy of other states, the new foundations of Messene and Megalopolis seem to have been democratic.

[10] At Argos there was a massacre of oligarchs (Diod. xv 57): at Sicyon a tyranny was established in the interests of democracy (Xen. *Hell.* viii 1 46); the democracy was probably restored at Mantinea (*ib.* vi 5 3) and at Tegea (vi 5 6).

[11] In Chios, Mitylene, Rhodes and many other states oligarchies were established probably at this time. See Dem. xv 19 and cf. Ar. *Pol.* viii 3 1302 b 22 and 5 1304 b 25—30 on Rhodes and Cos.

the termination of the brief Theban supremacy removed from Greek politics the influence of dominant powers and for a brief season there was a free competition of constitutions. But in the interval the power of Macedon had risen and Chaeronea put Greece beneath the heel of Philip. Greece was no longer independent, but her master was indifferent to the war of constitutions, by which she had for so long been distraught. To him oligarchy, democracy or tyranny were equal, so long as the government offered a sense of security and was ready to subserve his dominion[12]. The city state had reached the end of its development: the future was with monarchies and federations; and it is with mingled humour and pity that we read the poems of Isyllus, who, blind to all the real forces of the age, vaunts the power of the god in beating back Philip and looks for the salvation of Hellas in the return to a pious, mediaeval state of the Dorian type; and seeks a counterpoise to Macedon in those nobles of the Dorian tribes, who are to grow their hair long and establish a new festival in honour of the patron saint of Epidaurus, the god of health and fortune—Asclepius[13].

[12] Macedon interfered, if she had reason to fear the conduct of an existing government. Thus at Thebes Philip established an oligarchy of exiles (Justin ix 4): and in 322 Antipater established a moderate timocracy at Athens.

[13] See Wilamowitz-Möllendorff, *Isyllos von Epidauros*, where the poems are quoted.

APPENDIX A.

The formation of the united Athenian state[1].

The history of Athens down to the seventh century is based almost entirely on legends, supported by inferences drawn from later institutions or survivals. The time has gone by when the stories of Erechtheus, Cecrops, Ion and Theseus would be accepted as genuine accounts of the reign of real kings. But it may be possible to derive some historical results from legendary evidence, and it would be as unwise altogether to reject as implicitly to accept the help of myths and tradition[2].

Three stages in the unification of Attica are associated with the names of Cecrops, Ion and Theseus. The comparative method in its application to the origin of civilised communities, the tendencies at work in later Athenian

[1] In this Appendix I have endeavoured to present a credible account of the development of the Athenian commonwealth. I have not discussed all the theories that have been proposed, nor have I quoted all the evidence that makes for or against the theories I adopt. My object is to call attention to certain striking points, many of which escape notice in the ordinary textbooks. To deal exhaustively with the evidence and speculation on the subject would require a separate treatise of no inconsiderable length.

[2] The instance of Roman history shows what good results may be extracted from a rational treatment of the legends.

history[3] and the survival of religious festivals[4] show that the Athenian state was gradually developed by the combination of small tribal communities into larger groups; and it is entirely immaterial whether kings with the names of Cecrops, Ion and Theseus ever lived, if we can trace in the legends, however vaguely and indistinctly, some steps in the process.

In the first political system of Attica there was a number of village communities, the settlements of noble families with their followers and dependents[5]. The tendency towards union made itself felt, and partly by force, partly by voluntary cohesion, the villages gradually formed themselves into larger political communities, and legend attributed to Cecrops the combination of the κῶμαι into twelve πόλεις[6]. We may assume that at an early date the villages, feeling the need of common defence and common government, united in πόλεις, hill forts to which they could resort in time of danger[7], and which had each their king's house, council chamber and rulers[8]. Probably the πόλεις were joined in a loose federal system, such as existed in Boeotia and Latium, and in time of danger they

[3] For the tendencies to separation in later Athenian history see Appendix B.

[4] So Thucydides ii 15 quotes the festival of the ξυνοίκια as evidence for the union of Attica and bases a further argument on the buildings of the Acropolis. Cf. Harpocration on the Panathenaea.

[5] See above § 25 nn. 27—30.

[6] Strabo ix 397 quotes Philochorus. There were many reasons why the number twelve should be adopted and no stress need be laid upon it.

[7] The fortification was usually the first step in the foundation of a city.

[8] Thuc. ii 15 ἐπὶ γὰρ Κέκροπος καὶ τῶν πρώτων βασιλέων ἡ ᾽Αττικὴ ἐς Θησέα ἀεὶ κατὰ πόλεις ᾠκεῖτο πρυτανεῖά τε ἐχούσας καὶ ἄρχοντας. The πρυτανεῖα I take to be the residence of the chiefs.

recognised the sway of a single overlord, though they each had their separate governments and sometimes warred with one another[9].

The next stage in the progress towards unity was associated with the name of Ion, the eponymous hero of the Ionians, represented as the leader of a body of immigrants who settled in Attica[10], and gave their name to the people of the land[11]. In this way the legend suggests the spread of a feeling of unity, and Aristotle regards Ion as the first founder of the Attic commonwealth[12]. In other ways Ion's coming was important: he was said to have been made polemarch of Athens[13] by a division of the kingly power, which reminds us of the union of Ramnes and Tities and the consequent division of authority between Romulus and Tatius; he was said also to have founded the four Ionian tribes, each with a φυλοβασιλεύς as its head[14]. As to the origin, the composition or the purpose of these tribes there is still endless controversy, but if we conclude that they corresponded to local

[9] Thuc. *l.c.* continues καὶ ὁπότε μή τι δείσειαν, οὐ ξυνῇεσαν βουλευσόμενοι ὡς τὸν βασιλέα, ἀλλ' αὐτοὶ ἕκαστοι ἐπολιτεύοντο καὶ ἐβουλεύοντο· καί τινες καὶ ἐπολέμησάν ποτε αὐτῶν.

[10] Ar. *Ath. Pol.* 41 2 πρώτη μὲν γὰρ ἐγένετο κατάστασις τῶν ἐξ ἀρχῆς Ἴωνος καὶ τῶν μετ' αὐτοῦ συνοικησάντων· τότε γὰρ πρῶτον εἰς τὰς τέτταρας συνενεμήθησαν φυλὰς καὶ τοὺς φυλοβασιλεῖς κατέστησαν. Aristotle gave an account of Ion in the chapters lost from the beginning of the treatise: cf. *fr.* 381[3].

[11] Heracl. *Epit.* 1 συνοικήσαντος δὲ Ἴωνος αὐτοῖς, τότε πρῶτον Ἴωνες ἐκλήθησαν; cf. *fr.* 381[3].

[12] See the passage quoted in n. 10. The use of συνενεμήθησαν points to the establishment of a united state.

[13] See Ar. *Ath. Pol.* 3 2 and the other passages quoted by Dr Sandys in his note.

[14] See Aristotle quoted in n. 10.

divisions, we may trace in the legends the second great
step in the unification of Attica[15]. The πόλεις, with the
κῶμαι attached to them, were now grouped in four tribes,
each tribe having some unity of religion and government
and ruled by a φυλοβασιλεύς. It is not clear what place
Athens held at the time, whether her primacy was
recognised and whether the Athenian king exercised a
suzerainty over all Attica or ranked only as one of the
φυλοβασιλεῖς. But here we receive help from another
legend. Strabo says that all writers of *Atthides* were
agreed that the four sons of Pandion II. ruled over the
four divisions into which Attica was divided, and he quotes
a fragment of Sophocles to prove that Aegeus (who received Cecropia) was given the best share[16]. It seems
reasonable to connect these four divisions with the four
tribes, and the sons of Pandion with the φυλοβασιλεῖς.
On this assumption Athens (then called Cecropia) was
only the capital of one of the φυλαί, but its leading position
is shown by the title πρεσβεῖα given to it by Sophocles
and by its being the lot of Aegeus, presumably the eldest
son of Pandion ; while the assumption that Pandion was

---

[15] I omit the evidence for this conclusion. It is natural to assume
that the φυλοβασιλεῖς originally possessed real kingly power, and it is
difficult to conceive that any system of common government could at so
early a date be applied to tribes that were not local. Gilbert, *Handbuch* i[2]
p. 116 n. 1, quotes Ar. *Ath. Pol.* 21 3 to show that the τριττύες (which
were subdivisions of the φυλαί) corresponded to local divisions ; it would
follow that the φυλαί also were local. The identification of the tribes
with the four local divisions mentioned by Strabo (see n. 16) supplies a
confirmation of this theory.

[16] Strabo ix 392 (Megara and Euboea are included). Cf. also Heracl.
Epit. 1 Πανδίων δὲ βασιλεύσας μετὰ Ἐρεχθέα διένειμε τὴν ἀρχὴν τοῖς υἱοῖς
καὶ διετέλουν οὗτοι στασιάζοντες. If any stress be laid on this we must
assume that the four divisions tended to disunion.

able to make his four sons tribal kings, points to the dominant influence of the city. If this be correct the φυλοβασιλεῖς were sovereigns, ruling over large districts of Attica : their office survived after Athens had become the seat of government of a united Attica, and though they may at first have retained some power in the state[17], in course of time they lost all but certain ritual functions[18].

The existence of four separate kingdoms was likely to lead to rivalry and discord, and the next step was ascribed to Theseus, the son of Aegeus, who was said to have effected the συνοικισμός of Attica, to have put down the separate governments of all other πόλεις and made Athens the capital and seat of government of a united country[19]. There is less controversy about his work, and the only point that I wish to discuss is the division of the population into Eupatridae, Geomori and Demiurgi, which was said by Plutarch to be the work of Theseus[20]. But the division was obviously not an artificial institution : the three classes are such as are naturally found in all early societies. The most satisfactory explanation is that classes corresponding in their functions and privileges to these existed in the separate communities, that at the epoch associated with the name of Theseus these classes

---

[17] From their association with the βασιλεὺς in later times, Gilbert, *Handbuch* i² p. 120 n. 1, concludes that they formed a council of state assisting the king and representing the tribes.

[18] See Dr Sandys' n. to Ar. *Ath. Pol.* 3 2. The φυλοβασιλεῖς are generally supposed to be the βασιλεῖς mentioned in Plut. *Sol.* 19; Andoc. i 78.

[19] Thuc. ii 15.

[20] Plut. *Thes.* 25.

were made part of the political organisation of the united
state, and separate titles instituted to describe them[21].
From this time we trace the rise of Athens as a city state
and the rule of the men of the city over the country
people[22].

[21] This theory offers a satisfactory explanation of the names given to
the different classes. I suppose that similar class divisions existed in
the separate communities, but without common names. The Eupatridae
—which is an obviously artificial title—were the chieftains of the separate
communities (Bekker *Anecd.* Εὐπατρίδαι...μετέχοντες βασιλικοῦ γένους), who
doubtless had hitherto borne the patronymic names of their γένη. The
variety of titles under which the other classes were cited points to the
existence of such orders with varying titles in the different communities. Thus the Geomori are also cited as Γεωργοί, Ἄγροικοι,
Ἀγροιῶται, Ἄποικοι (?): while the Demiurgi are also called ἐπιγεώμοροι.

[22] See Meyer, *Geschichte des Alterthums* ii p. 336.

APPENDIX B.

The Athenian γένη and their importance in the early constitution[1].

In the preceding appendix I have traced in outline the gradual union of the people of Attica under one system of government. In the constitution thus formed privilege was restricted to the nobles[2], who possessed in other respects a dominant position, as society was organised on an aristocratic basis, the inhabitants of the country districts being dependent on the noble houses, whose members formed the ruling class in Athens.

The state was organised in γένη, φρατρίαι and φυλαί. The origin of the φυλαί I have already discussed; if the assumption that they formed local divisions of Attica be correct, we may assume that they included all classes of the people, but it is generally agreed that the φρατρίαι

[1] The following appendix, like the last, is intended to call attention to certain important questions without discussing the theories of others or quoting the evidence in full. The subject is exceedingly intricate and all conclusions must be more or less tentative. I have prolonged the Appendix in order to suggest an emendation in Ar. *Ath. Pol.* 22 4 which seems to me to involve some points of importance.

[2] For the early aristocratic Constitution of Athens cf. especially Ar. *Ath. Pol.* 2 and 3.

and the γένη, subdivisions based on birth, were originally closed to all but Eupatrids. Thus they formed the outworks of the aristocracy, if, as we may fairly conclude, membership of a γένος was a necessary condition of citizenship. Solon's legislation broke down the exclusive privilege of birth and substituted other qualifications for citizenship, but it did not abolish the tribal organisation of the state or deprive it of its political importance.

We have now to see how the admission of non-Eupatrids to citizenship was reconciled with the maintenance of the old birth organisations. We have no direct evidence to guide us and the greatest uncertainty still prevails[3].

There are several passages in the grammarians, all in substantial accord and probably ultimately derived from Aristotle, which describe the tribal organisation of Attica[4]. Two of these, both citing Aristotle[5], say that the whole

[3] Of recent textbooks Gilbert, *Handbuch* i[2] pp. 117—9, says 'Originally none but Eupatrids were counted as members of Phratries and γένη...... after the time of Draco at any rate, if not before, the burgess body, and therefore the phratries also, contained non-Eupatrid members'; Busolt, *Staatsaltertümer*[2] p. 126 n. 1, says 'In Solon's time at least the lower orders were admitted to the tribes' but he implies that they were not members of the γένη; Thumser (Hermann, *Lehrbuch*[6] p. 312) seems to think that the γένη did include non-Eupatrids, though he is uncertain whether there were special γένη for them or whether they were admitted to the old γένη; Meyer, *Geschichte des Alterthums* ii p. 311, thinks that at a comparatively early period the whole population was divided into γένη.

[4] The chief passages are Lexicon Dem. Patm. p. 152 Sakkelion (quoted by Dr Sandys in his edition of Aristotle's *Constitution of Athens* p. 252): Scholiast to Plato *Axiochus* 371 D; Pollux viii 111; Harpocration *s.v.* γεννῆται.

[5] Lexicon Dem. Patm. and Scholiast to Plato *l.c.* They are undoubtedly based on a lost passage in Aristotle's *Ath. Pol.*

population of Athens was divided into three classes; these were divided into four tribes, each tribe into three φρατρίαι, each φρατρία into 30 γένη, each γένος containing 30 men. Harpocration says that *all the citizens* were divided into φυλαί, φρατρίαι and γένη. Moreover the authorities show that Aristotle assumed a multitude of over 10,000 γεννῆται, and though the numbers are obviously fanciful and artificial, it seems clear that Aristotle could not have imagined that the Eupatridae alone included anything like that number. The only indication as to the date at which this elaborate system was drawn up is a statement that ' of old before Cleisthenes introduced his tribal organisation ' the population was so divided[6]. The system described in the passages cited, which assume, I think, the admission of non-Eupatrids, need not be put earlier than the reforms of Draco and Solon (which lasted until Cleisthenes), although the division of the Eupatrids into house, clan and tribe was probably a natural institution dating from the earliest times. This is the chief direct evidence and it might be supported by many inferences: but taking it alone the statements are explicit, and it does not seem reasonable to attach to them any other meaning than that the whole of the citizen population, whether Eupatrid or not, was admitted to γένος, φρατρία and φυλή.

We have next to discuss the means by which the γένη were opened to the Geomori and Demiurgi. The object might have been accomplished by the institution of new γένη, in which they should be enrolled. Of such a measure there is no evidence, nor is there anything to prove the existence of separate non-Eupatrid γένη in

[6] Lexicon Dem. Patm. *l.c.*

later times. Considering the imperfect character of the
materials for the history of the period, it would not be
safe to lay much stress on the silence of the historians,
but they are far less likely to have passed over altogether the creation of new γένη, than to have omitted to
mention the admission of new citizens to the different
divisions of the citizen body; for this step they might
regard as implied in the statement of their admission to
citizenship. Moreover the number of tribes and phratries
was not altered, as we might expect had there been a
large increase in the number of the γένη. Rejecting this
hypothesis we must conclude that the γένη already in
existence were opened to all citizens. It is true that
these γένη were supposed to be based on kinship, but
in early societies there is no legal fiction more frequently
and extensively employed, than ' that which permits family
relations to be artificially created[7].' The method would
be characteristic of primitive legislation. Moreover there
would have been a powerful motive for the inclusion of
the new citizens in the old γένη. Our whole conception
of early Athenian history requires us to assume the
division of Attica among a number of Eupatrid families,
each having attached to them in a patriarchal relation a
large number of dependents, belonging to the other orders
in the state. The power of the Eupatrids depended on
the allegiance of these vassals, and we may well imagine
that when it was felt necessary to extend the franchise,
the powerful nobles were more easily reconciled to it, if
citizen privileges and perhaps the exercise of citizen
powers were made to depend on the membership of or-

[7] Maine, *Ancient Law* p. 130.

ganisations in which they themselves were all-powerful. This theory of the γένη harmonises in every respect with what we know of Athenian history in the sixth century. The period was characterised by the struggles of great families and local factions. It was not a war of nobles against commons, but a war of factions, each of which had noble leaders and included all classes of the population.

The next question is whether there is any evidence in the constitution of the γένη of the admission of non-Eupatrid members. No subject is more difficult or has given rise to more controversy than this: the authorities, who after all tell us very little, are in conflict with one another and no safe conclusions can be drawn from them[8]. But the grammarians seem to have thought that the γεννῆται (in the general sense of members of the γένος) included two classes, ὁμογάλακτες and ὀργεῶνες. Many theories have been suggested to explain the distinction[9], and on the whole the most satisfactory is that which assumes that the ὁμογάλακτες (γεννῆται in a special sense) were the original Eupatrid members of the γένος, who could trace their common descent, while the ὀργεῶνες (signifying those who shared in the religious rites

[8] Pollux iii 52; viii 111; Suidas *s.v.* ὁμογάλακτες and ὀργεῶνες: Harpocration *s.v.* γεννῆται: Bekker *Anecdota* p. 227 9—15. The distinction is drawn most explicitly in Philochorus quoted by Suidas τοὺς δὲ φράτερας ἐπάναγκες δέχεσθαι καὶ τοὺς ὀργεῶνας καὶ τοὺς ὁμογάλακτας (possibly from an old law). The admission of non-Eupatrids to the phratries at least by the time of Draco is established by the law of Draco quoted in Dem. xliii 57 where ἀριστίνδην can scarcely bear any other meaning than 'from the nobles.'

[9] Thumser (Hermann, *Lehrbuch*[6] 319—20) assumes that the ὀργεῶνες were new members of the γένη admitted after the incorporation of Eleusis.

of the γένος and therefore including strictly *all* members of the γένος[10]) were, in a special sense, the non-Eupatrid members admitted to the γένος by the fiction of common religious rites. This fictitious method of admission tended to make the γένος into a political institution, and it is quite possible that before Cleisthenes it served as an artificial division of the population[11].

By the time of Solon then, if not before, the commons were admitted to citizenship. Solon's reforms had effected their political emancipation, but they had left the tribal organisation of Attica unaffected : the privilege of citizenship depended on admission to a γένος, an organisation dominated by noble influence. Thus Solon, if he took away the political privileges of the aristocracy, left their personal influence unimpaired. Hence his reforms made but little practical difference to Athenian history.

Factions and seditions broke out immediately after his departure from Athens[12], and his constitution seems never to have been actually realised, until Cleisthenes, by changes of organisation, made it possible for the institutions of Solon to do their work. Cleisthenes' reforms were not

[10] Bekker *l.c.* γένος ἐστὶ σύστημα ἐκ τριάκοντα ἀνδρῶν συνεστώς, οὗ οἱ μετέχοντες ἐκαλοῦντο γεννῆται (in the general sense of the word), οὐ κατὰ γένος ἀλλήλοις προσήκοντες, οὐδ' ἀπὸ τοῦ αὐτοῦ αἵματος, ἀλλά...κοινωνίαν τινὰ ἔχοντες...συγγενικῶν ὀργίων ἢ θεῶν, ἀφ' ὧν ὀργεῶνες ὠνομάσθησαν. From this it would appear that ὀργεῶνες was wide enough to include *all* γεννῆται, but it appears from other passages that it was especially used in opposition to ὁμογάλακτες.

[11] In Bekker *l.c.* the γένος is defined as a σύστημα ἐκ τριάκοντα ἀνδρῶν συνεστώς: Harpocration explains γεννῆται as οὐχ οἱ συγγενεῖς ἁπλῶς· ἀλλ οἱ ἐξ ἀρχῆς εἰς τὰ καλούμενα γένη κατανεμηθέντες.

[12] Ar. *Ath. Pol.* 13. The compromise effected after the expulsion of Damasias seems to point to some feeling between the orders, but the incident is too obscure to help us very much.

intended to introduce new principles into the constitution, to increase the power of the people or even to extend the franchise to any great extent. Their object and effect was to alter the social organisation, to break the personal influence of the Eupatrids, to divorce the conduct of the government from any connexion with the γένη. It would be beyond the province of this essay to discuss the reforms of Cleisthenes; but I wish to consider the accounts of his work, in so far as they throw light on the *aristocratic* organisation of the Solonian constitution.

The clearest account of his work is given in Aristotle's *Constitution of Athens* ch. 21. The introduction of ten new tribes needs no commentary. It was intended to 'mix (the population) in order that more might take part in politics' (§ 2). ὅθεν ἐλέχθη καὶ τὸ μὴ φυλοκρινεῖν, πρὸς τοὺς ἐξετάζειν τὰ γένη βουλομένους. The meaning of this passage is not obvious, but the last clause is most important. 'The saying arose "don't distinguish tribes" addressed to those who wanted to find out the γένος of anybody.' Under the new constitution the γένη were not connected with the local tribes, and membership of a γένος was no longer necessary to citizenship. New citizens had been created, who had not belonged to the old γένη: for their sake reference to the γένη was to be avoided, but the passage would be devoid of meaning if we supposed that only the Eupatrids had hitherto been admitted to the γένη. We need not discuss the local organization introduced by Cleisthenes (§§ 3 and 4): but at the end of § 4 there is a passage which needs explanation and also, I venture to think, emendation. The passage is as follows:

Καὶ δημότας ἐποίησεν ἀλλήλων τοὺς οἰκοῦντας ἐν

ἑκάστῳ τῶν δήμων, ἵνα μὴ πατρόθεν προσαγορεύοντες
ἐξελέγχωσιν τοὺς νεοπολίτας, ἀλλὰ τῶν δήμων ἀναγορεύ-
ωσιν· ὅθεν καὶ καλοῦσιν 'Αθηναῖοι σφᾶς αὐτοὺς τῶν
δήμων.

With the reading πατρόθεν the passage seems mean-
ingless to me. In the first place there is no reason why a
Greek of alien origin should declare his non-Athenian
birth by quoting his father's name: many of the same
names were found in different states: it would be impossible to say off-hand whether a name were of Athenian
origin or not. Secondly both before and *after* Cleisthenes
Athenians were called officially by their father's name,
and when the practice of adding a man's deme was introduced it did not drive out the custom of quoting his
father's name[13]. But if we assume that before Cleisthenes
a man was called by his *gentile* name[14], as he naturally
would be if his citizenship depended on his membership
of a γένος, then Cleisthenes did introduce a change and the
motive of citing the man's deme is obvious. It seems to
me that the exact sense required would be given by the
alteration of one letter, the substitution of the rare word
πάτραθεν, which has perhaps been driven out by the
more familiar πατρόθεν. Πάτραθεν in the sense of ' by
his clan name' would contrast the old organisation by
γένη with the new organization by δῆμοι, and the motive
assigned is 'citizens were no longer to be called by their
γένη, lest the new citizens (who had not been included in

[13] The practice was so constant that it does not seem necessary to
quote examples. If any were needed the tablets of ostracism, dating
only a few years after Cleisthenes (quoted by Dr Sandys, *Constitution of
Athens* p. 88), would be sufficient.

[14] There are many instances in which a man's γένος is quoted: Hdt.
v 55; v 66; Ar. *Ath. Pol.* 20 1.

a γένος) should be discovered at once; they were to be cited by their demes.' This agrees with the clause in the second section πρὸς τοὺς ἐξετάζειν τὰ γένη βουλομένους. Everything was done to prevent the γένος from having any influence whatever on politics: on the one hand the new citizens must be put on a level with the old, on the other hand men must exercise their political power simply as citizens not as members of a γένος, and every effort was made to prevent members of a γένος from acting together.

I have now to establish, as far as it is possible, the use of the word πάτραθεν. This form is found, I think, only once (Pind. Nem. 7 70), but in the exact sense required. Εὐξενίδα πάτραθε Σώγενες, says Pindar, honouring a man by citing his clan. Πάτρα, however, occurs more frequently. It bore two distinct meanings, fatherhood (i.e. clan, and so equivalent to γένος) and fatherland. In the former sense it is defined by Dicaearchus as identical with γένος, and inscriptions prove that it was so employed in Thasos, Rhodes and other places[15], and Pindar uses it constantly as an equivalent of οἶκος and γενέα[16]. Elsewhere (in old Ionic) according to the lexicons it was used almost always in the sense of πατρίς[17].

Is it not permissible to suppose that in the sixth century B.C. πάτρα was used in Attic, in a sense which might include both ideas (fatherhood and fatherland) and that πάτραθεν at any rate bore the special sense of ' by

[15] F. H. G. ii 238. The inscriptions are cited by Gilbert, Handbuch ii p. 302.
[16] Pind. Nem. 4 77; 6 41; 8 46; Pyth. 8 38; Isthm. 5 (6) 63 (all referring to Aegina): Nem. 11 20 (referring to Tenedos).
[17] In Il. xiii 354 it is used in the sense of fatherhood; and in Hdt. vi 126 it would give a better sense if we could translate it descent.

his clan'?   We know that the word was so used in other Ionic communities, and it was perhaps the archaic equivalent of γένος, possibly quoted by Aristotle from an actual law of Cleisthenes[18].

[18] Is it possible that πατρῷος is connected with πάτρα as the god of the clan, and may *patricius* in Latin have been connected with a word of similar meaning and denoted originally those who were the only true members of the original *gentes* (*gentiles*)?

CHAPTER IV.

VARIETIES OF OLIGARCHY.

§ 28. *Principles of Classification.*

WE have seen in the preceding chapters that whether we study the character of constitutions or whether we trace their historical development, there is a clear principle of separation between the aristocracy of birth and the oligarchy of wealth. But in discussing the organisation of government, the division of political functions and the details of political institutions, we can no longer keep the two constitutions apart: on the one hand the character of oligarchical institutions can only be understood by tracing their original type as it existed in the aristocratic state, on the other hand there is so general a similarity between the forms and method of the two governments that it would be idle to consider one apart from the other. Except in so far as different qualifications for citizenship or other variations of principle separate them, they will be treated in common.

We must first arrive at some principle by means of which different forms of oligarchical government may be distinguished. Oligarchy is the government of 'a part[1],'

---

[1] Cf. Thuc. vi 39 1, Athenagoras says ἐγὼ δέ φημι πρῶτα μὲν δῆμον ξύμπαν ὠνομάσθαι, ὀλιγαρχίαν δὲ μέρος. In ii 37 Pericles says of Athens ἕκαστος...οὐκ ἀπὸ μέρους...ἐς τὰ κοινά...προτιμᾶται.

not of the whole: by some principle of selection men,
otherwise on an equality, are divided into two classes:
those who belong to the minority possess political privileges and are defined as 'those within the constitution';
the rest have no political rights and are ' without the con-
stitution².' This characteristic offers a satisfactory test
for the subdivision of oligarchies, and they may be classified in accordance with the conditions required for citizenship, using that word to denote active political rights³.
The qualification for citizenship was not in all states the
same as the qualification for the magistracies⁴; but this
distinction is not of sufficient importance to affect our
classification.

In the following pages I discuss the different varieties
of oligarchies, in so far as this principle enables us to
distinguish them. The classification is of necessity em-
pirical and incomplete. I have collected the available

---

² The distinction into οἱ ἐν τῇ πολιτείᾳ or οἱ ἐν τῷ πολιτεύματι and οἱ
ἐκτὸς or οἱ ἔξω, which is characteristic of oligarchy, occurs again and
again in Aristotle. It is unnecessary to quote instances: both classes
are alluded to in *Pol.* viii 8 1308 a 6. The privileged body is often called
τὸ πολίτευμα and this is defined as τὸ κύριον τῶν πόλεων. Cf. *Pol.* iii 6
1279 a 25; 1279 b 11.

³ I have quoted Aristotle's definition of 'citizen' in § 4 n. 2. We
must remember that he uses ἀρχὴ to include all political functions, as he
explains in the same passage that participation in the assembly or law
courts is as ἀόριστος ἀρχή. Aristotle uses ἀρχὴ and ἀρχαί in two senses
(1) generally of citizenship: (2) specially of magisterial powers. But in
the definition of the different forms of oligarchy (discussed in the next
section) there is no doubt that he uses the word in its general sense.
The passage quoted in the next note contains an instance of the special
use.

⁴ Ar. *Pol.* viii 6 1305 b 30 ἐν ὅσαις ὀλιγαρχίαις οὐχ οὗτοι αἱροῦνται τὰς
ἀρχὰς ἐξ ὧν οἱ ἄρχοντές εἰσιν, ἀλλ' αἱ μὲν ἀρχαὶ ἐκ τιμημάτων μεγάλων εἰσὶν
ἢ ἑταιριῶν, αἱροῦνται δ' οἱ ὁπλῖται ἢ ὁ δῆμος. See below, § 41.

evidence on the different categories of oligarchies or aristocracies, but I have not been able to avoid cross divisions,
and many particular constitutions might be classed under
more than one of the subdivisions. The 'aristocracy of
birth and land' includes in some cases the 'aristocracy of
conquest' or 'the aristocracy of kingly family': aristocracies, when narrowed and degenerate, become 'dynastic
governments'; but it has seemed the best course to
discuss all the forms to which we find allusion made in
our authorities.

§ 29. *Aristotle's Division of Oligarchies.*

Aristotle enumerates and defines four forms of oligarchy[1], and distinguishes also aristocracy[2] and polity[3],
defined as mixed constitutions, the one inclining to oligarchy, the other to democracy[4].

The classification is neither scientific nor exhaustive;
its value lies in the recognition of the principle of degree[5]. 'The broad object which Aristotle had in view,'
as Mr Newman says[6], 'was to uproot the general impression that there are but two or three constitutions, and
that oligarchy and democracy have each of them only one

[1] The four forms are enumerated in *Pol.* vi 5 1292 a 38 and defined
with more detail *ib.* 6 1293 a 11. In this section I shall not quote more
particular references, and it must be assumed that I am referring to these
passages unless other references are given.

[2] Aristocracy in its different forms is defined *ib.* 7 1293 b 1 ff.

[3] Polity is defined *ib.* 9 1293 a 35 ff.

[4] *Ib.* 8 1293 b 35.

[5] Cf. Plato *Rep.* viii 551 B νόμον τίθενται ὅρον πολιτείας ὀλιγαρχικῆς
ταξάμενοι πλῆθος χρημάτων, οὗ μὲν μᾶλλον ὀλιγαρχία, πλέον, οὗ δ' ἧττον,
ἔλαττον.

[6] *Introduction*, p. 494.

form.' He is careful to lay stress on the superiority of
the moderate forms of either oligarchy or democracy to
the extreme forms; and his lesson was needed, for there
was a strong tendency in Greece to intensify the ruling
characteristics of the constitutions[7]. The extreme oligarchy was almost a tyranny, the most moderate form
was but little removed from a moderate democracy, and
Aristotle describes it in almost the same terms[8].

The first principle applied to the subdivision of oligarchies is connected with the conditions qualifying for
citizenship. A second test is afforded by the method
of admitting those who attained the qualification to the
active exercise of citizen rights. Political privilege might
be offered freely to all who fulfilled certain conditions;
it might be extended to the excluded only at the discretion of the ruling body; or the ranks of the privileged,
once fixed, might be closed against all without the pale.
This distinction is important. In sentiment and in
conduct there must have been the greatest difference
between governments constantly recruited by fresh blood
and close corporations which jealously guarded their
privileges against the rest. Lastly, Aristotle has another
means of distinction. Oligarchies are either ruled according to law or they are controlled by the caprice of
individuals, a criterion which also enters into his classification of constitutions in general.

[7] On the intensification of constitutions see Ar. *Pol.* vii 5 1319 b 32.
The champions of oligarchy and democracy were not content with the
moderate forms; they strove to increase their worst characteristics. Cf.
Thuc. v 81 (the Spartans) τὰ ἐν Σικυῶνι ἐς ὀλίγους μᾶλλον κατέστησαν.

[8] Cf. *Pol.* vi 6 1292 b 25—33 with *ib.* 1293 a 12—20. If neither
passage is corrupt, the repetition of the same phrases in both definitions
is strange.

The four forms of oligarchy described by Aristotle corresponded, no doubt, to the oligarchic governments with which he was most familiar. But there is a certain inconsistency in his method, and the enumeration cannot be regarded as complete. He distinguishes two moderate forms of oligarchy, based on the assessment of property, both ruled in accordance with law, and two extreme forms, based upon birth (a condition not involved in his definition of oligarchy), one observing the law, the other tyrannical and arbitrary. Now there can be no underlying principle, which should prevent oligarchies of birth from being moderate, or oligarchies of wealth from being extreme : and examples might be quoted to show the insufficiency of Aristotle's definitions. Moreover, in the governments of birth it is implied that wealth will accompany birth, but nothing is said as to how the diverse claims should be reconciled, if they are in conflict. We must not expect to find in Aristotle's classification an exhaustive description of all the oligarchies of Greece, but we may suppose that he included the types most familiar to his experience, which had been evolved in the development of constitutions. As such they must be considered.

The first form is a government 'based on a property qualification sufficient to exclude the poor (who form a majority), but admitting to citizenship anyone who attains the necessary qualification : while, owing to the large number of citizens, the law must be sovereign.' This form is very similar to the first form of democracy (which differs, however, in admitting a *majority* to citizenship) : it would be impossible to mark any distinction between this and the polity based on moderate property[9].

The second form is the government of 'a lesser number of men, having a higher property qualification, who owing to their greater power desire aggrandisement, and therefore they themselves choose from the many those who are to join the citizen body, but not being strong enough to rule without law, they give this function to law.'   Aristotle seems to have in his mind an 'oligarchy of fixed number[10]' in which vacancies are filled by co-optation on the part of the rulers.   This form supplies a link between the first oligarchy in which citizenship is always accessible and the other forms in which the ranks are altogether closed.

The third form is a close government in which 'son succeeds father,' and it is further defined as that in which 'a smaller number have still larger properties.' It is impossible to get any clear idea of the constitution which Aristotle has in view.   If he means that only the eldest sons succeed their fathers, he is describing the 'oligarchy of heads of families[11]'; but if it is simply a government based upon hereditary descent, in which all a citizen's sons are admitted, then they could not all have had the large amount of property that he seems to consider essential.

The fourth form is also a close hereditary oligarchy, constituted in a similar way to the third form, but ruled according to the caprice of the rulers and not in accordance with law.   It is tyrannical in character,

<hr>

9 See ch. i § 5.   10 See below § 38.
11 See below § 34.

and is further defined as occurring when men are excessively powerful owing to their property and their connexions[12].

To conclude Aristotle's classification, that government is aristocratic which is based on virtue as well as wealth; while the mixture of democracy and virtue is also defined as aristocratic. In this connexion virtue implies the qualification either of birth or of training[13]. Polity, regarded as the government of a minority based on a moderate property, is included in the definition of the first form of oligarchy.

§ 30. *Aristocracy of Birth and Land.*

We have seen that aristocracy was a stage of constitutional development through which all states passed, and it is obvious that it is not a form of government which can easily be established afresh in an old constitution. Except, therefore, for aristocracies based on conquest, we have only to consider the instances of states in which the ordinary aristocracy survived. These were naturally those in which industry and commerce never became of much importance; for the survey of the history of Greek constitutions shows that the rise of strong commercial and industrial classes must in the long run be fatal to the pretensions of an aristocracy of birth. Aristocracy, therefore, was found in states in which land was the only form of wealth, and the land was owned for the most

[12] This is the δυναστεία. See below § 35.

[13] See ch. i § 6. In *Pol.* vi 7 1293 b 10 (quoted in the next section n. 1) ἀριστίνδην probably does not connote more than the qualification of ἀρετή, but *ib.* l. 37 it is implied that the ideas of παιδεία and εὐγένεια are included under the term ἀρετή.

part by the nobles or (in an aristocracy of conquest) by
the ruling class. It follows from this that the qualification of birth in an aristocratic constitution included
also the qualification of wealth, whether a fixed minimum of property were required to be held by all the
citizens or not. The ordinary type of aristocracy was one
in which only the members of certain privileged families
were admitted to citizenship: the government was administered by a supreme council and such magistrates
as were required. Usually speaking the nobles were
all equally privileged to hold office, but many states
required their citizens to hold a certain amount of
property[1]. The possession of land, which was a natural
accompaniment of noble birth, became itself a qualification for citizenship. Such a condition involved certain
difficulties. Originally, no doubt, land was held by the
γένη in joint ownership, and, as long as population did
not increase too fast, there was no difficulty in providing
for the needs of all the members. But when once the
idea of separate ownership was established, there must
have been the greatest difficulty in maintaining anything
like an equal distribution of property. On the one hand,
the owner of a lot of land might have a number of sons
and yet be able to provide for only one of them. In
some states the difficulty was met by admitting only the
eldest son to privilege, and so the 'government of heads

---

[1] Aristotle in his definition of an aristocratic constitution (*Pol.* vi 7
1293 b 10) says it is ὅπου μὴ μόνον πλουτίνδην ἀλλὰ καὶ ἀριστίνδην αἱροῦνται
τὰς ἀρχάς. Cf. Ar. *Ath. Pol.* 3 1 (on the aristocratic constitution of
Athens) and Strabo x 447 of Chalcis προέστησαν...ἀπὸ τιμημάτων ἄνδρες
ἀριστοκρατικῶς ἄρχοντες (where ἀπὸ τιμημάτων corresponds to πλουτίνδην:
ἀριστοκρατικῶς to ἀριστίνδην).

of families' was established[2]. This was not a frequent
solution, and, as Aristotle saw, the whole question of population was involved[3]. Adoption offered a partial solution
of the difficulty[4], but there might still be too many sons
for the property to maintain, and it is possible that in-
fanticide and exposure were practised more frequently
in aristocracies than elsewhere in order to meet the difficulty[5]. There was also the opposite danger to be considered: if the transfer of property were allowed, many
of the nobles might become impoverished (while a few
got most of the land into their hands), and in this way
the number of the citizens would decline. The remedy
devised to meet this was the division of the land into

[2] See below § 34.

[3] Ar. *Pol.* ii 6 1265 a and b *passim*, especially *ib.* a 38 ἄτοπον δὲ καὶ
τὸ τὰς κτήσεις ἰσάζοντα τὸ περὶ τὸ πλῆθος τῶν πολιτῶν μὴ κατασκευάζειν.
The difficulty in the Spartan state was met at first by her continued
conquests. Afterwards the opposite danger befell the Spartans. Their
rigid system tended to the decline of population and the consequent
inequality of property.

[4] This was the legal fiction employed to prevent the extinction of a
γένος. Plato lays stress on adoption in the *Laws* v 740 c.

[5] There is very little evidence. Ar. *Pol.* ii 6 1265 b 12 says that
Phidon of Corinth τοὺς οἴκους ἴσους ᾠήθη δεῖν διαμένειν καὶ τὸ πλῆθος τῶν
πολιτῶν, but he does not say how this was secured. At Thebes (*ib.* ii 12
1274 b 3) Philolaus legislated περὶ τῆς παιδοποιίας, οὓς καλοῦσιν ἐκεῖνοι νόμους
θετικούς. Aelian *V. H.* ii 7 says the law at Thebes prohibited exposure,
but allowed a father to sell his children into slavery. Cf. Plato *Rep.* v
459 d where the exposure of the unfit is suggested, and *Laws* v 740 d
where the highest magistracy is to deal with 'the redundant or deficient,'
and various means are specified. Ar. *Pol.* ii 10 1272 a 21 (speaking of
Crete) alludes to another method: πρὸς δὲ τὴν ὀλιγοσιτίαν ὡς ὠφέλιμον
πολλὰ πεφιλοσόφηκεν ὁ νομοθέτης, καὶ πρὸς τὴν διάζευξιν τῶν γυναικῶν, ἵνα
μὴ πολυτεκνῶσι, τὴν πρὸς τοὺς ἄρρενας ποιήσας ὁμιλίαν. In Crete (and possibly elsewhere) παιδεραστία (a specially oligarchic vice) assumed a political aspect, as a check on redundant population.

fixed lots, which their owners were forbidden to alienate.
There was in many states what amounted to a law of
entail. A distinction was drawn between the lots which
were supposed to have been originally apportioned, and
land acquired subsequently: and the lots might not be
sold. To take examples[6]: at Sparta 'it was disgraceful
to sell land at all, but it was unlawful to dispose of the
ancient lot[7]'; at Thebes Philolaus is said to have taken
measures 'to preserve the number of the lots[8]'; in East
Locris, a place of strong aristocratic sentiment, a man
might not dispose of his land except in case of manifest
poverty[9]: in Leucas also there were provisions for the
preservation of the original lots[10], as there were at Elis[11].
We are told that the possession of citizen rights at
Leucas depended on the possession of the lot of land,
and we may suppose that similar provisions held in
other places. In spite of these provisions there was a
tendency for these close hereditary aristocracies to decline in numbers. At Sparta, some time in the fourth
century, the restraint on the sale of land was removed
with such disastrous consequences that in the third
century the land of Lacedaemon had got into the hands

---

[6] Ar. *Pol.* vii 4 1319 a 10 ἦν δὲ τό γε ἀρχαῖον ἐν πολλαῖς πόλεσι νενομο-
θετημένον μηδὲ πωλεῖν ἐξεῖναι τοὺς πρώτους κλήρους. Aristotle recognises
the benefit of such provisions in oligarchies: *Pol.* viii 8 1309 a 20 ἐν δ'
ὀλιγαρχίᾳ δεῖ...τὰς κληρονομίας μὴ κατὰ δόσιν εἶναι ἀλλὰ κατὰ γένος, μηδὲ
πλειόνων ἢ μιᾶς τὸν αὐτὸν κληρονομεῖν. οὕτω γὰρ ἂν ὁμαλώτεραι αἱ οὐσίαι
εἶεν.

[7] Heraclides, F. H. G. ii 211; Plut. *Inst. Lac.* 22.

[8] Ar. *Pol.* ii 12 1274 b 2.

[9] *Ib.* ii 7 1266 b 19. (It is probable that Aristotle is referring to *East*
Locris.)

[10] *Ib.* l. 21.   [11] *Ib.* vii 4 1319 a 12.

of a hundred rich men, while the rest were disfranchised and impoverished[12]. The philosophers accepted the aristocratic traditions about the ownership of land, and both Plato and Aristotle provided that each citizen was to have one or more lots of land[13].

There were probably many states in which citizenship was based upon a qualification of landed property, even after the aristocracies of birth had passed away[14]. Thus the earliest form of timocratic constitution took only landed property into account[15], and there was a tendency in the colonies to divide the land taken into occupation in lots among the first colonists, and to establish the rights of the original settlers. These formed in many states the governing body.

§ 31. *Aristocracy of 'Original Settlers.'*

Professor Freeman, in speaking of the Greek colonies[1], says 'Nowhere else is what we may call the aristocracy of original settlement so likely to grow up. The first settlers divide the land, and so long as the new settlement is weak, they may welcome new comers; but as soon as its numbers are large enough for the needs of an independent city, the

[12] Plut. *Agis* 5: cf. Ar. *Pol.* ii 9 1270 a 16 τοῖς μὲν αὐτῶν συμβέβηκε κεκτῆσθαι πολλὴν λίαν οὐσίαν, τοῖς δὲ πάμπαν μικράν· διόπερ εἰς ὀλίγους ἧκεν ἡ χώρα.

[13] Apart from the communistic scheme of the *Republic*, the citizens in the *Laws* are to have lots of land, divided into two parts, and these are to be inalienable (*Laws* v 740 A B : 745 c). Aristotle assigns to each citizen of his best state two lots of land (*Pol.* iv 10 1330 a 15).

[14] See below § 36 n. 4.

[15] Cf. the constitution of Solon, and of Leucas.

[1] *History of Sicily* ii p. 11: cf. Newman's *Introduction*, p. 375.

descendants of the elder settlers are no longer willing to
admit such new comers to any share in their hereditary
right.' This condition of affairs gave rise to the special
form of constitution in which privilege was limited to
those who claimed descent from the original landholders
of the colony. With this I think we should identify the
so-called governments of 'landowners' of which we hear
in Syracuse² and Samos³, and under another name in
Miletus⁴. In Apollonia on the Ionian gulf and in Thera
the government was in the hands of the first settlers, who
were of illustrious birth⁵. We chiefly hear of these governments in connexion with seditions: for the privileged
position of the landholders and the exclusion of new
settlers from the government were a most frequent cause
of discord. Aristotle says that the greater number of
cities which received new settlers were involved in
faction⁶, and among many instances we may mention
Apollonia on the Euxine⁷, Byzantium⁸ and Cyrene⁹,
where the mediation of Demonax was required to settle
the conflicting claims of the different elements in the
population.

---

² Diod. viii *fr.* on Ol. xi 4; Marm. Par. 37. Hesychius gives different
definitions of γαμόροι: the most correct seems to be οἱ ἀπὸ τῶν ἐγγείων
τιμημάτων τὰ κοινὰ διέποντες.

³ Plut. *Q. G.* 57: Thuc. viii 21.

⁴ Plut. *Q. G.* 32 gives an obviously aetiological explanation of ἀειναῦ-
ται. Gilbert, *Handbuch* ii p. 139, connects the word with ναίω.

⁵ Ar. *Pol.* vi 4 1290 b 11 ἐν ταῖς τιμαῖς ἦσαν οἱ διαφέροντες κατ' εὐγένειαν
καὶ πρῶτοι κατασχόντες τὰς ἀποικίας.

⁶ *Pol.* viii 3 1303 a 27 διὸ ὅσοι ἤδη συνοίκους ἐδέξαντο ἢ ἐποίκους, οἱ
πλεῖστοι διεστασίασαν.

⁷ *Ib.* l. 36.

⁸ *Ib.* l. 33.

⁹ Hdt. iv 159 ff.

§ 32. *Aristocracy based on Conquest.*

A special form of aristocracy, in which also the ruling class owned the best land of the state, was that arising from the conquest of one race by another invading race. Here we have not to deal primarily with the existence of a separate order of nobles; the conquerors as a whole constitute a class superior to the conquered, of whom some are reduced to serfdom, while others occupy a more favourable position. This special division of classes is typical of the aristocracy of conquest[1]. We find this aristocracy, on a more or less uniform plan, not only in the Dorian states of the Peloponnesus[2], in Crete, and to a certain extent in Thera, but also in Thessaly: while both in Boeotia and Elis the ruling class owed their position to the right of conquest. The rulers owned the best lands and these were cultivated for them by serfs.

These aristocracies may be divided into two classes. In some all members of the conquering race were equally privileged; in others there existed differences of rank within the circle of the conquerors, which gave to some families a superiority over the rest.

Thus in Thessaly the government of the different towns was held by a few noble families, all of them tracing their descent from Heracles, while so far as we can trace their followers had no share whatever in the government[3].

[1] These class divisions are discussed below § 50.

[2] There seem to have been similar constitutions originally in the Dorian states. The same class divisions can be traced in Argos, Sicyon, Thera, Crete, Epidaurus as in Sparta.

[3] The noble families, the Aleuadae, Scopadae etc., traced their descent from Heracles. The government is specially described as a δυναστεία (Thuc. iv 78): corresponding to the fourth form of oligarchy,

This special form of the government of birth the Greeks
called *dynasty*. In Boeotia also we may assume that the
nobles had complete control of the government, and in
process of time the Theban government assumed the
character of a dynasty[4]. The same appears to be true of
Elis[5] also and of Epidaurus[6].

On the other hand in Sparta and Crete, although we
can trace distinctions of birth within the circle of the
privileged[7], larger powers seem to have been given to the
conquering race as a whole; and the Spartiates were
considered, in themselves, to form a demos of equally
privileged citizens.

Another common characteristic of aristocracies of conquest was that they usually had a distinctively military
organisation. The conquerors had won their position by
force of arms ; they held sway over a population of subjects, immensely superior in number to themselves, usually
disaffected and often breaking into revolt. Such a rela-

described by Aristotle. Ar. *Pol.* viii 6 1306 a 10 attests the existence of
a strong, united but narrow oligarchy in Pharsalus: viii 6 1305 b 28
mentions an oligarchy at Larisa, in which the people elected the πολιτο-
φύλακες (the chief magistrates) and the constitution was overthrown at
some date not specified (viii 6 1306 a 26).

⁴ The aristocracy at Thebes was based on the lots of land (see p.
73 n. 3): but the commons do not seem to have been altogether excluded:
Hdt. v 79 (of the year 507 B.C.) mentions ἀλίη at Thebes. By the time
of the Persian wars the Theban government was a δυναστεία (Thuc.
iii 62).

⁵ See the description in Ar. *Pol.* viii 6 1306 a 15.

⁶ See Plut. in § 38 n. 14.

⁷ At Sparta the γέροντες were chosen from οἱ καλοὶ κἀγαθοί (Ar. *Pol.* ii
9 1270 b 24): these are assumed to be a class of nobles. This has been
disputed; for a discussion of the question see Gilbert, *Handbuch* i²
p. 13 n. 1. At Crete certain γένη were privileged: the κόσμοι were chosen
from them (Ar. *Pol.* ii 10 1272 a 33).

tion could only be maintained by the most unflagging
vigilance on the part of the rulers. The whole of the
Spartan and Cretan training was a preparation for war;
and the lives of the citizens were practically spent in
camp. It is not necessary to discuss the familiar details
of the Spartan and Cretan systems; it is sufficient to
point out that such methods of training and life were
essential to a constitution based on similar conditions.
This was formally recognised at Sparta, where it was
a condition of citizenship that the Spartiate should go
through the whole of the training[8]: there is no doubt
that the same rule held in Crete[9], and it may also have
been enforced elsewhere. These are the states which
made 'training' an essential condition of citizenship[10].
The 'practice' and 'training' of the Spartan system are
referred to again and again by Thucydides; their 'native
virtue' is praised, and above all their 'changeless ordinances' and their blind submission to the law receive
constant mention[11].

---

[8] Plut. *Inst. Lac.* 21 τῶν πολιτῶν ὃς ἂν μὴ ὑπομείνῃ τὴν τῶν παίδων
ἀγωγήν, οὐ μετεῖχε τῶν τῆς πόλεως δικαίων. Xen. *Resp. Lac.* 10 7 shows
that this constituted the difference between the ὅμοιοι and the disfranchised (ὑπομείονες).

[9] The Cretan system was as rigid as the Spartan and must have been
a necessary condition of citizenship, but I do not know that this is
anywhere expressly stated.

[10] Ar. *Eth.* x 9 1180 a 24 ἐν μόνῃ δὲ τῇ Λακεδαιμονίων πόλει <ἢ> μετ'
ὀλίγων ὁ νομοθέτης ἐπιμέλειαν δοκεῖ πεποιῆσθαι τροφῆς τε καὶ ἐπιτηδευμάτων.
There may have been other states which practised this training originally.

[11] Xen. *Resp. Lac.* 10 5 ἡ Σπάρτη μονὴ δημοσίᾳ ἐπιτηδεύουσα τὴν καλο-
κἀγαθίαν. Cf. Ar. *Eth.* quoted in n. 10; Thuc. i 84 (ὅστις ἐν τοῖς ἀναγ-
καιοτάτοις παιδεύεται). Thucydides also harps on ἀρετή, πόνος and μελετή
(see i 123; ii 39; v 69; vi 11). In Thuc. i 68 the Corinthians talk of
the ἀκίνητα νόμιμα of the Spartans: cf. i 77; iii 37 (νόμοι ἀκίνητοι); v 105

§ 33. *Aristocracy of the Kingly Family.*

I proceed to discuss some other special forms of aristocracy. Of these one of the most frequent is the aristocracy of the royal house. In tracing the extinction of kingship I called attention to one method by which the aristocratic government might be established. Power might be exercised not by a single king but by the whole of the royal race. This is due to the inherent similarity between aristocracy and the old monarchy. The ruling family might cease to give the supreme authority to a single man and resume the sovereignty themselves. In a large number of the Ionian colonies of Asia Minor and the islands, the ruling class traced their descent from the kings who were traditionally regarded as the leaders of the first colonists[1]. At Miletus the Neleids formed the ruling dynasty[2] : at Ephesus, Erythrae and Chios we find mention of Basilidae, who probably claimed descent from kingly families[3]. At Mitylene the aristocracy of the

(Λακεδαιμόνιοι γὰρ πρὸς σφᾶς αὐτοὺς καὶ τὰ ἐπιχώρια νόμιμα πλεῖστα ἀρετῇ χρῶνται). Cf. Xen. *Resp. Lac.* 10 7 τοῖς μὲν γὰρ τὰ νόμιμα ἐκτελοῦσιν ὁμοίως ἅπασι τὴν πόλιν οἰκείαν ἐποίησε. For their 'blind observance of law' cf. Thuc. i 84 (εὔβουλοι ἀμαθέστερον τῶν νόμων τῆς ὑπεροψίας παιδευόμενοι); ii 40; iii 37 and Xen. *Resp. Lac.* 8 1 ὅτι μὲν ἐν Σπάρτῃ μάλιστα πείθονται ταῖς ἀρχαῖς τε καὶ τοῖς νόμοις ἴσμεν ἅπαντες; cf. Hdt. vii 104.

[1] Hdt. i 147. Most of the colonies were said to have been governed by Proclidae or Glaucidae.

[2] Nicol. Dam. F. H. G. iii 388: other authorities are cited in Gilbert, *Handbuch* ii p. 139 n. 1.

[3] Strabo xiv 633 mentions βασιλεῖς at Ephesus, who even in his time had the *insignia* of kings. Suidas *s.v.* Πυθαγόρας mentions Βασιλίδαι. Ar. *Pol.* viii 6 1305 b 18 mentions ὀλιγαρχία βασιλιδῶν at Erythrae. Hdt. viii 132 and an inscription (*Bull. Corr. Hell.* iii 244 cited by Gilbert) mention βασιλείδης at Chios. From Strabo it appears that at Ephesus the γένος regarded themselves as kings.

Penthilids succeeded the monarchy of the same race[4]. In Thessaly the noble families who held sway claimed to be Heraclids[5]. Thucydides mentions the 'governing race' of the Chaones in Epirus[6]: and the instance of the Medontidae at Athens is familiar. Corinth also was ruled by a similar aristocracy. For two hundred years the clan of the Bacchiadae, claiming descent from Bacchis King of Corinth, numbering over two hundred members, ruled the city, choosing a yearly chief from their own number and excluding all others, both noble and simple, from the government. So close was the clan feeling that they only intermarried within their own order[7].

In many instances, no doubt, the assertion of royal descent was a fiction. The Greeks had a great talent for the composition of genealogies, and we know how many families claimed descent from gods or heroes. Many of the mythical founders of colonies belonged to the heroic period and doubtless received heroic honours, and the ruling class would naturally be proud to claim descent from them. The Basilidae (with whom we may compare the Archaeanactidae of Panticapaeum[8]) doubtless claimed royal descent, but such a title might naturally arise as a description of nobles, whose ancestors had borne the title of βασιλῆες. Even in Thessaly and Corinth it is difficult

[4] Ar. *Pol.* viii 10 1311 b 26.

[5] Pind. *Pyth.* x 1. There is of course plenty of other evidence.

[6] Thuc. ii 80 Χάονες ἀβασίλευτοι, ὧν ἡγοῦντο ἐπ' ἐτησίῳ προστασίᾳ ἐκ τοῦ ἀρχικοῦ γένους Φώτυος καὶ Νικάνωρ.

[7] On the Bacchiadae see Paus. ii 4 4; Diod. vii fr. referring to 1104 b.c. ; Strabo viii 378; Hdt. v 92.

[8] Diod. xii 31 οἱ τοῦ Κιμμερίου Βοσπόρου βασιλεύσαντες, ὀνομασθέντες δὲ Ἀρχαιανακτίδαι κ.τ.λ.

to believe that single clans, restricting marriage within their own circle, could establish a lasting government.

Whatever their origin these aristocracies must have tended to become narrow and 'dynastic' governments[9]. As long as they maintained their exclusive privileges, their numbers must have declined; and their rulers must have become tyrannical in temper and conduct; such aristocracies were provocative of discord and often led to a violent sedition in which they were overthrown[10].

§ 34. *Aristocracy of Heads of Families.*

The third form of oligarchy[1] defined by Aristotle is that in which son succeeds father[2]. If we take this to imply that only the eldest son succeeds to the political rights of his father, he is describing the 'aristocracy of heads of houses.' Such governments, in which if the father held power, the son was not admitted and of several brothers all but the eldest were excluded, are mentioned by Aristotle as having existed at Massalia, Istros, Heraclea and Cnidus[3]. The constitution in Plato's *Laws* is based on this principle, for in that there was to

[9] See below § 35.

[10] In many cases the only mention made of these aristocracies is in connection with their overthrow.

[1] To prevent confusion of phraseology, I may point out that I am using *aristocracy* in the conventional sense defined in § 6 above. Aristotle here uses oligarchy in its most general sense.

[2] See above § 29.

[3] Ar. *Pol.* viii 6 1305 b 4 and 12. The gradual reform of these constitutions was in the direction of first admitting the elder brothers, then the younger, so that it assumed the character of an ordinary aristocracy based on hereditary descent.

be a fixed number of citizens and privilege was to depend
on the possession of an hereditary lot of land, so that the
son could not succeed during the lifetime of his father.

Governments of this nature must have acquired a
representative character; for the privileged families, in
whose hands the wealth and power of the state rested,
would share in the government through their head. They
may have existed in many other states besides the ones
mentioned above: we lack evidence to prove their existence elsewhere, but I think it is probable that the
Opuntian Locrians were ruled under such a system.   We
hear of a hundred noble houses in Locris[4] and an assembly of a thousand[5], and it is open to us to suppose
that 'the hundred houses' were divided into smaller
divisions, and that the heads of each of such divisions
constituted the ruling body.

Another characteristic to notice in connection with
this type of government is the privilege that is indirectly
given to age.   If the sons were not admitted to political
power, as long as their fathers lived, there must have
been a preponderance of men of mature age in the government.   This was in accordance with the general principles
of oligarchy[6].

[4] Polyb. xii 5 7 in talking of the Locrians of Italy mentions τὰς ἑκατὸν
οἰκίας τὰς προκριθείσας in the mother city. (Cf. Thuc. i 108.)   Polyb. *ib.*
§ 6 says that in Locri in Italy descent was traced through women; this
was most probably the case in Opus.

[5] In this respect it formed an aristocracy 'of fixed number,' on which
see below § 38.

[6] See below § 41 n. 25.

§ 35.   *The 'Dynastic' Government.*

The two sorts of aristocracy last described, together
with the narrower forms of the aristocracy of conquest,
would be included in the definitions ascribed by Aristotle
to the two extreme forms of oligarchy, narrow governments
in which the sons succeed their fathers: and as it would
be natural for such governments to rule more by caprice
than by law they would most of them be described as
δυναστεῖαι[1].

The dynasty as a form of government needs a more
precise description.   It is the government of a few men,
strong in their wealth and connexions, who do not rule
by law.   In his definition Aristotle implies that such
governments are always based upon birth, but despotic
governments like those of the Thirty at Athens[2] or of the
decarchies established by Lysander[3] would naturally be
denoted by this title, and Aristotle himself applies it to
constitutions which do not rest on the qualification of
birth.   Thus he says that such a government results
when a number of men obtain an excess of power in the
state[4], or when large powers are entrusted to military
officers, who use them to establish an absolute government in their own interest[5]; he applies the term to the
rule of some ambitious men at Thurii who managed to
gain control of the state by re-election to the generalship[6].

---

[1] Ar. *Pol.* vi 1293 a 30.

[2] Ar. *Ath. Pol.* 36 1 does describe the government of the Thirty
as a δυναστεία.

[3] Xen. *Hell.* v 4 46 applies the term to the governments established in
Boeotia under Lacedaemonian protection.

[4] *Pol.* viii 3 1302 b 16.   [5] *Ib.* 6 1306 a 24.

[6] *Ib.* 7 1307 a 6 ff.

The word, like its cognates[7], had evil associations[8]. It denoted a narrow, despotic oligarchy of individuals, whose personal ascendency or connexions made them powerful. It was a tyranny of many tyrants, always regarded as closely analogous to real tyranny and naturally classed with it[9].

The term is applied to the close family governments in Thessaly[10] and to the narrow aristocracy of Thebes in the time of the Persian wars[11]: at Elis there was a narrow oligarchy and the privilege granted to certain families is described as δυναστευτική[12]. In this connexion it is interesting to remember that many oligarchies were described as 'tyrannies[13]' and that a tyrannical oligarchy

---

[7] It is perhaps worth while to point out that the cognate words δύναμις, δυνατὸς and δυνάστης are often used in a quasi-technical sense. I quote one or two examples. δύναμις often exactly corresponds to the Latin *potentia*, power due to wealth, connections etc., and as such was applied to the leaders in an oligarchy. Cf. Solon fr. 5 οἱ δ' εἶχον δύναμιν κ.τ.λ., Thuc. viii 73 3 where δύναμις is contrasted with πονηρία. Ar. *Ath. Pol.* 22 3 speaks of οἱ ἐν ταῖς δυνάμεσι. Cf. *Eth.* viii 10 1161 a 2 οὐ δὴ γίνονται κατ' ἀρετὴν αἱ ἀρχαί, ἀλλὰ διὰ πλοῦτον καὶ δύναμιν, καθάπερ ἐν ταῖς ὀλιγαρ-χίαις. Similarly οἱ δυνατοί often denotes the powerful oligarchs (cf. Thuc. viii 47 2; 48 1; 63 3; 73 2), while δυνάστης implies the additional idea of lawlessness (*Pol.* ii 10 1272 b 9).

[8] Plato *Politicus* 291 D uses it in a perfectly neutral sense of oligarchy in general.

[9] Thuc. iii 62 ὅπερ δέ ἐστι νόμοις μὲν καὶ τῷ σωφρονεστάτῳ ἐναντιώτατον, ἐγγυτάτω δὲ τυράννου, δυναστεία ὀλίγων ἀνδρῶν. So Aristotle in his definition calls it ἐγγὺς μοναρχίας. Ar. *Pol.* viii 3 1302 b 17; 6 1306 a 24 couples it with tyranny.

[10] Thuc. iv 78.

[11] Thuc. iii 62.

[12] Ar. *Pol.* viii 6 1306 a 15.

[13] And. i 75 alludes to the Four Hundred as οἱ τύραννοι. Isocr. iv 105 applies τυραννεῖν to the rule of δυναστεῖαι. Xenophon (*Hell.* ii 4 1) says of the Thirty ὡς ἐξὸν ἤδη αὐτοῖς τυραννεῖν. (They are first actually called

was generally regarded as the worst possible kind of
government.

§ 36. *Oligarchy of Wealth.*

Even in the aristocracies of birth the government of
the few was generally the government of the wealthy :
in the ordinary oligarchy wealth played a still more
important part : it was the only requisite qualification,
and it formed the 'defining principle' of the constitution[1].
We have seen the importance of landed property in the
early constitutions, and where the possession of land was
not restricted to the nobles the early timocratic governments were based on landed property[2]. In states, where
the land was of fairly uniform character, privilege probably
depended on the possession of a lot of land of a certain
size : Solon's system of taking the yearly return of corn
and oil into account was probably more complicated than
was generally necessary[3]. In later times it seems likely

'tyrants' by Diod. xix 32.) Strabo, viii 378, applies the same term to
the rule of the Bacchiadae at Corinth. In talking of the factions at
Mitylene Strabo, xiv 647, says ἐτυραννήθη ὑπὸ πλειόνων and mentions
among the rest the Κλεανακτίδαι. He probably refers not to individual
tyrants of this family but to a despotic oligarchy, as he says Pittacus
used his power εἰς τὴν τῶν δυναστειῶν κατάλυσιν. (See Gilbert, *Handbuch*
ii p. 162 n. 3.) Theopompus quoted by Athen. xii 526 refers to the
oligarchy at Colophon as a τυραννίς.

[1] Ar. *Pol.* vi 8 1294 a 11 ὀλιγαρχίας (ὅρος) πλοῦτος. See above ch. i § 4.
[2] See above § 30 n. 14: and cf. the description of the constitution of
Leucas Ar. *Pol.* ii 7 1266 b 21.
[3] Ar. *Ath. Pol.* 7 4. The elaborate provisions of Solon's constitution
were perhaps necessary in Attica, where the quality of the soil varied so
much. Even so it is strange that those who owned pasturage instead of
corn-fields or olive-yards should not be assessed on the proper value of
their property. Cf. Busolt, *Staatsaltertümer*[2] p. 146 n. 10. Meyer, *Ges-*

that in most of the oligarchies proper political privilege depended on the possession of a certain amount of wealth[4]. For oligarchy, as a form of government, was called into being by the rise of industry and commerce, and the diffusion of wealth; and wealth, apart altogether from the method of its acquisition, formed the condition of citizenship. Most of the Greek states, which did not remain petrified in aristocratic forms, developed at some time into oligarchies. Some passed into democracies, but many of them, including several of the most important mercantile states, preserved their oligarchic constitutions. And yet we have no account and no clear idea of the internal organisation of any timocratic government. What amount of property was usually required, when or how it was assessed, whether most states demanded a higher qualification for the magistracies than for ordinary citizenship[5], these and a hundred other questions must remain unanswered. We can only trace the general principles which characterised their institutions, and now and again find some fragment of evidence, which justifies us in forming conclusions about particular constitutions.

chichte des Alterthums ii pp. 653 ff., argues that the complicated system of assessment ascribed to Solon would not have been introduced at so early a period.

[4] Mr Wyse has called my attention to the rarity of evidence for a money qualification in oligarchies and suggests that as landed estate must always have been a favourite investment for capital, a certain qualification in real property may often have been required. I have referred at the end of § 30 to the possible survival of such a qualification, though I do not know of any certain instances. In the general description of oligarchy the wealth is not defined and I discuss in the next few pages what other evidence there is.

[5] See ch. v. § 41.

The first point for discussion is the method by which the conditions of citizenship were regulated in oligarchies. Oligarchies are usually described vaguely as the governments of the 'wealthy,' and even in official decrees we find vague phrases like 'those who are best equipped with property,' where a definite money qualification is implied[6]. But it is probable that in the ordinary oligarchy a census was taken at regular intervals, and from this census the roll of citizens was drawn up. It would be possible to make privileges depend on some other method, such as the amount of taxes paid by a man, but the evidence points to a regular assessment being normal. We do not know whether a man's capital or his income was usually assessed[7], but oligarchy was regarded as the government based 'on assessment,' and it is sometimes so defined[8]. Throughout the *Politics* 'assessment' is constantly associated with oligarchy[9], and Aristotle talks of the intervals at which the census is taken in oligarchies[10].

[6] In an inscription from Corcyra C. I. G. 1845 44 ἐλέσθαι δὲ τὰν βουλὰν ...ἄνδρας τρεῖς...τοὺς δυνατωτάτους χρήμασι seems from the connection to denote men having a certain property qualification. The phrase is used in a technical sense elsewhere. Cf. Thuc. viii 65 3; Ar. *Ath. Pol.* 29 5 (where the actual words of the decree may be quoted): Xen. *Hipparch.* 1 9 (quoted by Dr Sandys).

[7] In the Solonian constitution the value of the *produce* was taken into account. The method of assessment at Athens in later times is much disputed, but the constitutions of Antipater and Cassander seem to have been based on capital not income. Cf. Plato's *Laws* v 744.

[8] See above ch. i § 4 n. 9.

[9] Cf. the definitions of oligarchy in Bk vi and see also *Pol.* ii 6 1266 a 14; iii 5 1278 a 22; vii 6 1320 b 22.

[10] The intervals mentioned are one, three, and five years, *Pol.* viii 8 1308 a 39. It would be also possible to revise the list at irregular intervals, on the decision of the government. See Gilbert, *Handbuch* i[2] p. 412 n. 2.

Moreover it is clear that when Aristotle mentions the political privilege of the rich, he is thinking of those whose property has been ascertained by the census[11], and the same will probably be true of other writers. There are not many specific instances of particular constitutions being described as based on assessment[12], and there are very few in which we are told what amount of property was required. Generally speaking we may conclude that the amount of property required in an oligarchy was large[13]. The amount varied with the character of the oligarchy[14], but as a matter of experience oligarchies tended to make the qualification high. Where a low money qualification was required the constitution was defined as a 'polity[15].' Instances of such governments are those established by Macedonian influence at Athens at the end of the fourth century. Antipater required a census of 2000 drachmae[16]; Cassander a census of 1000 drachmae[17].

To take examples of important oligarchies, of whose

[11] In *Pol.* iii 12 1283 a 16 οἱ πλούσιοι is repeated in the phrase τίμημα φέροντες: in vi 13 1297 a 18 οἱ εὔποροι is repeated as οἱ ἔχοντες τίμημα.

[12] Strabo x 447 uses ἀπὸ τιμημάτων of the constitution of Chalcis, but landed property must have been in question. Aristotle mentions changes in the assessment at Ambracia (*Pol.* viii 3 1303 a 23) and Thurii (*ib.* 7 1307 a 28), and one of the qualifications for citizenship at Rhegium was a certain assessment. See below, § 38 n. 7.

[13] See above, p. 14 n. 6.

[14] Cf. the definitions of the different oligarchies in Ar. *Pol.* vi chs. 5 and 6.

[15] See ch. i § 5.

[16] Diod. xviii 18 προσέταξεν ἀπὸ τιμήσεως εἶναι τὸ πολίτευμα καὶ τοὺς μὲν κεκτημένους πλείω δραχμῶν δισχιλίων κυρίους εἶναι τοῦ πολιτεύματος καὶ τῆς χειροτονίας.

[17] Diod. xviii 74 τὸ πολίτευμα διοικεῖσθαι ἀπὸ τιμήσεων ἄχρι μνῶν δέκα.

constitution little definite information has come down to
us, I assume that there was an oligarchy of wealth at
Thebes in the fifth century, where, as Aristotle tells us,
'the rich' overcame the democracy[18]; and the same is
probably true of Megara, Corcyra and Corinth, as well as
of Chios and Lesbos, to mention the chief mercantile
states that were not under democratic government.

Megara was governed by a democracy from about the
middle of the fifth century to 424. An oligarchy was then
established, praised by Thucydides for its permanence[19], in
which the magistrates were appointed from those oligarchs
who had been in exile[20].

Corcyra, one of the most important mercantile states
of Greece, was said to have been originally colonised by
the Bacchiadae, and at first they probably controlled the
government. Their power must have been overthrown
and interrupted by Periander and was doubtless not
restored. We may conclude that an ordinary oligarchy of
wealth was established. In 427 the constitution was
democratic[21], but there are indications which point to the
existence of an oligarchy six years before when the alliance
with Athens was concluded. It is difficult otherwise to
explain the support given by the rulers to the oligarchic
exiles of Epidamnus, and their general conduct is consistent with this theory. Thus they seem to have sought

---

[18] *Pol.* viii 3 1302 b 28.

[19] Thuc. iv 74 ἐς ὀλιγαρχίαν τὰ μάλιστα κατέστησαν τὴν πόλιν. καὶ
πλεῖστον δὴ χρόνον αὕτη ὑπ' ἐλαχίστων γενομένη ἐκ στάσεως μετάστασις
ξυνέμεινεν. Plato *Crito* 53 praises Megara for εὐνομία.

[20] Ar. *Pol.* vi 15 1300 a 17 should probably be referred to this revolution. The arrangement was only temporary.

[21] Diod. xii 57.

the intervention of the Lacedaemonians and they told the
Corinthians that they would have to make allies of 'those
they did not wish[22],' a natural expression in the mouth of
oligarchs contemplating alliance with Athens. It was
natural that the alliance with Athens should strengthen
the democrats at Corcyra, and the capture of many of the
leading Corcyraeans by the Corinthians probably made
the democratic revolution all the easier[23].

But Corinth was the typical and preeminent oligarchy
of wealth. From the overthrow of the Cypselids to the
third century, with a brief interruption of five years,
Corinth maintained her oligarchic constitution, pursuing
on the whole a wise and prudent policy, seeking to maintain and extend her commercial relations and by the
permanence of her constitution attesting the moderation
of her rulers and their freedom from the usual faults of
oligarchs. The tyranny of the Cypselids overthrew for
ever the 'dynasty' of the Bacchiadae and doubtless served
the usual purpose of the tyranny in fostering trade and
industry and so promoting the rise of a prosperous middle
class[24]. The tyranny was overthrown by the Corinthians
themselves[25], and we can scarcely doubt that a moderate
oligarchy of wealth was established[26]. Pindar praises
Corinth for 'good order, justice and peace, stewards of

[22] Thuc. i 28.   [23] Thuc. i 55; iii 70.

[24] Cf. Busolt *Die Lakedaimonier* p. 211.   [25] *Ib.* p. 212.

[26] Busolt (p. 216) says 'whether all the nobles, as Duncker thinks,
were qualified to participate in the government or whether the rich
citizens, who were not noble, had such a qualification, cannot be
established.' He inclines to think that wealth was the only necessary
condition. Where the evidence is so scanty, none must be neglected,
and if any reliance may be placed on Cic. *De Rep.* ii 36 *Atque etiam
Corinthios video publicis equis adsignandis et alendis orborum et viduarum*

wealth to men²⁷.' Corinth was the great oligarchy of
trade as Athens was the great commercial democracy; and
we should doubtless gain a better idea of the principles
and method of oligarchic government from a study of the
Corinthian constitution than from any other source; but
unfortunately materials for such a study are altogether
lacking²⁸.

§ 37. *Oligarchy of 'The Knights' and of 'The Hoplites.'*

Two special forms of timocratic government were 'the
constitution of the knights' and 'the constitution of the
hoplites.'

The 'constitution of the knights' was doubtless
originally aristocratic, as Aristotle says it was the constitution that succeeded kingship¹: but the government
may have continued to exist in some states on a timocratic
basis.   Knighthood seems to have been a qualification at
Eretria, Chalcis, Magnesia² and Cyme³.

tributis fuisse quondam diligentes, the arrangements point to a timocratic
organisation.   Cf. E. Curtius in *Hermes* x p. 227.

²⁷ The description is conventional, as Εὐνομία, Δίκα and Εἰρήνα
mentioned in Pind. *Ol.* xiii 6 ff. are the three Ὧραι.   We find them similarly enumerated in a fragment of Isyllus, in Stob. i 5 11.

²⁸ Certain détails of the Corinthian constitution are discussed below.
So far inscriptions have given us practically no information.

¹ *Pol.* vi 13 1297 b 16 ἡ πρώτη δὲ πολιτεία ἐν τοῖς Ἕλλησιν ἐγένετο μετὰ
τὰς βασιλείας ἐκ τῶν πολεμούντων, ἡ μὲν ἐξ ἀρχῆς ἐκ τῶν ἱππέων.

² Ar. *Pol.* vi 3 1289 b 31 ἐπὶ τῶν ἀρχαίων χρόνων ὅσαις πόλεσιν ἐν τοῖς
ἵπποις ἡ δύναμις ἦν, ὀλιγαρχίαι παρὰ τούτοις ἦσαν...οἷον Ἐρετριεῖς καὶ Χαλ-
κιδεῖς καὶ Μάγνητες οἱ ἐπὶ Μαιάνδρῳ καὶ τῶν ἄλλων πολλοὶ περὶ τὴν Ἀσίαν.
At Chalcis the rulers were called Ἱπποβόται (Strabo x 447 ; Plut. *Per.* 23 ;
Hdt. v 77).

³ Cf. Heracl. F. H. G. ii 216 Φείδων...πλείοσι μετέδωκε τῆς πολιτείας,
νόμον θείς, ἕκαστον ἐπάναγκες τρέφειν ἵππον.

The 'constitution of the hoplites' is more important. Aristotle implies that many early constitutions assumed this form[4]: the hoplite qualification is the basis of the *polity* as it is most frequently described by him, and he refers so often to this form of government that it probably had a larger application than we have evidence to prove[5]. I have already discussed certain characteristics of this form of government: it would probably only admit a minority to power, and it seems practically to have been based on a property valuation, as hoplite service was usually obligatory on all who attained a certain census. Actual instances of such a constitution are few. The Draconian constitution gave power 'to all who provided themselves with a suit of arms[6]': the oligarchy established at Athens in 411 was intended to give power to five thousand, selected from those who were 'best able to serve the state in person and property[7]': the government which succeeded it was that of a fictitious body of five thousand, really composed of all who 'provided themselves with a suit of arms[8].' The Malians seem to have had a similar qualification for citizenship[9].

---

[4] *Pol.* vi 13 1297 b 22.

[5] See ch. i § 5 where the information bearing on the polity is collected.

[6] Ar. *Ath. Pol.* 4 2.

[7] Thuc. viii 65 3 ; Ar. *Ath. Pol.* 29 5. It was, I think, an oligarchy of limited number, based on a hoplite census. See Appendix C.

[8] Thuc. viii 97 1 τοῖς πεντακισχιλίοις ἐψηφίσαντο τὰ πράγματα παραδοῦναι· εἶναι δὲ αὐτῶν ὁπόσοι καὶ ὅπλα παρέχονται. Ar. *Ath. Pol.* 33 1 calls them οἱ πεντακισχίλιοι οἱ ἐκ τῶν ὅπλων. The number was a fiction.

Thucydides praises this constitution and it was the ideal of Theramenes (Xen. *Hell.* ii 3 48) τὸ μέντοι σὺν τοῖς δυναμένοις καὶ μεθ' ἵππων καὶ μετ' ἀσπίδων ὠφελεῖν διὰ τούτων τὴν πολιτείαν πρόσθεν ἄριστον ἡγούμην εἶναι.

[9] Cf. Aristotle quoted in § 41 n. 25.

§ 38. *Aristocracies and Oligarchies of Fixed Number.*

In some states participation in the active duties of citizenship was not made to depend directly on the attainment of a certain qualification, but was limited to a body of men, fixed in number, who themselves coopted others to vacancies on the roll. This is the second form of oligarchy described by Aristotle[1]. There were necessary conditions for the membership of these bodies: and any of the usual oligarchic qualifications might be required. Aristotle in the passage referred to, doubtless having certain instances in his mind, assumes that privilege will depend on a high assessment, but he corrects this by saying that if the choice be made from all the principle is aristocratic; if from any definite class, it is oligarchic[2]. The earliest form of such a government was that of the Opuntian Locrians, where a body of one thousand held supreme power[3]. I have already suggested that The Thousand should be connected with the hundred houses, and we may conclude that The Thousand represented the

---

[1] *Pol.* vi 4 1292 b 1 ὅταν ἀπὸ τιμημάτων μακρῶν ὦσιν αἱ ἀρχαὶ καὶ αἱρῶνται αὐτοὶ τοὺς ἐλλείποντας ; cf. *ib.* 14 1298 a 39.

[2] Ar. *l.c.* ἂν μὲν οὖν ἐκ πάντων τούτων (this word seems superfluous) τοῦτο ποιῶσι, δοκεῖ τοῦτ᾽ εἶναι μᾶλλον ἀριστοκρατικόν, ἐὰν δὲ ἐκ τινῶν ἀφωρισμένων, ὀλιγαρχικόν. In vii 7 1321 a 30 speaking of Massalia (which had such a constitution) and talking of the admission to citizenship, Aristotle describes them as κρίσιν ποιουμένους τῶν ἀξίων τῶν ἐν τῷ πολιτεύματι καὶ τῶν ἔξωθεν.

[3] Ὀπωντίων χιλίων πλῆθα is mentioned in an inscription (Roberts, *Epigraphy* 231 = I. G. A. 321), which is referred to about the middle of the fifth century, but the constitution was aristocratic and archaic; and the institution probably dated from a very early period.

noble families of Opus and that high birth and the possession of land were necessary qualifications for admission to the body[4].

The number of a thousand formed in early times the limit in many other states. Constitutions of this number can be traced in four of the Western Colonies (and they may have existed in many more, as the constitutions of the Greek cities in Italy and Sicily tended to assimilate); and their origin, I think, should be traced to Opus. Thus Locri Epizephyrii, where we hear of The Thousand and also of the hundred houses, probably derived its institutions from its metropolis, and the assembly of The Thousand may have spread from there to the other states[5]. At Croton we hear of such an assembly[6]: at Rhegium, where Charondas drew up the laws not long after Zaleucus had done his work at Locri, there was an assembly of The Thousand, chosen on a property qualification and controlling the whole administration[7]. At Acragas after the overthrow of the tyranny a moderate constitution was established and in connexion with it we hear of 'the gathering of The Thousand[8].'

---

[4] See § 34 above.

[5] Polyb. xii 16 10. Gilbert, *Handbuch* ii p. 240 n. 2, thinks that the assembly was instituted by Zaleucus and that it was timocratic. It is far more likely that it was derived from the metropolis, and if so it was probably based on birth.

[6] Iamblich. *De Pyth. vit.* 35 260. Val. Max. viii 15 1. Gilbert again assumes that this body was timocratic : Grote, iv 324, says that the Thousand were chosen from the original settlers. I can find no authority for either statement.

[7] Heracl. F. H. G. ii 219 πολιτείαν δὲ κατεστήσαντο ἀριστοκρατικήν· χίλιοι γὰρ πάντα διοικοῦσιν, αἱρετοὶ ἀπὸ τιμημάτων.

[8] Diog. L. viii 2 66.

At Colophon[9] and at Cyme[10] we hear of assemblies of the same number, while at Heraclea (probably the city of that name in the Pontus[11]), at Syracuse[12] and at Massalia[13] there were assemblies of six hundred in existence. At Epidaurus a hundred and eighty men formed the whole citizen body[14]. At Athens in the revolutionary oligarchy of the Four Hundred a pretence was made of establishing a privileged body of five thousand chosen from those who had the hoplite qualification[15], while the Thirty limited civic rights to three thousand[16].

This method of admitting men to citizenship seems to have commended itself to the Greek mind. Plato makes his constitution in the *Laws* consist of a 'perfect number' of citizens[17]. In some cases, and in constitutions other than oligarchies, a fiction of a fixed number was maintained. Thus at Aetna Hiero was said to have settled ten thousand citizens[18]; and at Megalopolis all citizens seem to have been admitted to the assembly of the Ten Thousand[19], while at Athens after the overthrow of the oligarchy of Four Hundred, a constitution of hoplites was

[9] Athen. xii 526 c quotes Theopompus and Xenophanes.

[10] Heracl. F. H. G. ii 217 Προμηθεὺς χιλίοις παρέδωκε τὴν πολιτείαν.

[11] Ar. *Pol.* viii 6 1305 b 11.

[12] Diod. xix 5 (of 336 B.C.).

[13] Strabo iv 179 ; cf. Dittenberger, *Sylloge* 200 42.

[14] Plut. *Q. G.* 1 τὸ πολίτευμα ὀγδοήκοντα καὶ ἑκατὸν ἦσαν.

[15] See Appendix C.

[16] Xen. *Hell.* ii 3 18: Ar. *Ath. Pol.* 36 1.

[17] *Laws* v 737 E. Plato seems to have had the constitutions of A Thousand in his mind more than once. Cf. *Politicus* 292 E ἐν χιλιάνδρῳ πόλει : *Rep.* iv 423 A.

[18] Diod. xi 49.

[19] Harp. defines the μύριοι at Megalopolis as συνέδριον κοινὸν ᾿Αρκάδων ἁπάντων. Diod. xv 59 thinks a definite number is implied.

established which bore the name of the Five Thousand,
although in all probability a larger number were admitted[20].

We know little about the method in which the actually
privileged citizens were chosen from the qualified body.
Aristotle assumes that it will be by cooptation, and the
assumption implies that the privilege would be held for
life[21]. In other states the privilege may have gone by
rotation to all the qualified[22]: or the assemblies may at
stated intervals have been dissolved, either wholly or in
part, and fresh members appointed. This is implied in
Aristotle's account of the government at Massalia[23]. The
conditions required must usually have included a property
qualification, but at Massalia we hear of different tests
being applied[24].

Something should be said about the place that these
bodies took in the constitution. Their political function
I discuss below[25]: for the present I wish to note that they

[20] See § 37 n. 8.

[21] Election seems to be contemplated from the use of the word αἱρετοί
which occurs in Ar. and Heracl.

[22] Such a method was sometimes employed in democracies, Ar. *Pol.*
vii 4 1318 b 23 παρ' ἐνίοις δήμοις, κᾶν μὴ μετέχωσι τῆς αἱρέσεως τῶν ἀρχῶν
ἀλλά τινες αἱρετοί κατὰ μέρος ἐκ πάντων κ.τ.λ. This principle was asserted
in the projected constitution of the oligarchs in 411. See Appendix C
n. 53.

[23] Ar. quoted in n. 2. I assume that Aristotle is referring to the
600 mentioned by Strabo *l.c.* The only discrepancy is that Strabo refers
to the 600 (called τιμοῦχοι) holding office for life, whereas Aristotle's
description implies elections at stated periods, with a sort of competition
of merit. But the change may have been made after Aristotle's time.

[24] Aristotle's account implies that the qualification was not timocratic. Strabo *l.c.* says τιμοῦχος δ' οὐ γίνεται μὴ τέκνα ἔχων, μηδὲ διὰ τρι-
γονίας ἐκ πολιτῶν γεγονώς.

[25] See § 47.

were not, so far as we can judge, mere organs of government: they composed the whole body to whom active political duties were allowed in the particular states. They were 'the assemblies' and not 'the councils,' and all outside the prescribed number, whether rich or poor, noble or base born, were equally excluded from privilege[26].

---

[26] This is implied in the definition of Aristotle as well as in the particular descriptions. Thus The Thousand are called at Opus πλῆθα, at Acragas ἄθροισμα; at Rhegium 'they control all things'; at Cyme ἡ πολιτεία is entrusted to them. At Heraclea ἡ ὀλιγαρχία...εἰς ἑξακοσίους ἦλθεν. The term συνέδριον which seems to be specially used of these bodies (Iamblichus, Diodorus and Strabo l.c.) is used elsewhere for the assembly of citizens. Diod. xvi. 65 (of Corinth) : Harp. s.v. μύριοι. Moreover a council of 600 or 1000 members would be out of place in an oligarchy.

CHAPTER V.

ORGANISATION OF OLIGARCHIC GOVERNMENT.

§ 39. *General Principles of Oligarchic Government.*

THE necessary elements in a government are defined by Aristotle to be the deliberative (a term which would include both council and assembly), the magisterial and the judicial[1]. Modern theory looks more to the functions of government than to those who exercise them, and Bluntschli for example enumerates Legislation, Administration, and Judicial power; he explains 'that Aristotle calls his first element deliberation, not legislation, because legislation proper was not exercised by the popular assemblies until late and only indirectly, while their deliberations were important[2].' Of course legislation was not so important in the Greek states as it is in the

---

[1] *Pol.* vi 14 1297 b 37 τὸ βουλευόμενον περὶ τῶν κοινῶν, τὸ περὶ τὰς ἀρχάς. These are μόρια τῶν πολιτειῶν. In vi 4 1291 a Aristotle, in enumerating the eight μόρια of a city, mentions τὸ μετέχον δικαιοσύνης δικαστικῆς, τὸ βουλευόμενον and τὸ δημιουργικὸν καὶ τὸ περὶ τὰς ἀρχὰς λειτουργοῦν. In iv 9 1329 a 3 the elements of government are described more vaguely as τὸ βουλευόμενον περὶ τῶν συμφερόντων καὶ κρῖνον περὶ τῶν δικαίων (cf. *ib.* 1328 a 23 and iii 1 1275 b 18). Thuc. vi 39 opposes βουλεῦσαι and κρῖναι.

[2] *Theory of the State* (Engl. Trans.), pp. 484—8.

states of modern Europe, but Aristotle expressly includes
legislation as one of the functions of the deliberative
element[3]. The correction of Aristotle seems to be a
mistake arising from a difference in the point of view:
for Aristotle, with the concrete method of thought natural
to a Greek, looks to the holders of political power and
not to the duties performed by them, and in the following
description of oligarchic government I shall follow his
classification.

It is characteristic of an oligarchy that 'some men
should deliberate about all[4],' and from the definition
of the deliberative element this principle involves the
corollary that some, i.e. a few men, should have supreme
power. For 'the deliberative element has authority to
decide war and peace, to make and dissolve alliance, to
pass laws, to inflict death, exile and confiscation, to elect
magistrates and to call them to account[5].' A body of
men possessing such authority must have been the
sovereign power in the state, and I proceed to consider to
what element in the oligarchic government sovereignty
was most often entrusted. In the aristocracy the chief
authority might conceivably be vested in the whole
body of the nobles, who would form in this way a small
assembly of the privileged, but it was generally wielded
by a council of nobles, who might be supposed to represent their order. So in the oligarchy proper 'the deliberative power,' though it might be exercised by a small

---

[3] τὸ βουλευόμενον is both legislative and administrative. Laws and
law-making are mentioned three times in *Pol.* vi 14 1298 a.

[4] Ar. *Pol.* vi 14 1298 a 34.

[5] *Ib.* 1298 a 4.

assembly of citizens[6], was generally entrusted to the
council, the special organ of oligarchic government.

The executive power in the early aristocracies was
usually entrusted to a single magistrate, whose powers
were as unlimited in scope as those of the king had been.
The division of power among a number of special magistrates was only gradually introduced with the growing
complexity of political life[7].

The powers both of council and of magistrates were
in the early constitutions undefined and unrestricted. In
this respect they recalled the king and the senate of
the Heroic age; and we have now to trace the development of the third element in the Heroic state, the
assembly of the commons. We saw that the commons,
though they had no definite authority, were called together in the agora to listen to the king or the nobles,
and expressed their approval or dissent in a primitive
fashion by shouting. The rise of aristocracy tended
further to reduce the slight importance which they had
hitherto possessed. The king was by his position raised
above the nobles and was thus better able to do justice to
all; but the people could expect but small consideration
from rulers, whose claim to political sovereignty was based
upon social superiority. Hence in many aristocratic states
the assembly of the commons had to submit to a still
further restriction of its powers, to be maintained on suffer-
ance or to be entirely removed from the constitution[8].

---

[6] This would be the case in some of the 'oligarchies of fixed number,'
for which see § 38. For the special case of the Oligarchy of the Five
Thousand at Athens see below, Appendix C.

[7] See Gilbert, *Handbuch* ii p. 323.

[8] For the reduction of the power of the assembly, we may compare

Oligarchies were unlikely to give a share in the constitution to any one outside the circle of the privileged few. It is probable that in most oligarchies there was an assembly of the qualified citizens, and in some, the poorer classes, who were in other respects debarred from exercising powers of government, were admitted to the assembly[9]; but, however constituted, the powers of the assembly were inconsiderable beside those of the council, and the oligarchs carried into effect their theory of specialisation of authority, of efficiency, secrecy and dispatch by delegating the duties of government to small councils or to the magistrates.

§ 40.   *Powers of Magistrates etc. in Oligarchies.*

'A ruler,' Sir James Stephen has said, 'may be regarded as the superior of the subject, as being by the nature of his position presumably wise and good; or he may be regarded as the agent and servant, and the subject as the wise and good master, who is obliged to delegate his power to the so-called ruler, because, being a multitude, he cannot use it himself.' Herein we have the antithesis of oligarchic and democratic sentiment, which may be abundantly confirmed from Greek literature.

the addition to the ῥήτρα at Sparta, by means of which the ordinary citizens lost the κυρία καὶ κράτος, which they had had before (Plut. *Lyc.* 6). In the aristocratic state at Athens there is no mention of the assembly: all power seems vested in the magistrates or council, and we know that the Eupatrids used it oppressively. It is obvious that the commons would have no voice in close governments like the δυναστεῖαι.

[9] See below, § 47.

Thus Plato draws almost the same distinction, when he says that the people in a democracy call their rulers 'magistrates' (ἄρχοντες), while in other states they are called 'masters' (δεσπόται)[1]. Demosthenes, whose evidence as that of a democratic advocate must be discounted, says that the subjects in an oligarchy are 'cravens and slaves[2],' all must be done sharply at the word of command[3], and it is a crime to speak evil of the magistrates, however bad they be[4]. It was characteristic of the oligarchic rulers to allow no criticism, brook no opposition and demand an instant obedience. This is the ground, no doubt, on which oligarchies claimed the character of being well governed and well ordered[5]: I have already called attention to the strict observance of the law that prevailed at Sparta[6], and, though there may not have been so ready a compliance in most oligarchies, the magistrates were doubtless swift to punish any insubordination or contempt for authority.

This idea of the competence and rights of government

[1] Plato, *Rep.* v 463 B. Ar. *Pol.* iii 4 1279 a 33 and b 8 contrasts ἀρχὴ δεσποτική with ἀρχὴ πολιτική.

[2] xxiv 75. Cf. [Dem.] lx 25, fear is a potent motive.

[3] xix 185 ἐν ἐκείναις ταῖς πολιτείαις πάντ' ἐξ ἐπιτάγματος ὀξέως γίγνεται. This is contrasted with democracy in which ἔστ' ἐν λόγοις ἡ πολιτεία.

[4] xxii 32 ἐν γὰρ ταῖς ὀλιγαρχίαις οὐδ' ἂν ὦσιν ἔτ' Ἀνδροτίωνός τινες αἴσχιον βεβιωκότες, οὐκ ἔστι λέγειν κακῶς τοὺς ἄρχοντας.

[5] εὐνομία and εὐταξία were commonly claimed by the oligarchs. It is doubtful whether the philosophers would give them credit for anything else than intense and despotic rule. So Ar. *Pol.* vi 3 1290 a 27 calls oligarchic governments συντονωτέρας καὶ δεσποτικωτέρας. In iv 4 1326 a 26 he argues that εὐνομία and εὐταξία can scarcely be found in an overpopulous city, although εὐταξία is the salvation of an oligarchy (vii 7 1321 a 3).

[6] See § 32 n. 10.

dominated in the oligarchic constitution, and we can best realise it by contrasting it with the democratic theory. In the fully developed democracy the people wanted to exercise their powers directly, they were jealous of all institutions in the state other than the assembly, and both council and magistrates were rendered in every way subordinate agents of the popular power. The duties of government were divided amongst a great number of magistrates whose authority was restricted as far as possible : the lot secured that ordinary men would be chosen (so that it was impossible to leave much to their discretion) : their tenure was short, reelection was usually forbidden, offices were intended to rotate and all who exercised the smallest authority did so with a full responsibility to the governing body[7].

In the oligarchies almost every one of these conditions is reversed. The functions of government were not so thoroughly divided, the magistrates had larger independent powers, they were appointed by and from a small privileged body, the same men might be reelected and they were most often irresponsible. These points must be discussed in detail.

§ 41. *Appointment and Qualification of Magistrates.*

It was characteristic of oligarchy to limit both office and the right of electing to office to privileged classes[1].

[7] On this characteristic of democracy, especially in so far as it is connected with the use of the lot, cf. Mr J. W. Headlam's *Election by Lot.*

[1] In the exceedingly corrupt passage in Ar. *Pol.* vi 15 1300 b it is clear that τὸ τινὰς (καθιστάναι) ἐκ τινῶν is oligarchic.

The electing body might be the same as the class eligible for office[2] or the candidates might possess a higher qualification than the electors[3]. On the other hand in oligarchies in which no assembly existed, or in those in which the powers of the assembly were altogether small and inconsiderable, election was entrusted to the council[4].

Election by vote was the usual method of appointment[5]. Lot was possible in an oligarchy[6]; it may have been sometimes adopted to check the powers of great families or cliques, but its use was probably rare: for the oligarch did not believe, as the democrat tended to believe, that all men were equally qualified for political duties. The lot was supposed to result in the appoint-

[2] At Sparta the Ephors γίνονται ἐκ τοῦ δήμου παντός (Ar. *Pol.* ii 9 1270 b 8), the γέροντες from the καλοὶ κάγαθοί. The κόσμοι at Crete were appointed ἐκ τινῶν γενῶν (ii 10 1272 a 34).

[3] Cf. Ar. *Pol.* viii 6 1305 b 30 ἐν ὅσαις ὀλιγαρχίαις οὐχ οὗτοι αἱροῦνται τὰς ἀρχὰς ἐξ ὧν οἱ ἄρχοντές εἰσιν, ἀλλ' αἱ μὲν ἀρχαὶ ἐκ τιμημάτων μεγάλων εἰσὶν ἢ ἑταιριῶν, αἱροῦνται δ' οἱ ὁπλῖται ἢ ὁ δῆμος, i.e. the power of election was entrusted to an assembly of hoplites, or presumably of the classes otherwise excluded from the government. Cf. also the passages in n. 2 and vi 15 1300 a 15 quoted in n. 14 below, and 1300 b 4.

[4] The Council of the Areopagus, according to Ar. *Ath. Pol.* 8 2, originally had power of election, and in the revolutionary governments at Athens the Council of the Four Hundred was to have power to appoint magistrates (*ib.* 30 2; 31 2), and the Thirty did so (35 1).

[5] Ar. *Pol.* vi 9 1294 b 8 δοκεῖ δημοκρατικὸν μὲν εἶναι κληρωτὰς εἶναι τὰς ἀρχάς, τὸ δ' αἱρετὰς ὀλιγαρχικόν.

[6] *Ib.* vi 15 1300 b *ad in.* Cf. also Anaximenes Rhetor quoted by Gilbert, *Handbuch* ii p. 319 n. 1, περὶ δὲ τὰς ὀλιγαρχίας τὰς μὲν ἀρχὰς δεῖ τοὺς νόμους ἀπονέμειν ἐξ ἴσου πᾶσι τοῖς τῆς πολιτείας μετέχουσι, τούτων δὲ εἶναι τὰς μὲν πλείστας κληρωτάς, τὰς δὲ μεγίστας κρυπτῇ ψήφῳ μεθ' ὅρκων καὶ πλείστης ἀκριβείας διαψηφιστάς. This is rather an ideal scheme than a generalisation of experience.

ment of the 'average' man[7], and the oligarch did not, any more than the philosopher[8], believe in the political capacity of the 'average' man. The method of appointment by acclamation which prevailed at Sparta and possibly at Crete was a 'puerile' method[9] in the opinion of Aristotle and little better than the lot[10]. In some cases there was a double process of election[11], or a combination of lot and election[12], and more rarely perhaps cooptation[13].

[7] Ar. *Ath. Pol.* 27 5 κληρουμένων ἐπιμελῶς ἀεὶ μᾶλλον τῶν τυχόντων ἢ τῶν ἐπιεικῶν ἀνθρώπων: Xen. *Mem.* iii 9 10 election by οἱ τυχόντες or the lot are classed together.

[8] Besides the passages in the preceding note, cf. Ar. *Pol.* ii 8 1269 a 5 (primitive man was like οἱ τυχόντες and οἱ ἀνόητοι); viii 8 1308 a 34 (ὁ τυχών opposed to ὁ πολιτικὸς ἀνήρ): viii 8 1309 a 9.

[9] Plut. *Lyc.* 26 describes the election of γέροντες at Sparta βοῇ γὰρ ὡς τἆλλα καὶ τοὺς ἁμιλλωμένους ἔκρινον. This is justly described as παιδαριῶδης in Ar. *Pol.* ii 9 1271 a 10, and as the election of the ephors is described in the same terms (ii 9 1270 b 28), we may infer that the same method was adopted.

[10] Ar. in the passage last quoted says οἱ τυχόντες were appointed ephors. So Plato, *Laws* iii 692 A, describes the power of the Ephors as ἐγγὺς τῆς κληρωτῆς δυνάμεως. The Cosmi at Crete are compared to the Ephors in terms which may apply to the method of election: γίνονται γὰρ οἱ τυχόντες (ii 10 1272 a 30).

[11] In criticising the appointment of magistrates in Plato's *Laws* Aristotle (*Pol.* ii 6 1266 a 26) describes it as τὸ ἐξ αἱρετῶν αἱρετούς. The appointment of generals and other army officers is conducted in this way (*Laws* vi 755) but most of the magistrates are appointed by a combination of lot and election. The constitution of the Four Hundred at Athens involved a double election of magistrates (see Appendix C). The Council of 500 under the Thirty was similarly appointed (Ar. *Ath. Pol.* 35 1).

[12] The principle is stated to be common to oligarchy and democracy (Ar. *Pol.* ii 6 1266 a 9). Under the Solonian constitution the magistrates were κληρωτοὶ ἐκ προκρίτων (Ar. *Ath. Pol.* 8 1).

[13] Ar. *Pol.* ii 11 1273 a 13 (of Carthage), and it is defined as

Passing to qualification for office, it was natural in oligarchies, in which the citizenship was at all extended, to require special conditions in the candidates for the different magistracies[14]. In some aristocracies special families were privileged above the rest[15]; and in oligarchies property and age were often made conditions for office. In the constitution attributed to Draco we find a special property qualification: while Solon (whose reforms in many respects were democratic in tendency) introduced an elaborate gradation of privilege[16]. We may assume that there were similar provisions in many oligarchies[17].

In some states the same object was attained indirectly by imposing conditions which would make a poor man loath to undertake office, or by debarring a rich man from renouncing an office to which he had been appointed[18]. This principle was applied to every exercise of political activity, and Aristotle describes it as an oligarchic device to impose a fine on the rich for not

oligarchic, τὸ τὰς πενταρχίας...ὑφ' αὑτῶν αἱρετὰς εἶναι. The process by which the Four Hundred were chosen described in Thuc. viii 67 3 is a sort of cooptation.

[14] See Ar. quoted in n. 3 and cf. Pol. vi 15 1300 a 15 καθιστᾶσιν...ἐκ τινῶν ἀφωρισμένων, οἷον ἢ τιμήματι ἢ γένει ἤ τινι τοιούτῳ ἄλλῳ.

[15] See n. 2.

[16] Ar. Ath. Pol. 4 2; 7 3 (of Solon) ἑκάστοις ἀνάλογον τῷ μεγέθει τοῦ τιμήματος ἀποδιδοὺς τὴν ἀρχήν.

[17] Cf. Ar. Pol. vii 6 1320 b 22 in a moderate oligarchy δεῖ τὰ τιμήματα διαιρεῖν, τὰ μὲν ἐλάττω τὰ δὲ μείζω ποιοῦντας, ἐλάττω μὲν ἀφ' ὧν τῶν ἀναγκαίων μεθέξουσιν ἀρχῶν, μείζω δ' ἀφ' ὧν τῶν κυριωτέρων. Cf. Plato Laws v 744 c.

[18] Cf. Ar. Pol. ii 6 1266 a 9 τὸ δὲ τοῖς μὲν εὐπορωτέροις ἐπάναγκες ἐκκλησιάζειν εἶναι καὶ φέρειν ἄρχοντας ἤ τι ποιεῖν ἄλλο τῶν πολιτικῶν, τοὺς δ' ἀφεῖσθαι, τοῦτο δ' ὀλιγαρχικόν.

attending the assembly or for not acting as judges[19]. Instances in which this principle is enforced are to be found in the constitution attributed to Draco by Aristotle and in the projected oligarchy at Athens[20]. Pay for public services on the other hand was a democratic institution[21] and was rarely found in oligarchies[22]. On the contrary it was oligarchic for the highest offices to involve such a burden of expense that the poor might be unwilling to hold them[23].

It was usual in all states, whether oligarchic or democratic, to set a higher limit of age for the exercise of official power than for the ordinary duties of citizenship; but the principle was carried further in oligarchies than in democracies. 'In an early stage of society age implies rule and rule implies age[24]'; and in the councils of the oligarchies (which were usually survivals from the aristocratic constitutions) old age was very often a necessary qualification, while in many the senators held office for life[25], so that there was bound to be a preponderance of old men.

Specific instances of advanced age as a condition of office are not frequent[26]. The magistrates appointed at

[19] Ar. *Pol.* vi 13 1297 a 16; cf. Plato *Laws* vi 764 A.

[20] Ar. *Ath. Pol.* 4 3; 30 6.

[21] Ar. *Pol.* vi 13 1297 a 36.

[22] The constitution of the Four Hundred maintained pay for the archons and πρυτάνεις (Ar. *Ath. Pol.* 29 5) but the government was an oligarchy disguised as a democracy.

[23] Ar. *Pol.* vii 7 1321 a 31.

[24] Freeman, *Comparative Politics* p. 72.

[25] See below, § 44, and cf. the title γερουσία applied to many of the old councils.

[26] Except for the constitutions considered in § 34 no certain instance

Athens after the Sicilian expedition to be a check upon
the democracy were a board of old men[27], and at Chalcis
an age of at least fifty was required for the magistrates[28].

§ 42. *Tenure and Responsibility of Magistrates.*

From the general conception of government formed by
the oligarchs we should naturally expect them to grant a
longer tenure of power to their magistrates than was usual
in democracies[1], and to allow them to hold their office
more than once. As specific instances we may cite those
constitutions in which hereditary kings survived, for these
formed 'life magistracies[2]': and the gradual transition

can be quoted in which a mature age was a necessary condition of citizenship. In Ar. *Pol.* vi 13 1297 b 14 ἐν Μαλιεῦσι δὲ ἡ μὲν πολιτεία ἦν ἐκ
τούτων (τῶν ὡπλιτευκότων), τὰς δ' ἀρχὰς ᾑροῦντο ἐκ τῶν στρατευομένων it is
doubtful whether οἱ ὡπλιτευκότες denotes those who are already released
from service or is meant to include also οἱ ὁπλιτεύοντες. In Plato's
Republic (vii 740 A) the guardians were not to be admitted to rule until
their fiftieth year, and in Aristotle's ideal state the younger men were to
be excluded from deliberative (i.e. political) power (*Pol.* iv 9 1329 a 13;
14 1332 b 35), and it is probable that some states actually had similar
provisions. The constitution of Draco (Ar. *Ath. Pol.* 4) indirectly made
a mature age a qualification for the στρατηγία.

27 Thuc. viii 1.

28 Heraclides F.H.G. ii 222 νόμος δὲ ἦν Χαλκιδεῦσι μὴ ἄρξαι μηδὲ
πρεσβεῦσαι νεώτερον ἐτῶν πεντήκοντα. (I do not know whether πρεσβεῦσαι
could mean *be a senator,* but its ordinary sense does not seem suitable
here.) It is difficult to believe that all magistrates (e.g. military officers)
had to be over 50.

1 Ar. *Pol.* ii 11 1273 a 15 a long tenure of office is defined as
oligarchic. Cf. also viii 8 1308 a 24.

2 Ar. *Pol.* iii 15 1287 a 5 describes kingship as στρατηγία ἀίδιος. It is
possible that the chief magistrates of Opus and of Epidamnus (mentioned
in this place) held office for life, but the passage is capable of another
interpretation.

from a life tenure to ten years and then to one year can
be traced in the case of the supreme magistrates at
Athens: but after the completion of constitutional development, even in oligarchies, we know no instances of
office conferred for more than a year, except in the case of
the council, the members of which often sat for life.

The idea of the responsibility of the magistrates which
is characteristic of democracy was never enforced to the
same degree in oligarchies. The oligarchic conception of
official power required that the magistrate should not be
liable to be called to account by the ordinary citizens:
the authority of government would have been impaired
had the magistrates been brought into collision with any
board of revision and audit. At the same time the success
of an oligarchy depended so absolutely on the intimate
cooperation of magistrates and council, that a magistrate
would be extremely unlikely to act against the authority
of the council: and the council, composed as it usually
was of past magistrates, would, from the age and experience of its members, be able to make its advice
equivalent to command and its censure to condemnation.
Hence the indefinite powers entrusted to the aristocratic
and oligarchic councils often included, no doubt, the
power to control the magistrates, to see that they did not
transgress the laws and to call them to account in case
they offended[3].

Sparta, whose constitution differed in most respects
from that of other states, left the supervision of all other

---

[3] It is recorded of the council of the Areopagus that they had to keep
the magistrates within the written laws (Ar. *Ath. Pol.* 4 4: in § 2 of
this chapter, which contains so many difficulties, εὔθυναι are mentioned
without a hint as to how they were conducted). Solon gave the power

magistrates to the Ephors[4]. In states in which stress was laid on the strict observance of the law the nomophylaces may have had the duty of seeing that the magistrates did not transgress the law and so have formed a board of control over them[5]. But in most states the magistrate was left a large amount of freedom. They acted on their own discretion and were not bound by written rules[6]: while oligarchies would be more inclined than democracies to entrust single magistrates or small boards of magistrates with absolute and omnipotent authority[7]. The powers of the Ephors and the Cosmi are well known, and another significant instance is afforded by the oligarchic constitution at Athens in 411. Under the provisional government the ten generals were to have absolute power and only to consult with the council at their discretion[8].

of calling the magistrates to account to the people, but the Areopagus remained the guardian of the laws (Ar. *Ath. Pol.* 8 4 it was ἐπίσκοπος τῆς πολιτείας entrusted with τὸ νομοφυλακεῖν) and so must have had some control over the magistrates. The council of the Four Hundred at Athens was to have power περὶ τῶν εὐθυνῶν (Ar. *Ath. Pol.* 31 1). Cf. Plut. *Q. G.* 2 on the 'nocturnal council' at Crete. The councils themselves were usually irresponsible.

[4] *Pol.* ii 9 1271 a 6. From Ar. *Rhet.* iii 18 1419 b 31 and Plut. *Agis* 12, Gilbert, *Handbuch* i[2] p. 59 n. 1, concludes that the Ephors were responsible and had to render an account to their successors.

[5] See below, § 43.

[6] Ar. *Pol.* ii 9 1270 b 29 says that the Ephors at Sparta decided αὐτογνώμονες and not κατὰ γράμματα καὶ τοὺς νόμους. Cf. *ib.* 10 1272 a 38.

[7] Cf. Theophr. *Charact.* 8; the oligarchic man is wont to say, when the appointment of magistrates is discussed, ὡς δεῖ αὐτοκράτορας τούτους εἶναι.

[8] Ar. *Ath. Pol.* 31 2.

§ 43. *Single Magistrates and Boards of Magistrates.*

The oldest type of aristocratic government is that
represented by the rule of the Bacchiadae at Corinth, in
which the clan of that name formed a council of government, jointly controlling the state and appointing every
year one of their number with the position and powers of
the former king[1]. We need not suppose that he was the
only magistrate[2], but in dignity he was the chief and he
doubtless held the chief administrative power. Gradually
in most states political functions were divided; military
command was separated from civil administration, which
was shared by a number of magistrates; but many oligarchies still kept one man at the head of the constitution[3] and entrusted him with the chief control of the
administration, while democracies tended to divide power,
to suspect the holders of it and therefore to create several
boards of magistrates. Single magistrates, who are described as supreme in the administration, were appointed
at Opus and at Epidamnus[4], in the different Elean com-

---

[1] Diod. vii fr. οἱ δὲ...Βακχίδαι...κατέσχον τὴν ἀρχὴν καὶ κοινῇ μὲν
προειστήκεσαν τῆς πόλεως ἅπαντες, ἐξ αὐτῶν δὲ ἕνα κατ' ἐνιαυτὸν ἡροῦντο
πρύτανιν, ὃς τὴν τοῦ βασιλέως εἶχε τάξιν.

[2] Nicol. Dam. F. H. G. iii 392 implies that there was a πολέμαρχος : if
so the πρύτανις was not commander in chief.

[3] Ar. *Pol.* viii 1 1301 b 25 ὀλιγαρχικὸν δὲ καὶ ὁ ἄρχων ὁ εἷς (of
Epidamnus).

[4] Ar. *Pol.* iii 16 1287 a 6 πολλοὶ ποιοῦσιν ἕνα κύριον τῆς διοικήσεως·
τοιαύτη γὰρ ἀρχή τις ἔστι καὶ περὶ 'Επίδαμνον καὶ περὶ 'Οποῦντα. In Locris
we may perhaps identify this magistrate with the ἀρχός mentioned in
I.G.A. 321 41 (Roberts *Epigraphy* 231, Hicks *Manual* 63). From the
passage of Aristotle quoted in n. 3 we might conclude that the magistrate at Epidamnus was called ἄρχων. Gilbert, *Handbuch* ii p. 237 n.,
suggests that he was called διοικητάς.

munities[5] and at Locri in Italy[6]. In most Greek states
there was one magistrate, who was formally at the head
of affairs[7], but apart from these merely titular chiefs we
may distinguish the πρύτανις as a magistrate found with
especial frequency in oligarchies[8].

Single magistrates of this sort were entrusted with
large powers; but a small board of magistrates, if acting
in concord, must have possessed still more authority.
The best examples of such boards are furnished by the
Ephors at Sparta and the Cosmi at Crete. The Ephors
enjoyed a high prestige[9], and the Cosmi (who are often
compared to the Ephors) had also the command in war[10].
Ephors were also to be found in the Dorian colonies of
Tarentum, Heraclea in Italy, Thera and Cyrene[11].

In Western Locris the damiorgi were the chief magis-

<hr/>

[5] Cauer *Delectus*[2] 112, Roberts *Epigraphy* 292 ὃρ μέγιστον τέλος ἔχει is
used to describe the different magistrates in the different towns (who
probably had different titles).

[6] κοσμόπολις Polyb. xii 16.

[7] Of eponymous magistrates without real power we may cite the ἄρχων
in Boeotia, the βασιλεύς in Megara.

[8] Besides Corinth cf. Miletus (πολλῶν γὰρ ἦν καὶ μεγάλων κύριος ὁ
πρύτανις Ar. *Pol.* viii 5 1305 a 16); Tenedos (Pind. *Nem.* xi 1): Mitylene
(Cauer *Delectus*[2] 472 20); Croton (Athen. xii 522 A—D).

[9] Ar. *Pol.* ii 9 1270 b 7 ἡ ἀρχὴ κυρία μὲν αὐτὴ τῶν μεγίστων αὐτοῖς ἐστίν.
He calls it λίαν μεγάλη καὶ ἰσοτύραννος. Cf. Plut. *Ages.* 4.

[10] Ar. *Pol.* ii 10 1272 a 9.

[11] Inscriptions prove the existence of ephors at a comparatively late
period in Thera and Heraclea; but as all these colonies had direct or
indirect connexion with Sparta we may assume that the ephorate was
an early institution. For Thera cf. Cauer *Delectus*[2] 148 1: Cyrene
Heraclides F. H. G. ii 212; Heraclea Cauer 40 1 (of about 400 B.C.), and
as Heraclea was a colony of Tarentum we may assume that this magistracy existed also in the metropolis.

trates[12]: magistrates with this title held the chief executive power in many states[13]. At Athens, in the early
constitution the gradual division of the king's powers can
be traced, while in the oligarchy of the Four Hundred the
chief authority was entrusted to a board of ten, and in
404 B.C. the Thirty seem to have directed the administration themselves.

Massalia shows us an artificial constitution, with a
gradual devolution of power. From the assembly of Six
Hundred, fifteen men were chosen to administer current
affairs; from the fifteen three presidents were elected and
from the three one man to have supreme power in the
state[14]. This system of ensuring that the magistrates
should be members of the assembly produced a well-
ordered government, which lasted for centuries. A similar
attempt to introduce unity into the administration was
made by the Four Hundred at Athens; for in the projected constitution all the magistrates were to be chosen
out of the council[15].

There were certain magistracies connected with special
constitutions. One class of these was entrusted with
censorial duties, with the supervision of women and
children and the control of the gymnasia: such magistrates Aristotle describes as aristocratic and not oligarchic[16]. In a luxurious oligarchy, he says, a magistracy

[12] Roberts *Epigraphy* 232 and 233 (I. G. A. 322 and 323).

[13] For instances see Gilbert *Handbuch* ii p. 327.

[14] Strabo iv 179.

[15] Ar. *Ath. Pol.* 30 2. See Appendix C.

[16] In vii 8 1322 b 37 ἴδιαι δὲ ταῖς σχολαστικωτέραις καὶ μᾶλλον εὐημερού-
σαις πόλεσιν, ἔτι δὲ φροντιζούσαις εὐκοσμίας, γυναικονομία, νομοφυλακία,
παιδονομία, γυμνασιαρχία. The states that 'care for good order' naturally
maintain the censorship.

of this sort would not be possible[17]; but the old-fashioned
aristocracies claimed to exercise a rigid control over their
members. The Spartan system involved the interference
of the state with every detail of private life, although it
did not succeed in chastening the women, and their conduct Aristotle regards as one of the great defects of the
state[18].

Of political magistrates the probuli are described as
oligarchic; the nomophylaces as aristocratic, while both
are contrasted with the large council of the democracies[19].
The probuli were most often a division or committee of
the council, and this magistracy will therefore be considered in the next section.

The nomophylaces on the other hand, though mentioned in connexion with the council and the probuli, seem
to have formed an independent board of magistrates[20].
They were entrusted with discretionary powers to see
that the laws were duly observed, and they were thus
able to exercise a sort of censorship over the private life
of the citizens. We may suppose that their powers were
very similar to those of the council of the Areopagus,
which is described as being the guardian of the laws.
They were especially natural in a state, whose constitution depended on the observance of fixed ordinances; and
their duties in this connexion were to take care that the
laws were duly obeyed, to see that no proposal in conflict

[17] Ar. *Pol.* vi 15 1300 a 4.

[18] Ar. *Pol.* ii 9 1269 b.   [19] Ar. *Pol.* vii 8 1323 a b.

[20] This is stated of the νομοφύλακες at Athens: see n. 24. In some
instances these magistrates may have been able to veto proposals made
in the assembly, and thus to exercise a function usually reserved to the
council.

with them should be made and to guard the state
archives, in order that proper records might be kept[21].

Such magistrates were appointed in Abdera, Chalcedon, Mylasa, and Corcyra, and with slightly different
titles in Andania, Elis and Thespiae[22].

To the thesmothetae at Athens at the date of their
institution Aristotle assigns duties very similar to those
ascribed to the nomophylaces[23], and in the reform of the
Athenian democracy at the end of the fourth century
seven nomophylaces were instituted as a check upon the
democracy[24]. Other magistrates who performed some of
the duties usually ascribed to the nomophylaces were the
registrars, who had the custody of private contracts and
of public documents, but these do not seem to have been
a specially oligarchic institution[25].

---

[21] The best general description of their duties is in Xen. *Oec.* 9 14
ἐδίδασκον δὲ αὐτὴν ὅτι καὶ ἐν ταῖς εὐνομουμέναις πόλεσιν οὐκ ἀρκεῖν δοκεῖ τοῖς
πολίταις ἢν νόμους καλοὺς γράψωνται, ἀλλὰ καὶ νομοφύλακας προσαιροῦνται,
οἵτινες ἐπισκοποῦντες τὸν μὲν ποιοῦντα τὰ νόμιμα ἐπαινοῦσιν, ἢν δέ τις παρὰ
τοὺς νόμους ποιῇ ζημιοῦσι. Cf. Plato *Laws* vi 754 D (of the νομοφύλακες in
his constitution) πρῶτον μὲν φύλακες ἔστωσαν τῶν νόμων, ἔπειτα τῶν
γραμμάτων ὧν ἂν ἕκαστος ἀπογράψῃ τοῖς ἄρχουσι τὸ πλῆθος τῆς αὐτῶν οὐσίας.
(Their duties in other respects seem more extensive than those of this
magistracy in general.) Cf. Cic. *de Leg.* iii 20 46. See also the description of these magistrates at Athens in n. 24.

[22] For these see Gilbert *Handbuch* ii p. 338 n. 1.

[23] Ar. *Ath. Pol.* 3 4.

[24] Their duties are stated in Lex. Rhetor. Cantab. 674 τὰς δὲ ἀρχὰς
ἠνάγκαζον τοῖς νόμοις χρῆσθαι καὶ ἐν τῇ ἐκκλησίᾳ καὶ ἐν τῇ βουλῇ μετὰ τῶν
προέδρων ἐκάθηντο κωλύοντες τὰ ἀσύμφορα τῇ πόλει πράττειν· ἑπτὰ δὲ ἦσαν
καὶ κατέστησαν, ὡς Φιλόχορος ὅτε Ἐφιάλτης μόνα κατέλιπε τῇ ἐξ Ἀρείου
πάγου βουλῇ τὰ περὶ τοῦ σώματος. It has been thought that the last
statement is mistaken, as there is no trace of the existence of this
magistracy before the reforms of Demetrius.

[25] Ar. *Pol.* vii 8 1321 b 34.

§ 44. *Constitution of the Council.*

Generally speaking the council formed the most important element in the oligarchical constitution. In the times of the Heroic Monarchy and of the Aristocracy it acted as the representative of the nobles, and in the constitution of the later oligarchies it continued to represent the privileged body. It was the sovereign power in the state as the assembly was in the democracy, and where the one institution was powerful, the other was bound to be subordinate[1]. But the oligarchic council differed from the democratic council not only in power and importance, but in size and constitution. The democratic assembly was obliged to delegate some of its powers to a council, but in order to minimise the power of the individual members a large number of citizens was admitted to it, usually appointed by lot, and the large council was regarded as essentially democratic[2].

The oligarchic council, on the other hand, was composed of a small number of members, which even in the most populous states rarely exceeded one hundred. At Sparta there were thirty, at Cnidus sixty, at Corinth[3] eighty, in Elis ninety; and in the Areopagus, which was made up of ex-archons sitting for life, it has been calculated that

[1] Ar. *Pol.* vi 15 1299 b 38 καταλύεται δὲ καὶ τῆς βουλῆς ἡ δύναμις ἐν ταῖς τοιαύταις δημοκρατίαις ἐν αἷς αὐτὸς συνιὼν ὁ δῆμος χρηματίζει περὶ πάντων. The converse is true of oligarchy. Cf. J. W. Headlam *Election by Lot*, p. 42 'It would be equally correct if we substituted for the Greek words 'Rule of the Many,' 'Rule of the Few' the expressions 'Rule by the Assembly,' 'Rule by the Council.'

[2] Ar. *Pol.* vii 8 1323 a 6.

[3] For Corinth see § 46 n. 2.

there would be not more than ninety members at a time[4]. In the few instances in which larger councils occur in oligarchies, we may assume that they practically took the place of the assembly, and that no more numerous body was entrusted with real power. Thus in the oligarchic revolution at Athens in 411, the Five Thousand were practically excluded from the government, while in the projected constitution, the acting council was apparently intended to be formed of one fourth part of the whole body of the citizens[5]. In the later oligarchy the Thirty nominated a council of Five Hundred, but this was the most numerous body in the constitution, and the Thirty themselves probably acted as a council[6]. In the oligarchies of fixed number, in which the Assembly was not so large as to preclude discussion, the council would not be so indispensable, and this may explain why we do not find it so much in evidence in these constitutions[7].

I proceed to discuss the method of appointing members of the council. In primitive times when government was of the patriarchal type the chiefs were probably convoked by the king to advise him[8]. When sovereignty

[4] Hermann *Lehrbuch der Staatsaltertümer*[6], p. 388 n. 6, where Titt-mann is quoted.

[5] In the provisional constitution the Four Hundred acted as the supreme authority. For the projected constitution see Ar. *Ath. Pol.* 30 3 and Appendix C below.

[6] Ar. *Ath. Pol.* 35 1. The 'Three Thousand' seem never to have had any power.

[7] Dicaearch. F.H.G. ii 244 mentions τὸ τῶν γερόντων ἀρχεῖον at Croton: at Locri we find the χίλιοι performing functions that usually belonged to an oligarchic council. At Massalia 15 προεστῶτες were chosen from the συνέδριον, who probably formed a sort of council, Strabo v 179.

[8] There is not, so far as I know, any evidence as to the method by which the council was selected in the heroic constitution.

passed from the king to the chiefs, the council either
included all the nobles of a certain age or it was formed
from the heads of the clans whose union made the state[9].

In later times some principle of selection had to be
applied. At Sparta[10], in Elis[11] and at Cnidus[12] the senators
were elected from certain privileged classes or families;
in Epidaurus sixty of the hundred and eighty citizens
were constituted a council[13]. In Athens[14] and Crete[15] the
chief magistrates were admitted to the council after their
term of office. We have not sufficient information as to
the constitution of the councils in ordinary oligarchies,
but we may infer that the highest qualifications required
for the magistracies were also exacted in the case of the
senators and that the most careful process of election was
usually enforced[16]. But the senators differed from the

[9] The title of the senators at Epidamnus φύλαρχοι may point to a
system in which the φυλαί and their subdivisions were represented: it is
possible that the Spartan γερουσία may have been originally representative of the thirty obes. In many states the numbers of the senators
suggest a connexion with the φυλαί, and originally the smaller divisions
may have been represented.

[10] Ar. Pol. ii 9 1270 b 24.

[11] Ar. Pol. viii 6 1306 a 18 says the αἵρεσις was δυναστευτική (I take
this to mean from certain families), and he compares it to the Spartan
method.

[12] Plut. Q.G. 4 πρόκριτοι ἐξ ἀρίστων. It is doubtful whether the καλοὶ
κἀγαθοί of Sparta and the ἄριστοι of Cnidus refer to certain privileged
families or merely to the claims of wealth and education. For Sparta
see § 32 n. 7.

[13] Plut. Q.G. 1.

[14] Ar. Ath. Pol. 3 6; Plut. Sol. 19.

[15] Ar. Pol. ii 10 1272 a 34 (αἱροῦνται...τοὺς γέροντας ἐκ τῶν κεκοσμηκό-
των) and Strabo x 484 both imply some principle of selection applied to
the ex-cosmi.

[16] From the few instances of which we have definite information it is

magistrates inasmuch as a higher limit of age was usually necessary[17] and in many cases they were appointed for life[18].

The commonest title used to describe the senate in an oligarchy was γερουσία, though βουλή was also found; and in constitutions in which the old oligarchic senate was preserved side by side with a democratic council, they were sometimes distinguished by the titles of γερουσία and βουλή[19]. The senators were often called γέροντες, but many other titles were used to describe them in different states, and we hear of the ζαμιωργοί in Elis[20], the τιμοῦχοι at Teos[21], the ἄρτυνοι at Epidaurus[22], the ἀμνήμονες at Cnidus[23], the φύλαρχοι at Epidamnus[24].

The oligarchic council was then, as a general rule, composed of a comparatively small number of men, who fulfilled the highest conditions in respect to birth and

clear that the conditions for election to the council were more stringent than for the election of magistrates.

[17] At Sparta an age of at least sixty years was required (Plut. *Lyc.* 26), and the frequent application of the title of γέροντες to the senators, of γερουσία to the senate, points to a high limit of age being necessary elsewhere.

[18] Examples of life senates are the councils at Sparta, in Crete, Elis, Cnidus (Plut. *Q. G.* 4) and the council of the Areopagus at Athens.

[19] Ephesus, Strabo xiv 640, Dittenberger *Sylloge* 134. At Crete the senators were called γέροντες (they are so described by Aristotle), the senate βωλὰ (Cauer *Delectus*² 121ᶜ).

[20] Gilbert, *Handbuch* ii p. 101, thinks the ζαμιωργοί were the senators of the separate states, and that they united to form the ζαμιωργία of the united state (mentioned in Cauer *Delectus*² 257).

[21] Dittenberger *Sylloge* 234 13.

[22] Plut. *Q. G.* 1.

[23] Plut. *Q. G.* 4.

[24] Ar. *Pol.* viii 1 1301 b 22.

wealth, who had usually held the most important magistracies, and who, in many cases, were appointed for life.

§ 45. *Powers of the Council.*

The members of the oligarchic council thus enjoyed the highest political privilege in their states, and the council could not fail to be imbued with an exclusive and aristocratic spirit. Its authority was great. The individual magistrate, holding a temporary office, usually without experience of its duties, was expected to seek and to follow advice from a council, composed of ex-magistrates, irresponsible and deciding on their own discretion, which often formed the only permanent organ of the constitution. Such an institution, whatever the theoretical division of political power may have been, was inevitably obliged to rule the policy of the state : the magistrates acted under its direction and thus became in a sense its responsible ministers.

Its powers could not be defined, for the very reason that they were unlimited[1]: there was probably no branch of the administration in which it had not sovereign authority, and even where the assembly possessed any importance, the council decided what business was to be brought before it and so exercised a veto on its proceedings[2].

[1] This point is brought out by Mr J. W. Headlam in an article on *The Council at Athens* (*Classical Review*, vi p. 296). 'The natural conclusion is that the Council (of the Areopagus in early times) never had any definite and limited duties. The archons were executive; the council superintended, directed and if necessary punished them.'

[2] Even in democracies the council was 'probouleutic': and this part

Hence we find the vaguest descriptions of the competence of the senate in oligarchies. The Council of the Areopagus 'administered most of the greatest things[3]' and was 'the guardian of the state[4].' At Cnidus the senators were 'guardians and counsellors in the greatest matters[5]'; at Crete the elders were 'irresponsible and absolute[6]' and 'advisers in the greatest matters[7],' while at Sparta, although the Ephors attained a power that was almost tyrannical, they only held office for a year and the senate was said to 'rule over all things' and to be 'sovereign in affairs of state[8].'

These instances are sufficient to show that the competence of the oligarchic council eludes definition. It was the sovereign body, the chief 'deliberative' element[9], just as the assembly was in the democracy : and the other elements in the state, whether assembly or magistrates, exercised their powers in subordination to the council.

Its judicial duties will be discussed below.

of its duties must have been of more real importance in oligarchies. See below § 46.

[3] Ar. *Ath. Pol.* 3 6; 4 4.

[4] *Ib.* 8 4.

[5] ἐπίσκοποι...καὶ πρόβουλοι τῶν μεγίστων Plut. *Q. G.* 4.

[6] Ar. *Pol.* ii 10 1272 a 36.

[7] Strabo xiv 480.

[8] Isocr. xii 154; Polyb. vi 45 5 δι' ὧν καὶ μεθ' ὧν πάντα χειρίζεται τὰ κατὰ τὴν πολιτείαν; Dionys. Hal. ii 14 ἡ γερουσία πᾶν εἶχε τῶν κοινῶν τὸ κράτος. Plut. *Ages.* 4 represents τὸ κράτος as shared between the senate and the ephors: and in the fourth century the ephors undoubtedly gained authority at the expense of the senate.

[9] Cf. the definition of the deliberative element in Ar. *Pol.* vi 14 1298 a 4. Some of the powers mentioned there were formally exercised by the assembly in some oligarchies.

§ 46. *Subdivisions of the Council.*

In discussing the constitution of the oligarchic council
I have laid stress on the small number of members which
it usually included.   But there was usually, also, a much
smaller committee, chosen generally from the council, on
which considerable power was conferred.   This committee
was entrusted with the duty of the preliminary consideration of measures before they came before the council or
the assembly, the duty of preparing motions and drawing
up proposals : and hence they sometimes bore the name
of πρόβουλοι[1], a magistracy which Aristotle describes as
especially oligarchic.   In democracies these duties were
generally performed by the council, but even in democracies,
the council was often divided into committees in order to
transact current business and to control meetings of the
council or the assembly.   But while in a democracy each
committee was appointed for a very brief period and given

---

[1] It is usually assumed that the πρόβουλοι denote a small board of
magistrates, often a subdivision of the βουλή itself. I think the term
was applied vaguely to the small oligarchic councils as well. Thus Ar.
Pol. vi 14 1298 b 26 describes πρόβουλοι as an ἀρχεῖον in oligarchies
entrusted with *probouleutic* duties, arranging all questions to be submitted to the people (there is no mention of any other kind of βουλή): cf.
ib. 15 1299 b 33 all constitutions must have a probouleutic magistracy:
if this is small, it is oligarchic, and called πρόβουλοι ; if large, democratic
and called βουλή: ὁ μὲν γὰρ βουλευτὴς δημοτικόν, ὁ δὲ πρόβουλος ὀλιγαρχικόν. (There seems here a contrast of the large consultative body of the
democracy with the small one of the oligarchy.)   So in vii 8 1322 a 12
the πρόβουλοι and the βουλή are described as similar institutions in different constitutions.   The term is used to describe the council at Cnidus
(Plut. *Q. G.* 4). At the same time in the instances in which we know of
the πρόβουλοι (as at Corinth and Athens) the term describes either a
committee of the βουλή or a magistracy independent of it.

as little real power as possible, we may assume that the corresponding oligarchic committees were appointed for a considerable period and possessed considerable power, securing the oligarchic ends of secrecy, efficiency and despatch.

At Corinth there was a council of eighty (in all probability) and a committee of eight[2] : at Chios[3] and Massalia[4] there were bodies of fifteen chosen from the larger councils. At Corcyra[5] and Eretria[6] magistrates called πρόβουλοι are mentioned in inscriptions, though we know nothing of the duties they performed ; and committees of the council, with special titles, can be traced in Delphi[7], Megara, and Chalcedon[8].

---

[2] Nicol. Dam. F. H. G. iii 394 (ὁ δῆμος) παραχρῆμα κατεστήσατο πολιτείαν τοιάνδε· μίαν μὲν ὀκτάδα προβούλων ἐποίησεν, ἐκ δὲ τῶν λοιπῶν βουλὴν κατέλεξεν ἀνδρῶν θ'. This is of course impossible. Busolt *Die Lakedaimonier* reads o' for θ'. He thinks that one φυλή appointed eight πρόβουλοι, and from the other seven φυλαί 70 senators were appointed. This seems extremely unlikely; is it not more probable that the source of the corruption lies in ἀνδρῶν? I suggest ὀκτάδων (perhaps ἀνδρῶν should precede προβούλων above, cf. Ar. *Ach.* 755 ἄνδρες πρόβουλοι): then we get a council of (9 × 8) + 8 = 80, i.e. 10 councillors chosen from each of eight tribes, and one from each made a πρόβουλος.

[3] Cauer *Delectus*[2] 496 a οἱ πεντεκαίδεκα seem to have formed a committee of the βουλή.

[4] At Massalia fifteen were chosen from τὸ συνέδριον of 600 (really an assembly, not a council) πεντεκαίδεκα δ' εἰσὶ τοῦ συνεδρίου προεστῶτες, τούτοις δὲ τὰ πρόχειρα διοικεῖν δέδοται Strabo iv 179.

[5] C. I. G. 1845 113. Both πρόβουλοι and πρόδικοι βωλᾶς are mentioned.

[6] See Gilbert *Handbuch* ii p. 67 n. 2.

[7] In Delphi two βουλευταί and a secretary are frequently mentioned in inscriptions. See Gilbert *Handbuch* ii p. 38.

[8] In Megara αἰσιμνᾶται (Dittenberger *Sylloge* 218) and in Chalcedon (a Megarian colony) αἰσυμνῶντες (C. I. G. 3794) occur. In the latter instance it is supposed that they act in the same capacity as the Athe-

§ 47. *The Assembly.*

In the heroic kingship, although no definite power or
privilege was assigned to the assembly of the commons, it
was still customary to convoke them to hear the decision
of their chiefs, that they might express in primitive
fashion their approval or dissent[1]. In this function lies
the germ of those powers of the people, which were afterwards developed in the sovereign assemblies of the Greek
democracy : but in the later aristocracies and in the
oligarchies the commons lost for the most part even the
small part which they had hitherto enjoyed in the constitution. The supreme council of government was the
political creation of the aristocracy, and the powers wielded
by it left small place for the assembly. In some oligarchies
the commons still retained their right of meeting, and an
assembly existed open to those who were otherwise politically disqualified[2]: but the powers of such an assembly
were neither independent nor important; and in most
oligarchies and aristocracies the commons had no place or
lot whatever; for these constitutions involved the creation
of a privileged class to which alone political rights were
given, and the distinction of ' those within ' and ' those

nian πρυτάνεις. It is therefore assumed that in both states they originally acted as πρόβουλοι.

[1] Cf. Freeman *Comparative Politics*, p. 206. 'There is no formal
reckoning of votes (in the Homeric assembly); but I suspect that any
formal reckoning of votes is a refinement belonging to a much later stage
of political life. To shout or to clash the arms is the primitive way of
declaring assent.'

[2] For the admission of the δῆμος (or a class otherwise unprivileged) to
the assembly in oligarchies see Aristotle quoted in n. 3 § 41 and n. 5
below).

without the constitution' arose. 'Those within the constitution' formed some sort of assembly, which met when
summoned and decided questions submitted to it, but
differed as widely as possible from the assembly of a
democracy.

In the aristocracies of conquest, the members of the
ruling race were alone qualified to take part in the
assembly ; the subjects were altogether excluded. In the
oligarchies of limited number, 'the Six Hundred' or 'the
Thousand' were the only privileged citizens. Their
number was not too large to preclude discussion, and the
assembly performed, therefore, some of the functions
usually entrusted to the council: and in this form of
constitution the institution was more important than in
any other kind of oligarchy. In the dynasty there was
probably nothing of the nature of an assembly[3].

Leaving these special forms of government out of
view, we may assume that the ordinary oligarchical constitution did include some sort of assembly[4]. But it was
characteristic of the oligarchy to make the council the
responsible and efficient element in the constitution and
to give but a minimum of power to the assembly. Its
action was restricted to such questions as were brought
before it by the magistrates or council[5]; the magistrates

[3] A δυναστεία ὀλίγων ἀνδρῶν probably held all power in their own
hands. Cf. the account of the rule of the Bacchiadae Diod. vii fr.

[4] Ar. Pol. iii 1 refers to some states in which there was no regular
assembly 1275 b 7 ἐν ἐνίαις γὰρ οὐκ ἔστι δῆμος, οὐδ᾽ ἐκκλησίαν νομίζουσιν
ἀλλὰ συγκλήτους. For the σύγκλητος we may cite Acragas and Melite.
See Swoboda, Griechische Volksbeschlüsse, p. 307.

[5] Ar. Pol. vi 14 1298 b 29 it is a good plan in an oligarchy to submit to the people what the πρόβουλοι have decided upon and to limit the
issue to the question submitted, οὕτω γὰρ μεθέξει ὁ δῆμος τοῦ βουλεύεσθαι

were alone qualified to speak, there was practically no discussion and the assembly had only the power to express approval or dissent; and legally, perhaps, their dissent might be disregarded. The meetings served to make the citizens acquainted with the will and purpose of the rulers; they secured, as far as possible, that the action of the government should not be in conflict with the feelings of the people; the assembly served also the purposes of publicity and registration⁶; it was an office of record for many formal acts which needed witnesses, such as the adoption of sons or the emancipation of slaves⁷. Lastly the assent of the assembly was especially called for in cases in which the state contracted responsibilities to other states. The decision of war and peace and treaties often took place in the assembly. It was doubtless felt that the honour of the state was more solemnly pledged by the united action of council and assembly. Even in the states in which the power of the assembly was very small, it was generally called upon to participate in the decision of the community⁸. The most important power that the assembly

καὶ λύειν οὐδὲν δυνήσεται τῶν περὶ τὴν πολιτείαν…ἀποψηφιζόμενον μὲν γὰρ κύριον δεῖ ποιεῖν τὸ πλῆθος, καταψηφιζόμενον δὲ μὴ κύριον. This is in a description of a moderate oligarchy in which the lower classes were admitted to the assembly; the ordinary oligarchy probably gave even less power.

⁶ This was its function in the heroic age, Grote ii p. 69 'The Agora was a special medium of publicity not including any idea of responsibility.'

⁷ For adoption see the Gortyn inscription x 33; for the emancipation of Helots at Sparta, Thuc. v 34.

⁸ Hence even in oligarchies the regular form of decree would be ἔδοξε τῇ βουλῇ καὶ τῷ δήμῳ (or some equivalent phrase). See Swoboda *Griechische Volksbeschlüsse*, p. 24, who quotes the usual forms.

exercised was the election of magistrates[9]: but in some cases they do not seem to have exercised even this power freely[10], and the example of Rome shows us how it was possible for an oligarchic council to interfere with the right of the citizens to appoint their magistrates. In some rare instances the council directly elected the officers of state[11].

In all other respects the assembly acted only in sub-ordination to the council, without power of initiative or independence of action. In the rare event of disagree-ment between different magistrates or between magistrates and senate the assembly might be called upon to decide[12], but usually the policy of the state was already resolved on, when the assembly was invited to assent[13]. It thus served generally to secure a general knowledge and pub-licity of policy and to register the divers acts of the state. In proportion as the power of the council rose, the importance of the assembly declined[14].

[9] This Ar. *Pol.* ii 12 1274 a 15 calls τὴν ἀναγκαιοτάτην δύναμιν that can be given to the δῆμος.

[10] The method of 'double election,' which is described as oligarchic, prevented the people from exercising an absolute choice. It involved the interference of council or magistrates with the choice of the assembly.

[11] Cf. Ar. *Ath. Pol.* 8 2.

[12] Cf. Thuc. i 87 where the assembly of Sparta decides between the king and the ephors.

[13] Cf. the gradual decline of the power of the assembly at Venice (*Encycl. Brit.* xxiv p. 142). 'It remained none the less true that the people had been left nothing more than the illusory right of approving by acclamation each new *doge* after his election.'

[14] There are many passages laying stress on the small powers of the assembly in the oligarchy. Cf. Ar. *Pol.* ii 10 1272 a 10 (of Crete) ἐκκλη-σίας δὲ μετέχουσι πάντες, κυρία δ' οὐδενός ἐστιν ἀλλ' ἢ συνεπιψηφίσαι τὰ δόξαντα τοῖς γέρουσι καὶ τοῖς κόσμοις; Plut. *Dion* 53 (of Corinth) ὀλιγαρχι-

We shall gain a better idea of the place that might be occupied by an assembly in an oligarchic government, if we briefly survey the powers of the Apella at Sparta. We must remember, however, that the Spartan government was unlike that of the ordinary oligarchy; for the theory that all Spartiates were equally privileged was maintained, and hence the assembly was entrusted with some considerable powers.

Originally the 'people' at Sparta was to have 'sovereignty and power': in later times the senate and the Ephors had obtained the supreme control of the state. Doubtless this had come to pass, to a great extent imperceptibly and unconsciously, by the natural working of political forces, but history records a formal change in the charter of the Spartan constitution by which the kings and senate were rendered competent to set aside a 'crooked' decision of the people. Plutarch says that the assembly had been affecting the power to amend or to add to the proposals submitted to them and the kings added this clause to prevent them. But whatever the original intention may have been, such a provision could be wrested to deprive the assembly of all authority: the magistrates and council might on occasion feel strong enough to neglect entirely the popular vote[15].

In any case the assembly was entirely subordinate to

κώτερόν τε πολιτευομένους καὶ μὴ πολλὰ τῶν κοινῶν ἐν τῷ δήμῳ πράττοντας; Dionys. Hal. vii 4 (of Cyme) ἦν δ' ἀριστοκρατία...καὶ ὁ δῆμος οὐ πολλῶν τινων κύριος.

[15] Plut. *Lyc.* 6. Grote and Gilbert think that the clause was intended to give the magistrates power to quash *any* decision of the assembly: others that the assembly was forbidden to vote except directly on the motion submitted. In any case the amendment was intended to check any encroachment of the Apella.

the senate and only possessed the right to listen to the magistrates and senators, without speaking against them[16], and to express their decision in the primitive fashion by shouts[17].

The assembly was called upon to decide war and peace, to sanction treaties and other matters of foreign politics; it chose the magistrates and voted on other important subjects submitted to it[18]. It also seems to have been the rule at Sparta for ambassadors to be received in the assembly[19].

§ 48. *Judicial Affairs.*

In the Greek constitutions legislation was a political function that was rarely exercised. The old aristocracies rested on the maintenance of traditional ordinances (sometimes unwritten) which had come down from a remote antiquity. Of the oligarchies and democracies of more recent creation many were the work of law-givers, who had newly ordered the whole of the institutions of the state, and who vainly hoped that their work would possess finality. But in all constitutions

---

[16] Plut. *Lyc.* 6 τοῦ δὲ πλήθους ἀθροισθέντος εἰπεῖν μὲν οὐδενὶ γνώμην τῶν ἄλλων ἐφεῖτο, τὴν δ' ὑπὸ τῶν γερόντων καὶ τῶν βασιλέων προτεθεῖσαν ἐπικρῖναι κύριος ἦν ὁ δῆμος.

[17] Thuc. i 87: Plut. *Lyc.* 26.

[18] The evidence is collected in Gilbert, *Handbuch* i² p. 57.

[19] Cf. Thuc. i 67 the conference of allies is held before ξύλλογος ὁ εἰωθώς: i 90 and vi 88 ambassadors go before the ἐκκλησία. This seems at variance with the usual oligarchic practice. At Melos the oligarchs receive the Athenians ἐν ταῖς ἀρχαῖς καὶ τοῖς ὀλίγοις (Thuc. v 84); and Cleon accuses the Lacedaemonian ambassadors τῷ μὲν πλήθει οὐδὲν ἐθέλουσιν εἰπεῖν, ὀλίγοις δὲ ἀνδράσι ξύνεδροι βούλονται γίγνεσθαι (Thuc. iv 22).

and at all times jurisdiction formed a most important branch of political activity.

Oligarchies were, perhaps, even more averse to changes of constitution than democracies; reform was likely to dissolve privilege and the oligarchs made a point of their respect for law and order. Jurisdiction was of course a necessity: legal processes were not so frequent as in a democracy, for the larger powers given to the oligarchic magistrates must often have obviated the necessity for a regular trial: and we may suppose that in many constitutions the magistrate's command had often the effect of a summary jurisdiction in inflicting punishment or redressing a wrong. But the ordinary oligarchies, with all the complexity of affairs arising from industry, commerce and navigation, felt the need of an efficient judicial system, and they probably paid almost as much attention to judicial organisation as the democracies.

No uniformity can be traced in the legal system of the different oligarchic governments. Jurisdiction might be entrusted to a single magistrate or to a board of magistrates; to the council, to special judges or courts, even to large jury courts composed of men, who in all else were excluded from the constitution.

To trace the subject historically; in the Heroic age there do not seem to have been any special judicial magistrates: trials were conducted either by the king or by the chiefs, always in public. The idea of a fixed law, defining in advance right and wrong, and prescribing penalties in case of violation, had not yet arisen. Each case was considered as if it stood entirely by itself: the 'dooms' were supposed to be inspired by the gods[1], but except for

---

[1] See Maine, *Ancient Law*, pp. 4 ff.

a vague respect for custom and precedent, there was no means of testing the equity of the sentence. In the aristocracies the nobles were 'the depositaries and administrators of law': they alone knew the principles of right and the customary rules of procedure: they monopolised the knowledge of the law². The duty of conducting the trial and pronouncing the sentence, passed either to the magistrate as the inheritor of the king's powers, or to the council as the representative of the chiefs. It was probably at this period that the jurisdiction of the whole privileged body arose: the magistrate whose most essential function was to give commands might enforce them by punishment: but all communities find it necessary to put some limit on the magistrate's power, and a frequent solution, when his authority was questioned, was to grant an appeal to the assembly. This was the origin of the jurisdiction of the assembly at Rome; it was the idea underlying the popular jurisdiction at Athens, and there are instances of a similar procedure in some oligarchies³. But the method was not altogether in accord with the oligarchic theory of the specialisation of political duties: it was characteristic of oligarchy that 'some classes should judge all causes,' and it was usual to entrust judicial duties to smaller bodies than the assembly⁴.

² *Ib.* p. 11.

³ Instances of trials by the whole governing body of the oligarchy occur at Syracuse (where the γεωμόροι decide a suit, Diod. viii 91): at Locri Epizephyrii (where the Thousand decide an appeal from the magistrate, Polyb. xii 16) and at Massalia (where the Six Hundred act as judges, Lucian *Toxar.* 24).

⁴ Ar. *Pol.* vi 16 1301 a 12 τὰ δὲ δεύτερα ὀλιγαρχικά, ὅσα ἐκ τινῶν περὶ πάντων, τὰ δὲ τρίτα ἀριστοκρατικὰ καὶ πολιτικά, ὅσα τὰ μὲν ἐκ πάντων, τὰ δ' ἐκ τινῶν.

Some states left all jurisdiction to the ordinary administrative magistrates and the council. Sparta, true to the traditions of the Heroic constitution, divided it between the kings, the council and the Ephors[5]: as Athens originally between the Archons and the Council of the Areopagus[6]; for some centuries such a division of judicial authority was normal, and even in later times the survival of the judicial powers of the council can be traced in some states[7]. Few however remained content with the primitive system of earlier times. Customary law almost everywhere gave way to written law[8], rules of procedure were published, magistrates were bound by the terms of the statutes and could no longer give inspired 'dooms.' This general development made law and justice scientific, and as a natural consequence special legal magistrates and special courts were instituted. Even in backward and semi-

[5] Generally speaking the senate had criminal jurisdiction: the Ephors most of the civil jurisdiction (cf. Ar. *Pol.* iii 1 1275 b 9; for other evidence see Gilbert, *Handbuch* i² pp. 89—90): the kings retaining the judgment of certain cases of family law, etc. (Hdt. vi 57). The system was altogether primitive; it is probable that there was no written law at Sparta; the judgments were θέμιστες.

[6] On the independent judicial powers of the Archons see Ar. *Ath. Pol.* 3 5. The Areopagus had an indefinite competence, and originally perhaps no distinction was drawn between its judicial and its administrative functions, but it is clear that from the earliest times it had an extensive jurisdiction (cf. *ib.* 3 6; 4 5; 8 4.

[7] At Thebes we find the βουλή trying a case of murder (Xen. *Hell.* vii 3 5—6). This is in the time of the democracy, but the power of the council was doubtless a survival. At Corinth βουλή and συνέδριον take part in the trial of Timoleon (if that is to be regarded as a judicial process) Diod. xvi 65.

[8] It is doubtful whether Sparta ever had any written laws other than the ῥῆτραι.

barbarous states we find an elaborate judicial organisation:
Aristotle in his section on the law-courts always assumes
that such institutions will be found in some form in
oligarchies and aristocracies, as well as in democracies[9],
and it is quite possible that Sparta was the only Greek
state with any pretension to civilisation in which no
special dicastic institutions were developed.

We have not sufficient evidence to enable us to trace
the difference of procedure in public and private causes:
but it is quite probable that private causes were often
left to the decision of a single judge or a small court, while
public causes, involving injury to the state, came before
some body, which represented the community, either the
council or the assembly[10]. This is one explanation of
the survival of the judicial powers of the council in later
times. We can also trace the existence of special dicasteries
in some oligarchies. Naturally the large popular jury
courts were rarely to be found except in democracies:
they were opposed to oligarchic ideas of proper government: they gave power to the many rather than to the
few: they required popular oratory and appeals to feeling
and the employment of irrelevant arguments. Hence it

---

[9] Ar. *Pol.* vi 14 1298 a 3 τὸ δικάζον is distinguished as a separate
element found in all constitutions. Cf. vi 8 1294 a 37, *ib.* 13 1297 a 21,
both of which assume the existence of δικασταί in oligarchies. Cf. the
passage quoted in n. 4 above. In the description of the Carthaginian
constitution, ii 11 1273 a 19, it is apparently defined as aristocratic, τὸ
τὰς δίκας ὑπό τινων ἀρχείων δικάζεσθαι πάσας, καὶ μὴ ἄλλας ὑπ' ἄλλων,
καθάπερ ἐν Λακεδαίμονι. This points to the institution of *special* legal
magistrates.

[10] Thus the Archons at Athens (to judge by their competence in
later times) were concerned with private law: the Council of the
Areopagus, like the senate at Sparta, and the Council at Thebes, had
public jurisdiction.

was a natural consequence both of oligarchic sentiment
and of the system of small courts, that in oligarchies the
speakers in trials should be kept to their subject and
should not be allowed to work on the emotions of the
judges[11]. One of the earliest acts in both oligarchic
revolutions at Athens was the suspension of the popular
jury courts[12].

In some oligarchies, however, we find traces of large
courts and even of the appointment of jurors from the
classes excluded in other respects from all political privilege. Thus at Chios we have evidence of a court of
three hundred at a time when the island was probably
under a close oligarchy[13], while in other states, of which
Heraclea on the Pontus serves as the example, the juries
were composed of men who were not on the citizen roll,
and this gave the orators an opportunity to make dema-

---

[11] Ar. *Rhet.* i 1 1354 a 17 τὰ τοιαῦτα πάθη τῆς ψυχῆς οὐ περὶ τοῦ
πράγματός ἐστιν ἀλλὰ πρὸς τὸν δικαστήν. ὥστ᾽ εἰ περὶ πάσας ἦν τὰς κρί-
σεις καθάπερ ἐν ἐνίαις γε νῦν ἐστὶ τῶν πόλεων καὶ μάλιστα ἐν ταῖς εὐνομουμέναις οὐδὲν ἂν εἶχον ὅτι λέγουσιν...οἱ δὲ καὶ κωλύουσιν ἔξω τοῦ πράγματος
λέγειν καθάπερ καὶ ἐν Ἀρείῳ πάγῳ. Cf. Plut. *de virt. mort.* 7 τοὺς ῥήτορας
ἐν ταῖς ἀριστοκρατίαις οὐκ ἐῶσι παθαίνεσθαι.

[12] In 411 the first step was to give the generals summary jurisdiction
with power of life and death (Ar. *Ath. Pol.* 29 5). We are not told to
whom judicial power was to be entrusted under the oligarchy. It was
perhaps included (with εὔθυναι) in the general administrative powers of
the βουλή (*ib.* 31 1). The Thirty τὸ κῦρος ὃ ἦν ἐν τοῖς δικασταῖς κατέ-
λυσαν (*ib.* 35 2). Trials were conducted in the βουλή of five hundred
with open voting and in the presence of the Thirty, but they put many
to death under their own order without trial (Lys. xiii 35).

[13] Roberts, *Epigraphy* 149 22. The inscription is referred to the fifth
century. The explanation of so large a court under an oligarchy may lie
in the alliance with Athens, as δίκαι ἀπὸ συμβόλων may have required
some such institution, which may have been generally used.

gogic appeals, which finally led to the overthrow of the oligarchy[14].

Three important inscriptions, referring to procedure in private causes in different oligarchies, have come down to us. These show that an elaborate organisation of judicial affairs prevailed even in the backward states, while they prove that the excellent judicial institutions which the Greeks developed were not confined to the democracies.

In the Gortyn inscription we gain an insight into the law regulating family relations, inheritance and slavery. In all disputes concerning these matters a single judge decides: and although much of the law is primitive, the system in some ways shows a comparatively high development[15].

The inscription concerning the colony at Naupactus sent out by the Eastern Locrians, at a date usually assigned to about the middle of the fifth century B.C., shows a separation of the duties of the presiding magistrate and the judges: the magistrate receives the charge and grants a trial, the judges decide by ballot[16].

An even more complicated system of jurisdiction is revealed in the semi-barbarous state of the Western Locrians. The fragments of the treaty between Oeanthea and Chaleion provide for suits between members of differ-

[14] Ar. *Pol.* viii 6 1305 b 34.

[15] On this see Zitelmann, *Das Recht von Gortyn*, pp. 67 ff. and J. W. Headlam (*Journal of Hellenic Studies* xiii 1 pp. 48—69).

[16] See Roberts, *Epigraphy* 231 l. 41 τὰν δίκαν δόμεν Mr Roberts says= grant a hearing. I should compare *iudicium dare* and translate 'grant a trial' (sc. a court); l. 45 ἐν ὑδρίαν τὰν ψάφιξξιν εἶμεν. Pindar, *Ol.* ix 15, praises Opus for εὐνομία and θέμις, and the praise was perhaps not merely conventional.

ent communities and prescribe the conditions for them[17].
Herein we have the distinction between local jurisdiction[18]
and what we should call to-day 'international' courts.   In
the latter courts there are different kinds of judges[19], and
the presiding magistrates choose jurymen to decide on
oath.

These instances, coming not from the highly civilised
commercial states of central Greece and the Aegean, but
from the backward tribes in the north and from Crete,
show us that the oligarchies did not neglect the proper
organisation of judicial institutions, and we may reasonably
conclude that the great commercial cities such as Aegina
and Megara and Corinth developed their legal system to
as high a pitch of perfection as the great trading democracies such as Athens[20].

§ 49. *Tribal Divisions.*

Having concluded the discussion of the powers of
government I proceed to consider the question of tribal
and class divisions in oligarchies. I have discussed in
a previous chapter the gradual break-up of the tribal
organisation and the substitution of local, political di-

[17] δίκαι ἀπὸ συμβόλων, cf. Roberts, *Epigraphy* 232 l. 35 δικάζωνται
κὰτ τὰς συνβολάς.

[18] l. 7 ἐπιδαμία δίκη.

[19] l. 10 τοὶ ξενοδίκαι (=*recuperatores*) and ἐπωμόται act in one event;
and δαμιοργοί and ὀρκωμόται in another.

[20] There must have been courts for the settlement of disputes between citizens of these cities and those of other states. This may
account for the praise lavished by Pindar on the respect which states
like Aegina and Corinth had for law and justice. Cf. *Ol.* xiii 6; *Pyth.*
viii 1; *Ol.* viii 21.

visions for the old tribes based on birth and religion, and
I have pointed out that it was only where this was
brought to pass that any government other than aristocracy was possible. But where aristocracy survived, where
birth and privilege remained united, it was necessary to
maintain the old divisions of tribe and phratry and house
uncorrupted and unassailed. It is strange that there is
scarcely any direct evidence for the existence of the
Dorian tribes at Sparta[1], but we can scarcely doubt that
they existed there, and we hear also of twenty-seven
phratries[2].

The Dorian tribes formed divisions of the population
in many other states: in some they lost their exclusive
privileges and other tribes of equal right were instituted :
in others, perhaps, they lost all political importance, but
some few probably still retained the old Dorian traditions[3].

Tribal divisions always point to the smaller groups out
of which cities are formed, and are usually associated with
the territorial influence of certain noble families. The
ideal of the noble was that he and his clan should be
absolute rulers in however small a domain. Hence some

[1] The most important evidence is in Pind. *Pyth.* i 62 Παμφύλου καὶ
μὰν Ἡρακλειδᾶν ἔκγονοι (as a description of the Spartans). It seems most
likely that the Dorian tribes arose before the Dorian migration and, as
they were found in many Dorian colonies, it is a natural inference that
they existed in Sparta.

[2] Demetrius of Skepsis in Ath. iv 141 E, F.

[3] There is a reference to the φυλαί in Epidauros in Isyllus B 6 (in
Wilamowitz-Möllendorff, *Isyllos* p. 9 : he identifies them with the Dorian
tribes and the Hyrnathii). The Ὑλλεῖς are mentioned in an inscription
from Thera. The Dorian tribes can be traced in Cos (see Gilbert, *Handbuch* ii p. 174 n. 1); Acragas (Cauer *Delectus*[2] 199).

states never advanced beyond the tribal stage of development[4]; in others the tendency to union and centralisation
was always resisted. Decentralisation was always a means
of establishing the supremacy of noble families and of
preventing or dissolving democracy.

Some states though formed by amalgamation still
retained local divisions, which hindered the union from
being complete[5], and some districts, though recognising
common race and forming loose federal leagues, left the
separate towns within their borders absolutely independent[6]. We may regard it as a frequent principle of
(aristocratic or) oligarchic policy to break up the larger
states into their constituent elements and so to restore
the influence of powerful men, while the supporters of
democracy saw in the union of smaller communities under
one strong government the only device for counteracting
this influence and so rendering popular government a
possibility. These tendencies might be carried out on a
larger plane, and we shall thus understand the constant
(although hypocritical[7]) assertion on the part of Sparta of
the principle of autonomy[8], which had so disastrous an

[4] Thuc. i 5.

[5] Although Sparta became a united state she retained the traces of
earlier institutions and the five villages of the Spartan plain were never
merged in a city (Thuc. i 10). They formed the basis of a political
division into five local tribes. (For the evidence see Gilbert, *Handbuch* i²
pp. 44—5. He connects them with the ὠβαί.)

[6] This was the case in Thessaly, Ozolian Locris (cf. the treaty
between Oeanthea and Chaleion in Roberts *Epigraphy* 232), and for a
long time in Boeotia.

[7] If we consider the control exercised by Sparta over the Peloponnesian states and her constant interference in the interest of oligarchy,
we realise the hollowness of her pretensions.

[8] Her pretended desire to restore autonomy was the great pretext with

effect on Greece, her hostility to leagues, whether of kindred peoples[9] or of cities of different race[10], and her policy of breaking up cities into the village communities by the combination of which they had been originally created.

The fate of Mantinea affords an illustration of the intimate connexion between oligarchy and decentralisation. A united state under a democratic government[11], it was broken into five villages in 385 and an oligarchic constitution introduced[12]. In 370 the state was united and democracy restored. Arcadia, as a whole, scarcely passed out of the stage of village communities till the fourth century, and the foundation of Megalopolis was intended to put an end to this disunion and decentralisation[13]. Elis, until a comparatively late period, consisted of a number of small communities governed by aristocracies with an elaborate tribal organisation[14]; but on their union in one state democracy was established.

One more illustration of this oligarchic principle is afforded by the history of the Thirty at Athens. They themselves tried to break up the state by dispersing the

which she entered on the Peloponnesian war. The principle is stated in the two treaties with Argos (Thuc. v 77 5; 79 1); it was asserted in the peace of Antalcidas and before Leuctra.

[9] As in Boeotia.

[10] As in the case of the Athenian and Olynthian confederacies.

[11] Thuc. v 29.

[12] Xen. *Hell.* v 2 7 describes the constitution as ἀριστοκρατία, probably in the sense of ὀλιγαρχία. The long period of democracy must have broken the power of the nobles and he says that οἱ ἔχοντες τὰς οὐσίας held the government.

[13] For the attempt of Sparta διοικίζειν τοὺς Μεγαλοπολίτας cf. Dem. xvi 30.

[14] See Cauer *Delectus*[2] 253.

population and by preparing Salamis and Eleusis for their own occupation. We learn for the first time from the Aristotelian treatise how directly the Spartans aimed at the dissolution of the Athenian state by making it part of the terms of peace that Eleusis should form an autonomous community, absolutely independent of Athens[15].

§ 50. *Class Divisions in Aristocracies and Oligarchies.*

In the old aristocracies there was a sharp line separating the privileged and the unprivileged; and the separation was nowhere more marked than in the aristocracies of conquest. Many of these maintained throughout the period of Greek independence the most rigid distinctions of classes, which were in fact fixed almost as definitely as castes. The victors were rulers, the vanquished were subjects. Generally speaking there was a triple division into the ruling race (the members whereof were often themselves divided into nobles and commons[1]), a class of serfs and an intermediate class of men free, but in political subjection[2].

Such class divisions can be traced in almost all the aristocracies of conquest and in several Dorian colonies, in

[15] Ar. *Ath. Pol.* 39. The settlers at Eleusis were to be κύριοι καὶ αὐτοκράτορες, to be separate contributories to the Spartan Alliance and in every way free from Athenian control.

[1] See above § 32. Meyer, *Geschichte des Alterthums* ii p. 272, raises a doubt about the origin of these classes: 'the ancients sought their origin in conquest: this is not tradition but inference: the Perioeci and Helots are, if not by descent, at least in sentiment no Achaeans but Dorians. The origin of serfdom was probably various and forgotten.' This last statement is no doubt true, but there does not seem sufficient reason for rejecting the general tradition.

[2] Plato *Rep.* viii 547 c speaks generally of περιοίκους τε καὶ οἰκέτας.

which, no doubt, the previous population had been reduced.

The serfs were a class of labourers attached to the soil[3] delivering the greater part of the produce to their masters, yet allowed to acquire private property themselves[4]. In states in which they were employed bought slaves were scarcely found at all[5]. There seems to have been no common title to describe them in Greece, but their position in other states seems to have been very similar to that of the Helots in Sparta[6]. They were generally treated with great harshness by the ruling class

---

[3] Cf. Athen. vi 264 A of the Penestae παρέδωκαν ἑαυτοὺς τοῖς Θετταλοῖς δουλεύειν καθ' ὁμολογίας, ἐφ' ᾧ οὔτε ἐξάγουσιν αὐτοὺς ἐκ τῆς χώρας οὔτε ἀποκτενοῦσιν· αὐτοὶ δὲ τὴν χώραν αὐτοῖς ἐργαζόμενοι τὰς συντάξεις ἀποδώσουσιν. Cf. ib. 263 D of the Mariandyni in the Pontic Heraclea. On the Helots see Strabo viii 365; Plut. Inst. Lac. 41.

[4] Cf. Athen. vi 264 B πολλοὶ τῶν κυρίων ἑαυτῶν εἰσιν εὐπορώτεροι. The ἀφαμιῶται of Crete (Ϝοικέες of Gortyn) might own property. See Zitelmann op. cit. p. 64. For the property of the Helots see Plut. Cleom. 23.

[5] There is scarcely any trace of bought slaves in Spartan ownership, but the Perioeci may have used them in their industries. In Crete χρυσώνητοι are distinguished from serfs in Athen. vi 263 E; they are probably the same as the δοῦλοι of the Gortyn inscription and are contrasted as οἰκέται κατὰ πόλιν with the serfs in the country.

[6] The Helots are generally taken as a type and the other serfs compared to them. Cf. Poll. iii 83. Serfs of this kind can be traced in Thessaly (πενέσται), in most of the Dorian states of the Peloponnesus besides Sparta, Argos (γυμνῆτες), Epidaurus (κονίποδες), Sicyon (κατωνακοφόροι or κορυνηφόροι), Corinth (possibly the κυνόφαλοι held this position). The serfs in these states were probably of Greek race. In the Dorian colonies of Heraclea in Trachis (Κυλικρᾶνες), Heraclea in Pontus (Μαριανδυνοί), Byzantium (προύνικοι), in Crete (μνῷται and ἀφαμιῶται), Syracuse (καλλικύριοι) they were probably barbarians. On the attempt to establish serfdom in Athens see above § 25 n. 9. On the subject generally see Gilbert Handbuch ii pp. 292—3, Hermann Lehrbuch der Staatsaltertümer[6] pp. 126—8.

and were in many cases permanently disaffected and ready to rebel[7].

The intermediate class of subjects were often described by Greek writers by the name they bore in Lacedaemon (περίοικοι)[8]. They were not found so universally in the Dorian states as the serfs. Isocrates explains that most of the Dorian invaders allowed part of the conquered peoples to dwell with them, although excluded from power and office, but that the Lacedaemonians deprived them of the best land and scattered them to live in small towns in absolute subjection to themselves[9]. In other Dorian towns part of the conquered population sometimes formed tribes separate from the three Dorian tribes, although they were not at first admitted to citizenship. A class similar to the *perioeci* can be distinguished in Thessaly and in Argos.

I have assumed above that the *perioeci* like the Helots

[7] Cf. Ar. *Pol.* iii 9 1269 a 36 of Helots and Penestae ὥσπερ γὰρ ἐφεδρεύοντες τοῖς ἀτυχήμασι διατελοῦσιν.

[8] Hdt. viii 73 uses the term of the Argive Ὀρνεᾶται; Sosicrates in Athen. vi 263 F says οἱ Κρῆτες καλοῦσι...τοὺς ὑπηκόους περιοίκους. On the other hand the term περίοικοι is not used consistently. Hesychius uses it to define the ἀφαμιῶται and Aristotle (in *Pol.* ii ch. 10) uses it three times of the Cretan serfs. (I should have pointed out in n. 6 that there are traces of many different terms being applied to the Cretan serfs, ἀφαμιῶται, μνῷται, κλαρῶται, ϝοικέες (at Gortyn) and περίοικοι. It seems probable that different titles were used to describe them in different towns of Crete.) Their position in the state made ὑπήκοοι appropriate as a general description of the class. Thucydides constantly applies the term to the subjects of the Thessalians (ii 101; iv 78; cf. Xen. *Hell.* vi 1 9). Gilbert, *Handbuch* ii p. 16 n. 1, assumes on insufficient evidence that the subject class in Thessaly bore the title of σύμμαχοι.

[9] Isocr. xii 177—8. It is not clear whether Isocrates regards the Perioeci as the conquered population: but I assume that he does, as he talks of the 'rightful owners of the land' (before the Dorian invasion).

originally belonged to the race conquered by the Dorian invaders. It is hard to explain the difference in the position of the two classes. Some writers assume a difference of race to account for the original difference of condition, but the balance of probability is on the whole against this assumption, although in the course of time no doubt both Helots and Perioeci included people of more than one race[10].

The theory that the Helots were the serfs of the 'Achaeans' who occupied the Peloponnese before the Dorian invasion and that the Perioeci were the conquered 'Achaeans' lacks evidence. Others assume that while the original Helots were the peoples subdued by the Dorians, the Perioeci were themselves originally Dorian: that in the Dorian invasion the invaders were divided into nobles (who afterwards became Spartiates) and commons who were made Perioeci[11]. Many of the ancient writers considered the Perioeci to be Dorian; they were included with the Spartiates in the term 'Lacedaemonians,' and no diversity of religion can be established[12]. But it is more probable that they were Achaeans; in favour of this assumption is the fact that there were noble families within the ranks both of the Spartiates and the

[10] Many Dorians must have been reduced to the condition of Helots after the conquest of Messenia.

[11] Grote ii p. 371 (who says: 'The Perioekic townships were probably composed either of Dorians entirely or of Dorians incorporated in greater or less proportion with the preexisting inhabitants') refers to Hdt. viii 73 and i 145.

[12] It is not possible to draw any conclusion from religion. Cf. S. Wide *Lakonische Kulte* p. 387—8 'Dorian and pre-Dorian cults cannot be distinguished. The Dorians probably took over most of their cults from the older inhabitants.'

Perioeci[13]; and above all the way in which the Spartan constitution was regarded. As I have already pointed out, the perioeci were entirely omitted from consideration, the Spartiates were regarded as forming the whole civic community, organised on an equal and democratic basis[14]. Such an idea would not have been so persistent had not the Perioeci been regarded as subjects of another race. If we assume that the Spartiates included all the original invaders, we can only suppose that the Perioeci got more favourable terms than the Helots when they submitted[15].

Similarly in Thessaly the Penestae were the inhabitants of the districts occupied by the Thessalian conquerors, while the Perrhaebi, Magnetes and Achaei, who occupied the more distant parts of Thessaly, had been granted better terms and were in a less galling subjection than the Perioeci of Lacedaemon, as they retained their tribe name and still remained members of the Delphian Amphictyony[16].

The existence of separate classes based upon birth usually involves a diversity of occupation and so effects a division of labour. Thus in Lacedaemon agriculture was

[13] The inference is doubtful: on the Spartiates see § 32 n. 7; Xen. *Hell.* v 3 9 talks of the καλοὶ κἀγαθοὶ τῶν περιοίκων.

[14] See above § 3 n. 15 and cf. especially Isocr. xii 178 who talks of the ἰσονομία and δημοκρατία of the Spartiates. Isocrates (xii 255) regards the original Spartan invaders as not being more than two thousand in number.

[15] Mr J. W. Headlam ingeniously suggests that the difference of status arose from the difference of occupation, the Perioeci living in the towns the Helots in the country. The distinction is so early, however, that we have no *data* to decide whether the difference of status was cause or effect.

[16] See Grote ii p. 279.

given over to the Helots, while commerce and industry were left to the Perioeci. The ruling class practised the arts of war and government. But the aristocracy usually went further than this : they not only felt a contempt for commerce and industry, but they made the practice of either pursuit an absolute disqualification for citizenship[17].

To consider particular instances, at Sparta the banausic arts were entirely forbidden to a citizen[18]; at Thebes, Aristotle says, a man must have 'held aloof from the market-place for ten years,' before he was eligible for citizenship[19]. At Thespiae even agriculture was considered dishonourable[20].

In Thessaly there was a 'freemen's agora' from which the farmer and the tradesman were excluded[21], while at Epidamnus, a colony which must have had a most important trade with the barbarians of Western Greece, industry was carried on by state slaves[22], the citizens were precluded from actually taking part in commerce, and a public magistrate superintended sales to foreigners[23].

Naturally oligarchies in which privilege was based on wealth and the wealth was mainly derived from commerce could not inflict disabilities on the trader. In this respect

[17] I have discussed the general aspects of this question above in § 12. See n. 3 there.

[18] Aelian *V. H.* vi 6 βάναυσον δ' εἰδέναι τέχνην ἄνδρα Λακεδαιμόνιον οὐκ ἐξῆν. Plut. *Lyc.* 4. We may compare, as characteristic of the same intolerant spirit, the exclusion of foreigners (ξενηλασίαι) which prevailed in Sparta and Crete.

[19] *Pol.* iii 5 1278 a 26: cf. vii 7 1321 a 28.

[20] Heracl. Pont. F. H. G.

[21] Ar. *Pol.* iv 12 1331 a 32.

[22] Ar. *Pol.* ii 7 1267 b 17.

[23] Plut. *Q. G.* 29.

they differed radically from the aristocracies, but they
inherited from them the contempt for the classes excluded from the government, and Corinth was distinguished for despising handicrafts less than any other
state[24].

§ 51. *Summary.*

I have brought to a close my study of the political
organisation of aristocracies and oligarchies. In both
constitutions we may notice the action of the same principles : both believed in the unwisdom of the multitude,
in the justice and necessity of limiting privilege to a few,
and in letting these rule the rest of the population, as
subjects excluded from citizen rights. Both had the same
scheme of government, in which the mean was struck
between the single dominion of a tyrant and the sovereignty of a large assembly, by the creation of a council,
in which a few able men, acting in concert, were to direct
the policy of the state. In both the magistrates had
considerable independent authority ; the theory of specialisation of functions was realised and the rulers were left
free of control and generally irresponsible. Throughout
the constitution the theory of 'some men' being qualified
and 'most men' unqualified was carried out; and law-
courts and assemblies were both filled by members of the
privileged minority.

But the points of difference between the aristocracies
of birth and the oligarchies of wealth were almost as great

[24] Hdt. ii 167 (after discussing the general attitude of the Greeks)
ἥκιστα δὲ Κορίνθιοι ὄνονται τοὺς χειροτέχνας.

as the points of similarity. The end of the aristocrat was success in war: the end of the oligarch wealth: the former (at least in Crete and Sparta) passed his life in military training and martial exercises, the latter in commerce and industry, pursuits which were either forbidden or put under a grave social stigma in aristocracies. The common system of Sparta and Crete led to a uniformity of life, and demanded an ascetic abstinence; the rich oligarchies were noted for their luxury and extravagance. The aristocracies rested on the maintenance of fixed ordinances and customs: they were conservative, slow to move and cautious. The oligarchies were keen and enterprising, anxious never to be displaced in the struggle for wealth and honour.

The aristocracies of birth were found in states in a backward stage of civilisation. Setting aside Crete and Sparta, aristocratic constitutions survived mainly in the semi-barbarous states of northern Greece. Had they been affected by the general advance of civilisation, their constitutions must have submitted to the inevitable progress, which elsewhere produced oligarchy or democracy. Even Sparta cannot be regarded as an altogether civilised state: in many respects the Spartiates resemble rather a host of savage warriors than the citizens of a Greek city. The Spartan system is an instance of the truth, that social uniformity, especially when combined with a narrow military ideal, must be purchased at a ruinous cost. It requires a good deal of imagination to conceive what the ordinary Spartiate was like, but Plutarch's statement that 'he wore one shirt all the year round, was filthy of body and for the most part abstained from washing,' is a strong corrective to the unmeasured panegyrics pronounced upon the race.

From his earliest years the individual at Sparta was sacrificed entirely to the state. An education, which stunted all his faculties, prepared him for the practice of war; and as a consequence Sparta produced scarce ten men who were eminent in aught else than the art of war. 'The whole scheme of their laws,' says Aristotle, 'is directed only to a part of virtue, to martial valour. So while they warred they were saved, but were ruined when they ruled, for they knew not how to be at leisure and had never practised any art more sovereign than the art of war.' No part of Aristotle's indictment is truer or more damning than that 'they knew not how to be at leisure.' All that constitutes the glory of the Greeks is entirely lacking in the Spartan: there is not a trace of Spartan literature and to have practised the fine arts would have disfranchised a citizen.

Lastly, they failed even in following their own ideal. Empire was the end of their national life: empire they attained by false professions of bringing liberty to the oppressed, and by a sacrifice of Greek interests to the barbarian. Empire they maintained by means of a crushing tyranny and a violation of justice; and empire they lost, as soon as another race rose to military preeminence. Lastly the very system on which the Spartan fortunes rested became itself corrupt and effete: it was intended to abolish private wealth and to make the citizens superior to money: it succeeded eventually in impoverishing the state, making the citizens greedy of lucre and finally in disfranchising all but a hundred, in whose hands wealth was concentrated.

At their best the Spartans were harsh soldiers; ruling so oppressively over their subjects, that they were always fiercely hated: in their private life not touched by the influences of Hellenic culture, living in a barrack with the ideals of a barrack: politically well disciplined and obedient, cautious, stupid and conservative.

The oligarchy of wealth differed from the aristocracy of the Spartan type alike in its virtues and its vices. Its character was more normal: it was Hellenic and not barbarous: its interests were diverse: literature and art were practised and formed no disqualification for citizenship.

In itself the oligarchic ideal of government was good: the intimate combination of a small council with the magistrates, acting in harmony themselves and commanding the willing allegiance of their subjects, forms one of the strongest and most efficient constitutions that can be imagined. Such was the cause of Rome's greatness, such the foundation of the glory of Venice. But the government of an oligarchy, to be successful, must rest on the contented obedience of the excluded classes; and the narrower the basis of the government, the more important this condition becomes.

The Greek oligarchies, to judge by the sentiment of Greek literature about them, rarely came near this ideal. Moderate oligarchies tended to become extreme, and in the fourth century, at least, every piece of evidence points to the ordinary oligarchies being narrow and oppressive. They were class governments and class governments of a particularly odious type. Governments of birth, though they may often prove vicious and tyrannical, are as often controlled by a sense of honour and by traditions of virtue. But a class government founded on wealth, in which wealth is the aim of the citizen and the standard of privilege, tends to become a government of brute force, treating its subjects with harsh injustice, exploiting the many at the expense of the few, making every possible abuse of absolute power.

Democracy at its worst is an evil tyranny: but keenly as the Greek writers (most of whom wrote in Athens with all the faults of the degenerate Athenian demos before their eyes) realised the evil character of democracy they have worse terms of condemnation for oligarchy. 'Men,' says Aristotle, 'who have excess of power and wealth and friends neither wish nor know how to be ruled.' 'A few men rule and base men in place of the best, for democracy is least base of governments.' Corruption, treachery and aggrandisement are the three characteristic vices of the oligarch : and in the awful war of factions, in which Greek states were at all times engaged, the historians have no hesitation in putting the blame on the oligarchs. An oligarchy is a city of slaves and tyrants, says Aristotle : oligarchy makes one city into two cities, always at war with one another, says Plato: and the oligarchic oath, 'I will be ill-minded to the demos and contrive what ill I can,' was a declaration of relentless war, waged by every means, in which peace and armistice were impossible. Στάσις was the bane of the city state of Greece, it was the overthrow of the social contract; and there is no doubt that if we strive to apportion the blame, the greater share must be assigned to the selfish greed for power and the sacrifice of state interests to private aggrandisement which characterised the oligarch.

APPENDIX C.

The oligarchic revolution at Athens: the provisional and the projected constitution[1].

For the study of the theory and practice of oligarchic government we have no material more interesting or important than the accounts of the brief rule of the Four Hundred at Athens and of the permanent constitution which they projected. Our knowledge of the revolution and of the revolutionary government is based almost entirely on Thucydides and Aristotle[2]: these authors are not always in agreement, and while Thucydides, as a contemporary, is more likely to have had a better knowledge of the inner workings of the conspiracy and of such matters as depended on hearsay, Aristotle, who used later historians in addition to Thucydides, probably availed

[1] The length of the following appendix is due in part to the importance of the subject and in part to its uncertainty. The new information given us by Aristotle is not yet incorporated in the text-books, and I have therefore made a careful study of the account given by him and compared it throughout with Thucydides. I have derived much help from Professor von Wilamowitz-Möllendorff's *Aristoteles und Athen* ii ch. 4, especially from his discussion of the projected constitution.

[2] The light thrown by Lysias xx is discussed in the course of the Appendix. Citations of Thucydides are from Book viii and those of Aristotle from the *Constitution of the Athenians.*

himself of documentary evidence, and is more precise in
quoting the terms of laws and decrees[3]. In some cases
the two authorities supplement one another, but it must be
admitted that their differences cannot always be reconciled.
This is the less to be wondered at, if we consider the circumstances of the revolution, the brief duration of the
government and the partial fulfilment of the proposals
made. These facts will serve to explain also the uncertainty concerning the body of the Five Thousand, which
played so large a part in the professions of the oligarchs
and yet was never constituted. Aristotle, moreover, gives
us, what is entirely passed over by Thucydides, a sketch
of the projected constitution which did not come into
existence. As an illustration of oligarchic theory this
scheme is of more importance than the provisional government of the Four Hundred, which, after all, was little
better than an organised reign of terror.

It would be beside my purpose to study the motives
which induced the Athenians to accept the change of
constitution. In one aspect, however, the professions of
the oligarchs are important. The revolution was carried
out in form of law; it established a close oligarchy under
the disguise of a moderate democracy[4], it was professedly
based on the hoplite census (the ideal of many political
thinkers[5]), and it assumed the pretence of a return to
the 'ancestral' constitution[6]. In the distress of their

[3] On Aristotle's materials see Gilbert, *Handbuch* i[2] p. xxxi.

[4] See the discussion concerning the Five Thousand below and cf.
Ar. 29 3.

[5] See above, § 37 n. 8.

[6] See above, § 20 nn. 12, 13. It is worth noting that the democrats
at Samos claimed that they were really maintaining the πάτριοι νόμοι

fortunes and the disappointment of their hopes the Athenians might look back with sentimental longing to the days of Solon and Cleisthenes, and envy the old balanced constitutions which existed in their time or before them[7]. The pretence, hollow as it was, was aided by the profession that the constitution was to be only a temporary expedient until the end of the war[8], when presumably the old democracy was to be restored.

The machinery by which the change of government was effected may be briefly considered. Down to the end of the sixth century the work of reform was usually entrusted to a single lawgiver: in the fourth century the normal process of legislation required the assent of the assembly, the council and a large court of Nomothetae; there is no evidence that this practice prevailed in the fifth century[9], and so far as we can trace, in the period of the Peloponnesian war, at least, important reforms were carried out by legislative commissions[10]. In 411

(Thuc. 76 6) against the oligarchs. The same pretence was made on the institution of the Thirty Tyrants. (Xen. *Hell.* ii 3 2; Ar. 34 3.)

[7] For Solon and Cleisthenes see Ar. 29 3. The limitation of the franchise went further than Solon, and in this as in other respects the oligarchic constitution has many resemblances to that ascribed to Draco in ch. 4 of Aristotle.

[8] Ar. 29 5 ἕως ἂν ὁ πόλεμος ᾖ. The same idea is vaguely suggested by Thuc. 53 3 'Athens has her life at stake, the constitution can be changed afterwards.'

[9] See Gilbert, *Handbuch* i[2] p. 336 n. It is a possible inference from Lysias xxx 28 (οἱ μὲν πρόγονοι νομοθέτας ᾑροῦντο Σόλωνα καὶ Θεμιστοκλέα καὶ Περικλέα) that the procedure of the sixth century was employed also in the fifth, and that individuals like Themistocles and Pericles were entrusted with powers of revision.

[10] The procedure in 411 B.C. is discussed in the text. On the overthrow of the Four Hundred νομοθέται were appointed (Thuc. 97 1). There is no reason for identifying them with the heliastic commission

the formal initiative for the revolution was entrusted to a committee of thirty[11]; and after the preliminary measures proposed by them had been carried a hundred men were chosen to revise the constitution[12]. The first proposal of the Thirty Commissioners ensured immunity to any one proposing any change in the constitution[13]. This required probably the suspension not merely of the γραφὴ παρανόμων, the great safeguard against revolution, but of all the special laws and processes designed to protect the democracy[14]. Thucydides, whose account is somewhat vague, implies that their proposals went no further[15], but we may accept Aristotle's account that they formally published the two great principles, which had already been

of the fourth century, and from Lysias we should conclude that they formed a special legislative commission. (Lys. xxx 2 Nicomachus was chosen as τῶν νόμων ἀναγραφεύς and held office for six years. He is referred to as νομοθέτης. Cf. also And. i 96 where ξυνέγραψεν is used, probably of a member of such a commission.) The Thirty Tyrants were appointed as a legislative committee (Xen. *Hell.* ii 3 2 τριάκοντα ἄνδρας ἑλέσθαι, οἳ τοὺς πατρίους νόμους ξυγγράψωσι). After the overthrow of the oligarchy in 403 And. i 82 refers to the appointment of five hundred νομοθέται. These, however, seem to have been special commissioners, for Lysias xxx 4, 5 shows that the revision of the different laws was divided between them, and he charges Nicomachus with spending four years over his share of the work.

[11] Ar. 29 2 corrects Thucydides 67 1, who mentions only ten ξυγγραφεῖς, saying that twenty ξυγγραφεῖς were added to the ten πρόβουλοι. He is confirmed by other authorities (quoted in Dr Sandys' n.).

[12] Ar. 30 1.

[13] Thuc. 67 2; Ar. 29 4.

[14] The process of εἰσαγγελία (Ar. 29 4) was especially adapted to meet attempts against the democracy. If, as has been suggested, the law of Demophantus passed in 410 (And. i 95) was based on a law of Solon, the necessity of a special ἄδεια in 411 is explained.

[15] Thuc. 67 2 ἐσήνεγκαν οἱ ξυγγραφῆς ἄλλο μὲν οὐδὲν κ.τ.λ.

mooted, the abolition of pay for political services and the
limitation of the franchise[16]. These two principles carried
with them the overthrow of the democratic constitution.
The Thirty then proposed the election of a board of one
hundred to draw up a register of the Five Thousand
and to draught the new constitution[17]. This board was
responsible for both the provisional and the projected
constitution[18], and the work of the Thirty Commissioners
was limited to the enunciation of general principles.

For this account of their proceedings we are indebted
to Aristotle: Thucydides, on whose divergence from it I
have commented above, here contributes some new matter.
The changes attributed by Aristotle to the initiative of
the Thirty Commissioners he describes vaguely as 'openly
proposed,' and he adds to these the appointment of five
proedri, who were to choose a hundred, each of whom
again was to coopt three others, and the council of the
Four Hundred constituted in this manner was to be
entrusted with absolute authority[19]. The appointment and

[16] Ar. 29 5 τὴν πολιτείαν διέταξαν; 30 1 οἱ μὲν αἱρεθέντες ταῦτα συνέ-
γραψαν.

[17] Aristotle does not positively identify the hundred appointed to
draw up the list of citizens (29 5) with the hundred legislators (30 1).
But I think it is probable that there was only one body of a hundred.
οἱ ἑκατὸν ἄνδρες without any other description are referred to several
times, and in 30 3, 31 3 the legislators are entrusted with the duty
of dividing the citizens into 'lots,' a duty that would naturally fall
to the καταλογεῖς. Against the identification may be urged that Aristotle
refers to the καταλογεῖς being elected by the φυλαί, the legislators by the
Five Thousand : but the passages may be reconciled, if we suppose that
the Five Thousand voted by tribes. Lysias xx does not help us. The
point is obscure and not important.

[18] Ar. 30 1; 31 1.

[19] Thuc. 67 3.

powers of the Four Hundred must be reserved for later consideration : for the present we must consider whether the hundred mentioned by Thucydides are to be identified with the board of legislators mentioned by Aristotle. In favour of the identification we may urge the order of the narrative : after describing the preliminary proposals of the Commissioners both authors tell us of the general principles on which the government was to be based, both then refer to the appointment of a hundred men. They are in conflict, however, as to the method of their appointment and the purpose for which they were appointed. The first discrepancy I discuss below : with regard to the second Thucydides describes the hundred as forming a fourth part of the council of government, Aristotle assigns to the hundred legislators certain specific duties and implies that part at least of their work was carried into effect before the Four Hundred were constituted[20]. If we can reconcile the divergent statements about the mode of their election, there is nothing which precludes us from supposing that the Hundred Commissioners of Aristotle were afterwards incorporated in the council of the Four Hundred. There is every ground of probability for supposing that the promoters of the revolution would be anxious to pack both the legislative commission and the ruling council with their own friends and supporters[21].

[20] If Aristotle's account of the establishment be accepted it would seem that Thucydides in his narrative anticipates the appointment of the Four Hundred.

[21] Professor Goodhart in his edition of Thucydides p. xxiv suggested this argument. He identified the hundred mentioned by Thucydides with the hundred legislators of Aristotle, and he pointed out that Polystratus, one of the καταλογεῖς, was also a member of the Four Hundred (Lys. xx 1). It must be noticed that Polystratus was only

They were establishing a government of false pretences; they must avoid at all hazards the effective fulfilment of their promises, and in order that the active organs of government should aid this project, they must be sure of their support. It was therefore to the interest of the conspirators to limit the active participation in the government to as small a circle as possible. There was always a danger of inconvenient suggestions that a constitution in accordance with the programme which they avowed should supersede the revolutionary oligarchy. They could not afford to run the risk of internal dissension, if it could be prevented: they must avoid, if possible, the presence of opponents on their commissions and councils and to this end control the elections. We may therefore regard it as probable, though absolute proof is lacking, that the Hundred Commissioners were afterwards included in the Council[22].

The duties of the Hundred were twofold[23]. They were to draw up a list of the Five Thousand, who were to form the citizen body; they were also to draft a constitution in accordance with the principles already accepted. It is scarcely to be doubted that the oligarchs, who had for many months been working for the revolution, had their scheme of government fully prepared, and that the projected constitution was in as forward a state as the provisional government, which they adopted[24]. But the

a member of the βουλή for eight days. He was probably elected as a substitute both as καταλογεὺς (§ 9) and βουλευτής.

[22] A higher limit of age (forty years Ar. 29 5) was required for the καταλογεῖς than for the council (thirty years Ar. 31 1), but many members of the council must have been over forty.

[23] I assume the identification suggested in n. 17.

[24] Apart from the general probability and the brief rule of the Four Hundred, which would have allowed little time for drawing up a

projected constitution involved changes too radical to be immediately accepted, and it probably seemed easier to adopt for the immediate present a temporary system, more in accord with existing institutions[25].

The place taken or intended to be taken by the Five Thousand in the constitution, is of the utmost importance to our understanding of the purpose of the conspirators. The pretence of entrusting them with power formed a cloak to disguise the absolute character of the government[26]; it conciliated the support of the moderates, who wished to make them a real and decisive force in the state[27]. It was an element of compromise, which rendered easier the acceptance of the government. But the extreme oligarchs who got power into their hands did not intend that the Five Thousand should be a reality, at least in the

constitution, Aristotle (c. 30) describes the projected constitution before the provisional government (c. 31). His narrative (31 1) implies that the two were drawn up together, and in the terms of the provisional government there is a reference to the written provisions of the permanent constitution (31 2 τὸ δὲ λοιπὸν τὴν αἵρεσιν ποιεῖσθαι τούτων τὴν βουλὴν κατὰ τὰ γεγραμμένα).

[25] It is possible that the two schemes corresponded to the aims of two different parties. The extremists no doubt were content with the provisional government. (Cf. Von Wilamowitz-Möllendorff *op. cit.* p. 116 'the definite constitution depended on the army at Samos. Antiphon and Phrynichus were in no hurry.') It is a possible inference from Ar. 31 2 that the provisional constitution was only to last for a year; see n. 46.

[26] Thuc. 72 1, 86 3 the envoys of the oligarchy lay stress on the Five Thousand. Cf. Plut. *Alc.* 26 οἱ πεντακισχίλιοι λεγόμενοι, τετρακόσιοι δὲ ὄντες. Ar. 29 1 gives the government the name it usually bears ἡ ἐπὶ τῶν τετρακοσίων πολιτεία.

[27] Thuc. 89 2 Theramenes and his party consider τοὺς πεντακισχιλίους ἔργῳ καὶ μὴ ὀνόματι χρῆναι ἀποδεικνύναι. The oligarchy was overthrown by the pretence of entrusting power to them Thuc. 97 1.

provisional government, and hence no list of them was ever published[28]. We are therefore left in perplexity about the constitution of this body. We are not told whether it was to contain a fixed number of citizens, or if so, how the Five Thousand were to be chosen from the larger number of the qualified.

It is thought by some that the number of Five Thousand was intended to serve as a fictitious description of all qualified for the duties of citizenship, as it certainly did on the overthrow of the oligarchy[29], and we learn from Lysias that when at last the Four Hundred were compelled to draw up the list, the register contained nine thousand names[30]. But there are other indications in the accounts of Thucydides and Aristotle, which make it probable that the oligarchs, whatever their intentions, proposed to limit power to a fixed number[31]. We lack all

[28] See n. 33.

[29] Thuc. 97 1; Ar. 33 1.

[30] Lys. xx 13. We cannot form any certain inference from this. The Four Hundred were compelled by the revolt of the moderates to consent to make the Five Thousand a reality. The list was drawn up in a hurry and the nine thousand may have represented the full number of the qualified from whom the Five Thousand were to be selected.

[31] Thuc. 65 3 says that not *more* than five thousand were to be admitted, Ar. 29 5 not *less*. If we accept these statements, they exclude the possibility of all the hoplites being admitted. Moreover had this been so there would have been no need for a special list, as the roll of hoplites might have been used (see n. 35 below), but Thuc. 92 11 implies that a special list was required. In the projected constitution, in which the Five Thousand were to play a most important part, the evidence points, I think, to a fixed number. If the number were indefinite there would be no reason for giving them the title of the Five Thousand (after the overthrow of the oligarchy it was a survival). I think we may conclude that an ' oligarchy of fixed number ' was intended, on which see § 38 above.

evidence to determine by what method the Five Thousand were to be selected[32]. It is probable enough that this point was purposely left vague and undecided.

No attempt was made to draw up a list of the Five Thousand until the Four Hundred were all but over-thrown[33]; at the same time, Aristotle mentions them as if they were really constituted and taking action[34]. The explanation seems to lie in a confusion between the citizens qualified to belong to the body and the actual register of Five Thousand, which was never published. The Five Thousand were to be those 'best able to serve the state in person and property,' that is they must belong to one of the first three classes, who were liable to hoplite service. For the immediate purposes of government old institutions had to be adapted, and on the few occasions on which the leaders of the revolution left anything to the decision of the citizens they allowed the right of voting to all who possessed the hoplite quali-fication, that is, to all on the roll of hoplites[35]. These

[32] Of the different methods by which the selection might be made (see § 38 nn. 21—24) we find no trace in our narratives. It would be possible to lay stress on the definition in Ar. 29 5 (τοῖς δυνατωτάτοις κ.τ.λ.) and to infer from the use of the superlative that the five thousand wealthiest hoplites were to be chosen. The phrase seems stereotyped, see § 36 n. 6.

[33] Thuc. 92 11; 93 2; Ar. 31 3. Polystratus began the work of drawing up the list eight days before the overthrow (Lys. xx 14).

[34] Ar. 30 1; 31 2; 32 1.

[35] The expedient was so natural, that this conjecture may be accepted. The κατάλογος contained the names of the hoplites of the first three classes, *arranged by tribes* (Gilbert, *Handbuch* i[2] p. 353). The θῆτες even if they served as hoplites were not included in the κατάλογος (Thuc. vi 43). The election by the tribesmen (Ar. 31 1; Lys. xx 2) meant elec-tion by the hoplites on the roll of each tribe, i.e. by the 'Five Thousand' voting by tribes.

did in certain cases exercise the powers nominally reserved for the Five Thousand[36], and as the number voting may easily have fallen short of that number[37] Aristotle speaks carelessly as if they were members of that body.

To the Five Thousand, he says, was entrusted the appointment of the hundred commissioners[38], and to them apparently the preliminary choice of candidates for the council of Four Hundred was left[39]. Aristotle does not tell us how the final choice was to be made, and we may perhaps supplement his account by the narrative of Thucydides and suppose that the method of cooptation described by him[40] was combined with a preliminary selection by the Five Thousand. In any case we must assume that the popular election was a mere form, in some way controlled in the interests of the oligarchs, who had rendered opposition dangerous by terrorism and assassination.

When the Four Hundred was once constituted, little more was heard of the Five Thousand[41]. The provisional government thus assumed the form of an extreme oligarchy and combined two specially oligarchic features, the

[36] Besides the instances in n. 35 cf. Thuc. 93 1 where the hoplites constitute themselves an assembly.

[37] Thuc. 72 1, the assembly rarely included as many as 5000.

[38] 30 1.

[39] 31 1 ἐκ προκρίτων οὓς ἂν ἕλωνται οἱ φυλέται; see n. 35.

[40] 67 3.

[41] Except for the powers of election entrusted to them, which I have already discussed, the Five Thousand took no part in the Constitution. In the first proposal they were represented as a sovereign power (Ar. 29 5 τὴν δ' ἄλλην πολιτείαν ἐπιτρέψαι πᾶσαν κ.τ.λ.; cf. Lys. xx 13); but Thucydides implies that they were subordinate to the βουλὴ (67 3 τοὺς πεντακισχιλίους ξυλλέγειν ὁπόταν αὐτοῖς δοκῇ). In the projected constitution they were entrusted with all powers of government.

sovereignty of the council[42] and an executive magistracy
with absolute power[43]. The council was not qualified to
change the laws[44], but in other respects its powers were
unlimited. It had the whole of the state business in its
control[45]. It was to appoint the magistrates and to call
them to account. The generals had important powers
but they were chosen by the council[46], doubtless from
its own members[47], the other magistrates were not to
hold office more than once, though no such restriction was

[42] Thuc. 67 3 ἄρχειν ὅπῃ ἂν ἄριστα γιγνώσκωσιν αὐτοκράτορας; Ar. 31 1.

[43] Ar. 31 2, the generals were to be αὐτοκράτορες and to consult with
the βουλή at discretion.

[44] The laws made περὶ τῶν πολιτικῶν were to be observed without
change (Ar. 31 1); i.e. the laws of the constitution, which had been
drawn up by the legislative commission, were to be observed by the
provisional government, i.e. it was to rule μετὰ νόμου.

[45] A few details are given in Ar. 31 1. Dr Sandys in his n. to Ar. 33
1 calls attention to C.I.A. iv 3 179 d in which the βουλή authorizes certain
expenditure. Nothing is said about the law-courts : the popular juries
had of course gone with the abolition of pay ; probably judicial powers
were divided between the executive and the council.

[46] The account of the election of generals in Ar. 31 2 is confused.
Apparently three occasions are referred to and a different process
prescribed for each : (1) for the immediate present ten generals are to be
chosen from all the Five Thousand (i.e. as the revolution took place in a
state of war, it was necessary to appoint without delay before the provisional constitution came into force generals superseding the former
board, most of whom were at Samos): (2) as soon as the βουλή is
appointed it is to choose ten men with full powers after a review of the
troops under arms (these must be the generals ; the method of election
would exclude those with the fleet at Samos): these were to hold office
for a year, and (3) for the future (τὸ λοιπὸν i.e. in the projected constitution) the election is to take place in accordance with the conditions prescribed.

[47] The inference, which is probable, is confirmed by the fact that
Theramenes (Thuc. 92 9), Aristarchus (98 1) and Alexicles (94 4), described
as στρατηγὸς ὢν ἐκ τῆς ὀλιγαρχίας, were all generals.

placed on the generals or the members of the council[48].
We do not learn any other details of the constitution.
It is possible that the five proedri mentioned by Thucydides acted as presidents of the council[49]. Thucydides
also mentions the appointment of prytaneis[50], whom we
may take to be a standing committee. The provisional
government, thus constituted, entrusted absolute and unlimited power to the Council of Four Hundred, who soon
established a reign of terror[51], which led to dissensions
within their own ranks and finally to their overthrow.

And so the government, which was intended as a
temporary expedient to prepare the way for a definite
and elaborate constitution, was swept away, and the projected scheme, a sketch of which is preserved by Aristotle[52],
was never realised. The scheme is of great interest, as
an instance of oligarchic invention, but it throws little
light on actual oligarchies, for it is unlike any known
constitution and its character is fantastic and unpractical.

[48] Ar. 31 3.

[49] The title of these officers and the analogy of the five presidents in
the projected constitution (Ar. 30 4) makes this probable. If the proedri
were the leading spirits of the revolution, as the part ascribed to them by
Thucydides 67 3 implies, I should be inclined to identify them with
Pisander, Antiphon, Phrynichus, Theramenes and possibly Aristarchus.
It is characteristic of Thucydides not directly to mention the names
of the proedri, but in ch. 68, immediately after relating their appointment, he proceeds, as if by a natural association of ideas, to describe
the chief agents of the revolution (Pisander, Antiphon, Phrynichus and
Theramenes). In 90 1 Aristarchus is associated with Phrynichus, Antiphon and Pisander as one of the leaders of the oligarchs.

[50] 70 1.

[51] Thuc. 70 1 ἔνεμον κατὰ κράτος τὴν πόλιν.

[52] c. 30. The projected is distinguished from the provisional government by phrases such as εἰς τὸν λοιπὸν χρόνον (30 3, cf. 31 2), εἰς τὸν
μέλλοντα χρόνον (31 1), εἰς τὸν ἄλλον χρόνον (31 3).

Its most important principle is the rotation of political duties[53]. The Five Thousand qualified for citizenship were to be divided into four 'lots[54],' and those over thirty years of age in each lot were to serve as a council[55] for the year while the rest were excluded from almost all the duties of government[56]. From the council thus constituted, which would contain about a thousand members[57], all the more important magistrates (about a hundred

[53] This we see clearly in the account of Aristotle; there are indications in Thucydides also that the principle was put forward by the oligarchs. The envoys at Samos assert (86 3) τῶν πεντακισχιλίων ὅτι πάντες ἐν τῷ μέρει μεθέξουσιν (sc. τῶν πραγμάτων), a passage which only becomes comprehensible in the light of the projected constitution. On the eve of their overthrow the Four Hundred promise (93 2) to appoint the Five Thousand καὶ ἐκ τούτων ἐν μέρει ᾖ ἂν τοῖς πεντακισχιλίοις δοκῇ τοὺς τετρακοσίους ἔσεσθαι. For the principle of rotation we may compare the 'Draconian Constitution' in Aristotle (4 3) and Ar. Pol. quoted in § 38 n. 22.

[54] Ar. 30 3 βουλὰς δὲ ποιῆσαι τέτταρας ἐκ τῆς ἡλικίας τῆς εἰρημένης εἰς τὸν λοιπὸν χρόνον, καὶ τούτων τὸ λάχον μέρος βουλεύειν, νεῖμαι δὲ καὶ τοὺς ἄλλους πρὸς τὴν λῆξιν ἑκάστην. τοὺς δ᾽ ἑκατὸν ἄνδρας διανεῖμαι σφᾶς τε αὐτοὺς καὶ τοὺς ἄλλους τέτταρα μέρη ὡς ἰσαίτατα καὶ διακληρῶσαι, καὶ εἰς ἐνιαυτὸν βουλεύειν. In this passage the hundred men are to divide all the Five Thousand (τοὺς ἄλλους as opposed to σφᾶς αὐτούς) into four equal lots (λήξεις); in each of these lots the citizens over thirty years of age are to form a βουλή for a year; those under thirty years of age (described by τοὺς ἄλλους in opposition to ἐκ τῆς ἡλικίας τῆς εἰρημένης) are to be included in the λήξεις. Cf. also 31 3 (this passage is difficult and probably corrupt).

[55] This is the necessary inference from the passage quoted in the last note. Dr Sandys in his commentary assumes that there were to be 'four councils of 400 each'; I can find no justification for this assumption. The whole scheme of government was directed to the concentration of power in the hands of a large βουλή, superseding both council and assembly.

[56] They would be eligible for the minor offices of state, which were filled from outside the βουλή.

[57] Each λῆξις would be a fourth part of 5000; the βουλή, after ex-

in number[58]) were to be chosen by a process of double election, while the minor magistracies were to be appointed from outside the council by lot. In case of need each member of the council might call in another citizen, himself qualified for the council, to take part in its deliberations. Regular sittings were prescribed: the archons were to call the council together, and five members chosen by lot, with one of their number as actual president, were to superintend the voting and the order of business. Lastly attendance at the council was enforced by a fine[59].

To the council thus constituted all powers of government were entrusted: there was no other power of state except the magistrates, and they were chosen from and by the council and were probably responsible to it. Of the duties of the council few details are given: nothing is said of the law-courts, but special mention is made of the control of finance[60]. The system of divided control and responsibility which ruled in the democratic exchequer was to be abolished, and the council was to have authority, aided by all the important financial officers, although the Hellenotamiae, who were actually on duty, were not to attend its meetings[61].

cluding the members between 20 and 30, would probably number something less than a thousand.

[58] Ar. 30 2. The magistrates mentioned there would be more than 100.

[59] These details are derived from Aristotle c. 30.

[60] Ar. 30 4 βουλεύεσθαι δὲ ᾗ ἂν δοκῇ αὐτοῖς ἄριστα ἕξειν περί τε τῶν χρημάτων...καὶ περὶ τῶν ἄλλων ὡς ἂν δύνωνται ἄριστα.

[61] Von Wilamowitz-Möllendorff op. cit. p. 119 explains the apparent inconsistency in the mention of the ἑλληνοταμίαι in 30 2 by the assumption that the duties of the Hellenotamiae were divided between the different members of the board, and those acting as treasurers were not on the

The special dangers of the democratic system were recognised and an attempt made to remedy them. The division of power between council and assembly was swept away. The new council was a compromise between the two : but as a deliberative body it could only have proved helpless and unwieldy. Another democratic defect, the separation of the executive from the sovereign power, was remedied by the inclusion of all magistrates in the council, while the principle of rotation secured the active participation in the government of all citizens in turn, and prevented the continuation of military office in the same hands. In its blend of oligarchic and democratic ideas we recognise the work of a somewhat fantastic theorist, and we may reasonably doubt whether his paper constitution would have worked with any measure of success.

But alike in the provisional and in the projected schemes of government we may notice certain ruling oligarchic principles : the exclusion of the lower classes from all political rights ; the abolition of pay ; the concentration of power in the hands of a council, entrusted with sovereign authority, and the creation of a strong executive appointed by and from the ruling council.

βουλή for the time, in order that their responsibility might be enforced. It is therefore unnecessary to omit καὶ ἑλληνοταμίας.

GENERAL INDEX.

[The large figures refer to sections, the small figures to notes, the letters A, B, C to the Appendixes.]

14

Qualification for office in oligarchies 41 14 ff.

Religion and constitutions 15; 25 *ad fin.*

Serfs 50 2 ff.
Social power determining form of government 14 3
Solon, his reforms B 12; his system of assessment 36 3, 7; his constitution 41 12, 16
Sparta, her constitution defined 3 16 ff.; influence of, on constitution of other states 16 4; 18; 19 2; 26 1, 6, 8, 9; decline of 27; population of 30 3; character of 51
Subject class in oligarchies 50 2, 8 ff.

Theognis 25 7, 16 ff.
Theseus A 19
Thetis in Homer 22 4

Thirty, The, 35 2, 13; 38 16; 41 4, 11, 13; 44 6; 48 3; 49 15
Thousand, constitutions of a 38 3 ff.; in Plato 38 17
Thucydides as a political philosopher 1 11
Tribal communities 21; 23 9, 10; 49
Tribe and city, conflict between 21; 23 9, 10; 25 27 ff.
Tribes, in Athens A, B; Dorian 49 1, 3; local in Sparta 49 5
Tyranny 3 3; 25 22 ff.; analogy of oligarchy to 35 9

Union of states, resisted by Sparta, 49 5 ff.

Village settlements, account of in Aristotle 21; in Attica A 5

Wealth, the principle of Oligarchy 4; 7; 36 1

GEOGRAPHICAL INDEX.

GREEK INDEX.

For EU product safety concerns, contact us at Calle de José Abascal, 56–1°, 28003 Madrid, Spain or eugpsr@cambridge.org.

www.ingramcontent.com/pod-product-compliance
Ingram Content Group UK Ltd.
Pitfield, Milton Keynes, MK11 3LW, UK
UKHW012328130625
459647UK00009B/134